University Leadership

University Leadership

The Role of the Chief Executive

Catherine Bargh
Jean Bocock
Peter Scott
David Smith

The Society for Research into Higher Education
& Open University Press

Published by SRHE and
Open University Press
Celtic Court
22 Ballmoor
Buckingham
MK 18 1XW

email: enquiries@openup.co.uk
world wide web: www.openup.co.uk

and

325 Chestnut Street
Philadelphia, PA 19106, USA

First published 2000

A catalogue record of this book is available from the British Library

ISBN 0 335 20487 2 (pb)   0 335 20488 0 (hb)

Library of Congress Cataloging-in-Publication Data
   University leadership: the role of the chief executive / Catherine Bargh . . .
   [*et al.*].
      p.   cm.
   Includes bibliographical references (p.) and index.
   ISBN 0–335–20488–0 – ISBN 0–335–20487–2 (pb)
   1. Universities and colleges–Administration.   2. Education, Higher–
Administration.   3. College administrators.   I. Bargh, Catherine, 1960–
LB2341 . U57 2000
378.1′01–dc21   99–088068

Typeset by Graphicraft Limited, Hong Kong
Printed in Great Britain by St Edmundsbury Press, Bury St Edmunds, Suffolk

Contents

Preface

This book continues our exploration of the 'top people' in contemporary higher education which we began in our earlier work *Governing Universities* (SRHE/Open University Press, 1996). In that book the composition, roles and functions of university governing bodies were discussed. Our conclusion was that changes in the culture of governance in higher education were less dramatic than might have been supposed in the light of the expansion of the system and transformation of institutions.

In our new book we switch our attention to another leadership group: the senior managers most closely identified with the fortunes of universities, vice-chancellors. The book examines some of the myths that have grown up about university leadership since the Jarratt Report in 1985, the most prominent of which is that vice-chancellors have been reborn as chief executives. The reality we have discovered is both more complex and more ambiguous. Although the managerial and political pressures on vice-chancellors have undoubtedly increased (as have expectations of the institutional leadership they can provide), there is substantial evidence of significant continuity – not simply in who vice-chancellors are and what they do (what we call 'the pattern of their days') but also in how they conceive their roles; the donnish monopoly of the top jobs in universities remains virtually unchallenged despite the development of mass higher education.

The scope of this book also extends beyond the United Kingdom. A parallel study of Swedish university rectors was undertaken by Professor Lars Engwall of Uppsala University, and the Centre for Higher Education Policy Studies (CHEPS) at the University of Twente helped us to undertake a survey of Dutch university rectors. The origins and attitudes, roles and functions of the presidents of universities and colleges in two American states, California and Georgia, were also studied as part of our research. The simple question we set ourselves initially – were patterns of university leadership worldwide converging or diverging? – also proved to be too simple. On the one hand, growing similarities can be observed as global perspectives and pressures bite; on the other hand, universities continue to be rooted in local environments which condition and shape the response of their leaders to these wider influences.

We would like to express our thanks to those vice-chancellors who agreed to help us with this research, especially to those who bravely agreed to be 'shadowed'. We would also like to thank the other senior academics and administrators, and members of councils and governing bodies, in universities who helped us to gain a more rounded picture of the role of their vice-chancellors. Above all, we would like to express our gratitude to the Leverhulme Trust which made the grant that enabled this research to be undertaken, and this book to be written.

Catherine Bargh
Jean Bocock
Peter Scott
David Smith

1
The Transformation of Higher Education

The subject of this first chapter is the wider context in which institutional leadership is exercised in higher education. That context is rapidly changing. The core mission of higher education is being transformed – compromised according to some critics – both by the addition of new roles, especially in the arenas of lifelong learning and technology transfer, and by the emergence of new training-and-researching organizations that threaten to invade the space traditionally occupied by universities and colleges. National systems of higher education are also being transformed – again, degraded in the eyes of some critics – by the abandonment of traditional planning regimes and the adoption of new market-like principles for allocating roles and resources. As a result of both transformations, of mission (or roles) and of systems, the organizational culture of universities too has been substantially modified. Loose-knit but coherent collegial institutions, middle-range in size, have been superseded by more tightly managed but diverse and mass institutions.

In the UK, university vice-chancellors (or principals in Scottish universities and also in colleges of higher education) have been at the heart of all three transformations: as initiators, or certainly as interpreters, of the much wider mission adopted by higher education; as mediators between national systems (and market forces operating on a global as well as a national level) and their institutions; and as managers of large and heterogeneous organizations. This chapter concentrates on the first two of these three transformations, and the emergence of new missions and the impact on organizational cultures. It is divided into three sections. The first considers the evolution of the core purposes of higher education in the context of the development of a knowledge society; the second the dialectic between differentiation and convergence of institutional missions at the level of national systems; and the third the impact of both on how universities are organized and managed. Chapter 2 considers the third transformation: of the role of the vice-chancellor as institutional leader.

Higher education and the knowledge society

The university is, pre-eminently, a knowledge institution. It produces knowledge in many different forms – credentials, skills, research. Other higher education institutions are also knowledge-producing institutions, although they have a more limited stake in the production of 'headline' knowledge in the shape of research. Society-at-large is now permeated by knowledge – most obviously, of course, in the form of the often incestuous links between advanced research and high-technology industry but also, just as significantly, in terms of greater knowledgeability, a fundamental social consequence of the growth of mass higher education, of knowledge artefacts, notably computers, and of knowledge images and symbols. It is in this generic sense that it is reasonable to refer to the 'knowledge society'.

But pervasive knowledge is knowledge transformed. The autonomous and discipline-denominated science of the twentieth century is being part-supplemented and part-superseded by more open and contextualized forms of knowledge production (Gibbons *et al.*, 1994). The social, economic and cultural forms characteristic of industrial twentieth-century society are being modified in analogous ways: its grand demarcations, conceptual and organizational, such as 'state', 'market' and 'culture', are becoming increasingly fuzzy; and its key institutions transformed, hollowed out, even abolished. There appeared to be intriguing affinities between the growing reflexivity of the knowledge production system on the one hand and on the other the transgressive quality of contemporary society (Nowotny *et al.*, 2000). It is important to consider what these changes mean for those organizations most directly implicated in the knowledge production system and therefore, it might be expected, most radically affected – in particular, universities and other higher education institutions.

The university is a key knowledge-producing institution. Indeed, in the past hundred years the university has become *the* key knowledge-producing institution, at any rate in large parts of Northern and Western Europe and in North America. Other institutional foci of scientific production have been unable to match the more demanding standards of professionalization set, or more generous resourcing enjoyed, by post-war higher education; the 'freelance' scientist has disappeared and even the autonomous intellectual is a threatened species. Or these other foci have been effectively incorporated in the wider higher education system; once-independent research establishments have been 'captured' by it for a mixture of academic and administrative reasons. Or such intimate alliances have been established between university science and military, civil and corporate R&D that they have coalesced into archipelagos of like-minded knowledge-producing institutions.

These changes are commonly regarded as unambiguous evidence of the increasing domination of the university. But it is also possible to argue that they are evidence of the transformation of the university itself into a new kind of institution. The university capturing but also captured. A generation ago the first interpretation was uncontested – the university as an triumphant, even imperialist, institution. It is still deeply ingrained in the thought and policy processes of politicians, civil servants and, of course, university leaders. But today the second interpretation is becoming plausible. In its 'take-over' of other, more democratic and more vocational, forms of higher education and its involvement in more contextualized forms of research the university has taken on new and more diverse roles that, some argue, may well be incommensurable and even incompatible. The boundaries between the university and other knowledge-producing institutions (such as think tanks or management consultants) and between the university and other types of post-secondary education and other parts of the R&D system have been eroded.

The traditional view of the university's fundamental purposes emphasized two aspects: its role as a producer of knowledge, whether in the form of scientific results (and other knowledge products) or of scientifically trained people; and as a producer of 'knowledgeability', in the shape of both a more highly educated, and presumably more scientifically rational and literate, population and, more generally, a more enlightened society. In these respects there was a close correspondence between the discourses of science and scholarship and of elite higher education. In the first the university (and quasi-university institutions) exercised scientific hegemony through the production of 'pure' research, which was the foundation on which society's capacity for innovation, and the economy's ability to exploit technological advances, ultimately depended. Even if a naive linear account of knowledge production was explicitly rejected, the key role of disinterested (i.e. university) science was still asserted. There was a similarly powerful but more subtle articulation between university scholarship and intellectual culture – or, wider still, 'public doctrine' in Maurice Cowling's phrase (Cowling, 1980). In the second the university played a leadership role in stimulating 'knowledgeability' through its formation of future elites, social and technical. Scientific literacy (and also, perhaps, cultural authority) would trickle down to, or be imposed upon, the general population with the help of university-educated school teachers, state officials, members of established professions and (more doubtfully) private-sector managers within a framework characterized by social and intellectual deference.

The accuracy of this traditional view, of course, can be challenged. First, the university's scientific hegemony is a comparatively recent phenomenon (and is still incomplete). Its culmination came only after 1945, and especially after 1960, when the elite university was already under attack. Indeed, two peaks of university success coincided. The scientification of the university culminated in the 1960s and 1970s just when higher education was becoming a mass system. Second, there was always tension between the university's aim to reproduce a cultivated elite, sometimes associated with anti-scientific (or, at any rate, anti-positivistic) notions of liberal education, and its development as a scientific institution. This tension took the form both of 'culture wars' (during the 1880s between Arnold and Huxley, and in the 1950s between Leavis and Snow) and of disputes about how universities should be organized. Educators emphasized the 'college'; researchers the department. Third, just as 'society' is suffused with 'knowledge', so 'knowledge' is suffused with the 'social'. This has important implications for the university. Its social and scientific roles, instead of being in tension (whether between the stasis of the elite university and the dynamism of progressive science, or between the open engagement of a democratic higher education and the disengagement of 'disinterested' science), may be converging.

Segregation or transgression?

However, most higher education policy makers, and many institutional leaders, remain reluctant to acknowledge this possibility. Their world-view is dominated by two secular trends. The first is a drive towards institutional segregation – or, to adopt policy-speak, diversity – because they see a growing contradiction between the university's role as a producer of scientific knowledge on the one hand and on the other its responsibility to satisfy democratic or market demands for mass participation, which they see as attenuating the university's scientific base and/or undermining academic standards. They also argue that far from producing a more scientifically literate population, the expansion of higher education has gone hand-in-hand with the growth of an anti-scientific spirit, even of a culture of irrationality. In their eyes the relationship between the scientific – or, more broadly, 'knowledge' – and social roles of the university amounts to a zero-sum game (the more 'scientific', the less 'social' and vice versa).

The second is the retreat from planning – at any rate in a bureaucratic mode. The normative authority of the welfare state has been eroded by free-market rhetoric, and the legitimacy of national planning has been seriously compromised. Far from being regarded as the highest good, the 'public interest' is now more likely to be interpreted as the self-interest of bureaucrats and professional experts, both of whom lack appropriate entrepreneurial values and skills. At the same time the functional effectiveness of the welfare state has been reduced by the perceived reluctance of affluent citizens to pay higher taxes and by the rise of symbolic sound-bite politics. These two trends, of course, are in tension. The challenge facing national policy makers is how to produce a more segregated system – but by sleight-of-hand. They must retain control over the direction of change without overtly planning it. Hence the rash of 'initiatives' (in essence, national planning disguised as quasi-market competition) and growing emphasis on quality assurance (which, again, can be used to steer the system covertly). For institutional leaders the challenge is more straightforward; they, too, must pursue policies of differentiation, but they have no inhibitions about exercising 'leadership' and espousing 'management', although these are merely the institutional analogues of system-wide 'planning'.

The first trend is more important than the second. The 'retreat' from planning has been exaggerated, because covert planning continues. Despite the messianic convictions of free-marketeers, it is not irreversible. The drive towards segregation, however, is more fundamental. The development of higher education and research policies in many countries has been based on the belief that it is necessary to insulate the scientific (and elite?) functions of the university from its social (or mass?) functions. The intention often has been to create a clearer separation between research and scholarship and the higher education (or, at any rate, socialization) of mass student populations where such a separation does not exist, and to reinforce it where it does exist, by encouraging the emergence of more differentiated systems. The separate funding of research and teaching by the higher education funding councils in Britain reflects this intention, which is reinforced by the highly selective (elitist?) distribution of research funding through the Research Assessment Exercise (RAE). A similar agenda has often been pursued at an institutional level. Research centres and graduate schools have been created to produce a clearer separation between these activities, which are regarded as inherently selective/elitist, and mass undergraduate education.

Three main systemic strategies have been pursued to protect science from the 'social' in the modern university. First, higher education systems have been formally stratified with a small number of research-oriented universities being granted a monopoly of PhD programmes. The best known example is the California master plan first promulgated in 1962 and revised on several occasions since, which created a three-tier system consisting of the eight-campus University of California, the California State University (CSU) campuses and the community college sector, each with its own entry standards and range of academic programmes. Second, binary systems of higher education have been maintained in much of Europe. A clear separation has been maintained between traditional universities and higher vocational education institutions, such as *Fachhochschulen* in Germany and Austria and HBO schools in the Netherlands. In some European countries another form of differentiation has also been maintained: between universities (and higher vocational institutions) and independent (or, at any rate, semi-detached) research institutions, such as the Max Planck, CRNS or Academy of Sciences institutes. Third, in those countries with unified higher education systems (for example, Australia, Sweden and the United Kingdom), efforts have been made to encourage institutional diversity by selective funding policies, especially for research, and through market pressures.

None of these strategies has been without its difficulties. Even within planned systems political pressures have tended to dissolve hard demarcations within tiered systems. For example, the University of California's monopoly of PhDs has been breached and substantial research programmes have developed on CSU campuses, while credit transfer systems to facilitate 'upward' student mobility have been emphasized. In Europe, even where binary systems have been maintained, higher vocational institutions are now generally embraced within the same legal frameworks as universities. Upward academic drift, although discouraged, has not been prevented. In any case, these binary systems had originally been designed not to produce a clearer separation between research-led and teaching-oriented institutions, but to cater for the further education of the separate streams of 'academic' and 'vocational' students within divided secondary school systems. As such they have come under attack as being incompatible with democratic entitlements to higher education.

In the past, institutional differentiation was the product of historical variation between different types of higher education broadly defined as 'academic' or 'vocational', 'scientific' or 'professional' (the precise language has varied over time and between nations). This variation, of course, was closely aligned with social-class hierarchies. Universities typically enrolled students from more socially privileged groups than higher vocational or teacher training institutions. Today institutional differentiation is more likely to be driven by the perceived need to protect, and enhance, research excellence. For example, a recent study commissioned by the Higher Education Funding Council for England suggested that in those countries where research and teaching were separately organized, whether this separation takes the form of independent research institutes on the Max Planck or CRNS model or of clearly delineated research universities, there was a stronger correlation between the number and impact (as measured by citation indices) of scientific publications than in countries where these conditions did not apply – for example, England. The conclusion drawn by some policy makers was that research funding should be even more selectively targeted, perhaps by abandoning the dual-support system entirely (Adams *et al.*, 1998).

This tension between the desire to preserve or enhance 'excellence', now defined in terms of scientific quality and productivity but formerly in terms of broader cultural (and social class?) considerations, and the need to satisfy popular pressures for increased participation, appears to confirm the existence of an inescapable contradiction between the university's scientific and social roles. Certainly policy responses have often been predicated on this assumption. In Britain, where traditionally universities received undifferentiated block grants from the state for both teaching and, at any rate core, research support, there has been a trend towards separate earmarked teaching and research budgets – partly in order to promote improved value-for-money and greater accountability, but also partly to prevent the dilution of research budgets by the demands of mass teaching (and to produce *de facto* research universities?). Furthermore, the growth of earmarked – and competitive – research funding has tended to reinforce the division of university staff into teachers or researchers. In effect, freestanding research institutes with independent budgets and separate staffs have been created within universities otherwise engaged in teaching mass student populations.

Yet these attempts to segregate higher education systems into research-led universities and access-oriented institutions have met with only limited success. Part of the reason is the difficulties any selective public policies encounter in open societies; they appear to go against the democratic grain. Part is the growing disinclination to 'plan' higher education (or any other) systems – at least overtly. These inhibitions may help to explain the tendency to seize on quasi-market, or actual market, solutions. Yet, in the case of the university (although the United States may be an exception), the market has also failed to produce the desired segmentation. Instead there has been a marked reluctance on the part of elite universities to concentrate on their scientific functions at the expense of their wider social responsibilities – a reluctance that can only be partly explained by either political expediency (the need to maintain, and mobilize, popular support) or the stubborn persistence of archaic notions of universality. At the same time, it has proved difficult to contain research within the emergent elite sector; it has spread into other, newer and more open, sectors of higher education, which again cannot be wholly explained in terms of institutional ambitions. Indeed, the containment of research (outside a few very high-cost subjects) has proved to be a failure. Not only has the number of 'researchers' within higher education systems increased as a result of the expansion of these systems since 1960; research is now undertaken in a wider range of non-university settings which extend far beyond free-standing research institutes or dedicated R&D departments into government, business, community and the media.

One response has been to try still harder. The failure to produce a suitably differentiated system is attributed to political timidity, a refusal to acknowledge that the claims of 'science' must take precedence over the clamour of the 'social'. The solution, therefore, is to depoliticize higher education and research policies – by (re?)asserting the autonomy of the university (or, at any rate, re-establishing its privileged position within the state) and by strengthening the authority of 'expert' elites, whether scientists themselves or state officials with a compatible orientation. However, in the context of the knowledge society, these difficulties appear in a very different light. While it was (and is) possible to contain 'professional' science, 'objective' and 'disinterested' science in the sense that it was (or supposed itself to be) decontextualized, within a restricted number of institutions, including elite universities, dominated by equally restricted scientific communities, it is not possible to contain contextualized knowledge production in the same way. It pervades society-at-large through not only the wide distribution of research-like activities but also the production of mass graduate populations.

So an alternative response has been to swim with the tide. The production of knowledge – 'research' in the old language – and of knowledge-ability – 'teaching' – is now so widely distributed that traditional processes of institutionalization, which typically have taken place in and through elite universities, are weakened. Scientific communities have become diffused and transgressive, with the result that the traditional structures of faculties and departments, institutes and centres, that create and sustain these communities become less relevant. The number of research, or knowledge, actors has exploded. Because of the contextualization of knowledge, the producers of research have become a less privileged group – and, even, a problematical category. Other actors, once dismissed as mere 'disseminators', 'brokers' or 'users' of research results, are now more actively involved in their 'production' (which itself has become a more capacious, and ambiguous, category). Further, the emergence of a knowledge society means that a much wider range of social, economic and even cultural activities now have 'research' components. Many institutions are now learning-and-researching organizations – because they trade in knowledge products and because they employ many more 'knowledgeable' workers.

The impact on institutions

For higher education institutions, and how they are managed, these changes have important consequences. They will find it difficult to delineate, and so demarcate, their activities according to anachronistic divisions between research and teaching, scientific and social roles. They may also have to acquiesce in a process of deinstitutionalization, because the boundaries between 'inside' and 'outside' now make no better sense than those between research and teaching. The most difficult task facing higher education leaders in the twenty-first century will be how to reconcile the university's increasingly open intellectual engagement with its enveloping environment(s) and its need to retain normative focus and managerial coherence.

The organizational culture of higher education is shaped by a dialectic between continuity, the conservation of traditional forms of scientific and intellectual (and social) authority, and 'movement', the reconfiguration of knowledge as a result of dynamic (and transgressive) science and of society as a result of the impact of mass participation. The enduring influence of tradition continues to be felt. Most universities still enjoy exceptional autonomy – by the prevailing standards of their societies. Those standards may have changed, typically through the invasiveness of the state (once preoccupied with its social functions in the shape of the 'welfare state' and now more concerned to promote national competitiveness within a global economy) and the intrusion of the market through the more vigorous exercise of consumer choice by students or by 'purchasers' of university research. But the relatively high degree of autonomy enjoyed by higher education institutions has probably not changed. Even where universities continue to be incorporated in state bureaucracies, the state has often reconceptualized – and reoperationalized – its relationship with them as that of, in effect, an 'external' contractor.

This has happened in both Sweden and the Netherlands, and in many other European countries the language of contracting has subtly supplemented the language of supervision and regulation. Intermediate bodies may no longer be formally constituted as 'buffers' between universities and the state, but they continue to provide a layer of operational insulation from direct political and administrative pressures which few other 'public' institutions in modern societies enjoy. Although the abolition of the University Grants Committee in 1988 was a blow to the pride and status of British universities, the new higher education funding councils still allow them exceptional room for manoeuvre – in terms of both academic strategy and institutional management. There is probably a danger of overestimating the political subordination of modern universities. Certainly in Europe a more plausible explanation is that the 'state' systems of higher education characteristic of continental Europe have been liberalized, while the 'autonomous' systems that prevailed in Britain and Ireland have become more constrained, and both have converged on a new model of state–university relations best described as one of 'state-supervision' and/or 'state-entrepreneurial' (Maassen and van Vught, 1994).

This political (and public) acceptance, however grudging, of higher education's claim to constitute an autonomous space may help to explain the persistence of traditional forms of internal organization, governance and management. Most higher education institutions still regard themselves – and are regarded – as professional rather than industrial organizations in which academic reputation is as important as managerial competence. This is reflected in patterns of institutional leadership, in a preference for collegio-hierarchical rather than line-management relationships and in distinctive modes of planning and budgeting. In continental Europe rectors continue to be selected from among the university's professors. But even in countries where, notionally, a freer choice is possible, most presidents and vice-chancellors are still drawn overwhelmingly from the ranks of the academic class. The evidence of our research confirms the reluctance to appoint outsiders to leadership roles in higher education, despite the growing complexity of institutional management and permeability of institutional (and system) boundaries.

Decision making in universities remains predominantly collective and collegial, and it is dominated by senior professors and their peers. Individual teachers and researchers still enjoy considerable autonomy in their work – to such an extent, in fact, that it can be argued that a university's core activities are the least amenable to being managed. A high value continues to be placed on participation, by both staff and students, despite greater emphasis on managerial values and structures (especially in more recently established universities and other higher education institutions). Typically academic planning is decentralized. Where more dynamic budgeting systems have been developed to relate more directly to such planning, they too have often devolved responsibility to faculties, departments and other sub-institutional units. These remain the 'basic units' of most higher education institutions (Becher and Kogan, 1980). The influence of tradition and the claims for continuity are still sufficiently powerful to ensure that the university continues to be a special kind of organization which cannot easily be assimilated to a generic 'industrial' model.

However, the forces of 'movement' have stimulated significant changes in the way higher education institutions are organized, governed and managed. Four such forces – or 'change drivers' – can be identified (Scott, 1995). One is the growth of wider higher education systems incorporating new kinds of universities and also non-university institutions. Very rapid rates of overall growth have been achieved over the past two decades; it was estimated that by the year 2000 there would be 66 million students, or 1 per cent of the world's population (Blight, 1995: 22). In Britain at the time of writing there were 1.8 million students, more than double the total a decade earlier. But the traditional universities' global market share has shrunk; most students are now enrolled in non-university institutions. In Britain this global trend has been disguised by the redesignation of the polytechnics as universities in 1992.

This growth, quantitative and qualitative, has led to a double transformation. First, the organizational exceptionalism of the university has been diluted by this accretion of other institutional types. Although it is wrong to exaggerate the differences between traditional universities and 'new' or non-universities in terms of academic structures and management cultures, the attachment of the latter to institutional autonomy and professional collegiality was originally much weaker. Whether it has remained so following their incorporation in the higher education sector (in contrast to their former location in further or higher technical education sectors) is less clear. Clearly some convergence of organizational cultures has taken place. Second, the creation of these wider higher education systems has had an impact on the traditional universities. Not only have they acquired new, and arguably more vigorous, rivals (as in Britain during the currency of the former 'binary system' of universities and polytechnics), they have also been obliged to consider their 'positioning', and so goals and missions, within these larger systems (which has been necessary even when non-university institutions have remained firmly subordinated to universities, as has typically been the case in the rest of Europe).

The second is that nearly all higher education institutions have taken on novel roles. Statistical analyses only capture part of this novelty. For example, more than a third of students in British higher education are now part-time, a 50 per cent increase in a decade. Thirty-two per cent of new entrants are aged 21 and over, although the introduction of tuition fees has depressed demand from mature students (Higher Education Statistics Agency (HESA), 1999: 5–11). Conventional notions of 'research' and 'teaching' are now being stretched to incorporate radically new activities. Elite research universities have developed science parks to serve as incubators for high-technology enterprises which, in return, fertilize their scientific research, and also to act as agents through which their intellectual property can be commercialized. Other higher education institutions have become more deeply involved in less traditional academic activities, such as continuing professional development for mid-career workers or work-based learning programmes in partnership with other public-sector organizations and private-sector companies. Developments in communications and information technologies, modes of presentation (and persuasion?) and patterns of marketing have stimulated the growth of interactive and distance learning – and also of 'distributed' research. The university has become a transgressive institution: literally so in temporal and spatial terms; normatively in the context of its spreading mission and proliferating roles; and organizationally in terms of its governance and management. The three are connected. Off-campus provision requires new control mechanisms which are more likely to be 'industrial' than 'collegial' in their basic orientation, while partnerships created to develop novel forms of provision cannot readily be managed within an autonomist institutional culture rooted in traditional academic norms.

The third is the impact of new forms of accountability. This takes many forms. One is that, as higher education has expanded, the strain on public finances has increased, with the result that budgets have been reduced (certainly on a unit-cost basis) and greater emphasis is now placed on value-for-money. A second is that, again because of the expansion of higher education and its adoption of novel roles, it is less evident that academic self-regulation is sufficient. At the very least it must be supplemented by other forms of review and regulation. The degree of collusive trust possible within an elite system has been dissipated. Academic quality now has to be managed rather than assumed. The general growth of more sceptical, and critical, attitudes towards 'experts' (a complex phenomenon linked to notions of the so-called risk society) has strengthened demands for more effective external accountability. These demands have been further strengthened by a fundamental shift in public policy in many developed societies. The planning of resource inputs, from which higher education was traditionally insulated by its successfully maintained autonomist claims, has become less dominant, while greater emphasis is now placed on the auditing of policy outcomes, from which higher education is no more exempt than any other system.

A third form of accountability has been imposed by the emergence of much broader higher education systems. Individual universities, loosely grouped in elite systems, could be shielded from scrutiny in a way in which a much larger number of higher education institutions, now constituting mass systems, cannot be. However, the emphasis on accountability can also be attributed to a contrary movement, the development of a so-called audit culture in which external controls have been internalized as forms of self-evaluation, or peer evaluation (Power, 1997). The emerging audit society is closely but curiously aligned with the parallel development of a knowledge society. Not only do knowledgeable systems make audit, internal or external, more effective by enhancing accuracy and enabling transparency, there are also more fundamental affinities between the audit and knowledge societies in their conceptualizations of access, expertise and risk.

The fourth 'change driver' reflects the changing characteristics of higher education institutions themselves. Most have grown greatly in size, whether measured by their student numbers or total budgets, and in scope, as measured by the range of their teaching and research programmes. The 'average' British university has approaching 17,000 students and a budget of almost £100 million. Because of the decline of larger-scale industrial organizations universities are now often the most significant economic units in their cities or regions. Notions of the knowledge, or learning, society that emphasize the centrality of knowledge production in the post-industrial economy have tended to underline (and even exaggerate?) their economic significance. In addition, the changing relationships between higher education, state and market have added to the burdens placed on university managers. Because of declining budgets they are forced to make the university's assets (whether human, physical and financial) 'work harder'. Higher education increased its 'efficiency' by more than 30 per cent from 1992 to 1999 measured in terms of expenditure per student, no mean feat in a people-based 'industry' which generally has been unable to exploit new productivity-enabling technologies to substitute for costly academic labour. Because of a closer engagement with the market they have to develop new entrepreneurial skills – and matching control systems. Because of the state's operational withdrawal from university administration in many countries they must undertake new managerial functions with regard to personnel, buildings and financial planning. This combination of greater size and increased complexity has led to far-reaching changes in how higher education systems and institutions are organized, governed and managed.

The cumulative influence of these four 'change drivers' has been to transform the organizational culture of the modern university. But it is important to emphasize two important qualifications. First, the undertow of more traditional assumptions about the abiding purposes, and so essential characteristics, of universities is still powerful. Their organizational culture, and consequently management structures and practices, can still only be properly understood by reference to these assumptions. Second, this new culture has not been produced by a simple linear process, involving the abandonment of the 'professional' model of the university and its replacement by an 'industrial' model. Instead, it is the result of complex process of internal and external changes which have produced a new kind of university – but still an organizational model that is in significant respects exceptional. As academic organizations, universities are still perhaps *sui generis*. Even when they no longer resemble, in A.H. Halsey's resonant phrase, a 'donnish dominion', universities are still professional bureaucracies – and, as in other professional bureaucracies such as hospitals, members of key professional groups will always have a significant voice in institutional management (Mintzberg, 1990).

New organizational models

If there has been any convergence between 'professional' and 'industrial' organizational models, it has taken the form of the latter apparently adopting some of the features of the former as well as – or, possibly, more than – the other way round. Much of the academic literature about the management of organizations, and good industrial practice too, now emphasizes the need for 'flat' rather than hierarchical management structures, for loosely coupled rather than tightly managed organizations, for quasi-collegial team-working rather than lengthy line-management (e.g. Handy, 1994). It has been argued that the modern university can serve as a model for how creative, or learning, organizations of all kinds should be managed. However, this argument should be used with some care – because of the still-strong elements of continuity and tradition in the university's organizational culture. Some of the similarities between, for example, the relationship between the university and its 'basic units', in the shape of faculties and departments, and the relationship between the corporate headquarters of a global corporation and its operating companies may be more apparent than real, although there may be a stronger case for greater organizational correspondence between universities and some new high-technology enterprises. But, even here, caution should be exercised. Universities, despite their ability to transform and regenerate themselves, are characterized by longevity. Many of the corporate organizations with which they are being compared are characterized by extreme volatility. This fundamental difference suggests that it is easy to exaggerate the synergy between their organizational cultures.

Perhaps a better way in which to conceptualize emerging models of higher education organization and management is to emphasize competing strategies for coping with complexity. The traditional university's strategy was to adopt a form of radical decentralization (decentralization may be a misleading word in this context because it implies a prior state of centralization, which did not obtain). The university, whether as an autonomous institution or as part of the state bureaucracy, was deliberately weak, even vestigial, in terms of its management responsibilities, although it possessed significant normative and symbolic influence. Operational decisions were taken by deans, professors, even students – and, moreover, were regarded as private rather than public decisions (and so largely exempt from external review). Within this (anti?) structure a reductionist science was able to flourish.

The modern university's strategy for coping with complexity has been different. It has been to develop planning and control systems, in order explicitly to establish and review academic priorities. Such systems could only be established by creating better management structures, although generally still influenced heavily by collegial values and practices. But managerial discourses have been needed as well as management structures, because the modern university's normative and symbolic influence has been reduced by the decay of the common 'academic' culture typical of elite university systems ('academic' because it owed as much to the solidarity of elite social groups as it did to shared intellectual agendas) and the widening of higher education's social base. An additional factor is that the complexity faced by the modern university is not simply the product of a reductionist science, and, therefore, essentially an 'internal' problem; it is also the result of increasingly complex relations with a growing number of stakeholders, which make it difficult to distinguish 'internal' from 'external' dimensions of complexity.

Of course, these complexities could run out of control. The diversification of higher education systems is now proceeding at such a pace that the very category 'higher education' is in danger of becoming redundant and being replaced by an even more expansive category, such as 'lifelong learning'. Such an extension of higher education's scope is implied in the notion of a learning society. But it also shifts the emphasis from a system of institutions to an aggregation of learning (and researching) activities. It is possible that the privatization of the late twentieth century, which was seen at first merely as a managed retreat from the welfare state and then later under the label of 'individualization' as a more profound cultural change, may lead in the twenty-first century to a much more radical process of deinstitutionalization. New communications and information technologies may undermine traditional institutions, perhaps as postmodernism and its lesser relativisms may dismantle traditional intellectual structures. Under these new conditions the university could be radically challenged, as both a material and symbolic institution. But even if deinstitutionalization is avoided (or, rather, reinstitutionalization around global media and information corporations), it may become more difficult to regard the university as the model higher education – or lifelong learning – institution.

Until now its hegemony has been maintained. New types of higher education institution, however rivalrous their behaviour, have largely conformed to an organizational culture recognizable as that of the university. The proliferation of virtual and corporate universities so far has been limited. Many are parasitic on the research and teaching resources of conventional universities and focus heavily on business education and information technology; others amount to little more than a rebranding of current corporate training and R&D activities (and their adoption of the 'university' title is a demonstration of the potency of this ancient brand). The distinctiveness of academic organizations has survived, even if the detailed interpretations of that distinctiveness have proliferated and diverged. But their survival cannot be taken for granted – not without radical adaptation. New kinds of 'knowledge' institution may emerge in the learning society, modelled not on universities but on management consultancies, market research companies and media organizations.

Even if higher education rises to the challenge posed by different kinds of learning-and-teaching organizations, it will be transformed in the process. The growth of a highly distributed knowledge system; the increasing permeability of institutions (in both operational and normative terms); the explosion of technologies that are both convergent and transgressive; the 'retreat' of the welfare state and the irruption of 'markets'; the contradictions between desires and risks – all these trends, and many others, have created an entirely new environment. To survive and thrive in such an environment, Burton Clark argues, universities need a stronger central core to steer the enterprise and manage appropriate control systems, an expanding periphery in which new development opportunities are incorporated into the university's mission and diversified funding (partly to reflect their increasing pluralism and partly to make good the deficiency in public funding). In their organizational culture they must be both entrepreneurial and collegial (Clark, 1998). Alan Wilson offers a similar analysis. His vision of the twenty-first century university is of an academic core with what he calls 'a recognisably ecological trace back to the present' and a periphery of entrepreneurial partnership-based activities (Wilson, 1999). There are clearly affinities between the Clark/Wilson visions of the future and the dialectic between continuity (= core?) and 'movement' (= periphery?) that has shaped the organization and management of higher education in the past.

Conclusion

This larger context needs to be kept in mind when one is discussing more detailed issues relevant to the management of higher education institutions and the management of change, and the role of institutional leadership which is the subject of this book. But the immediate concern must be how higher education institutions can successfully manage complexity, on the assumption that they will remain recognizable as such and that they will continue to be key players in the learning, or knowledge, society of the future. Three broad issues are especially important.

- The first is the extent to which the roles of higher education institutions will be transformed. In the 'distributed' university its core functions may no longer be the direct provision of teaching, in the form of (fairly) traditional academic programmes, or even of learning opportunities more liberally defined. Instead, these core functions may be to validate, accredit and quality-assure the outcomes of teaching and learning organized by other agencies. Such a change would have implications not only for the size and scope of higher education institutions, but also for their organizational culture and management. The university could become a rather less complex institution if many of its existing core functions were to be, in effect, subcontracted. Managerially it would be simpler, although its symbolic power might be increased.
- The second concerns the nature of leadership in academic organizations (and is most relevant to the theme of this book). Is it grounded in some notion of intellectual authority, which, in turn, probably implies a shared, if essentially symbolic, academic and scientific culture? Or is it to be based on operational competencies? This question, of course, can only be answered by reference to the purposes of the university, its future roles and its (increasing or reducing?) complexity, which have been sketched in this chapter. It also raises fundamental issues of organizational culture. Are higher education institutions best managed by a cadre of professional

(and presumably permanent and full-time) managers, or through collegial processes?
- The third is the balance between strategic and operational management. It can be argued that, with sophisticated management information systems (at both system and institutional levels), the day-to-day management of higher education has been made much simpler. Control systems control themselves. But the complexity, and volatility, of higher education's roles have made strategic management much more difficult. But should the strategic direction of higher education institutions be set by their 'external' stakeholders (which would imply a reform of governance structures), or by their 'internal' communities, or by creative managers able to mediate between these various interests?

This introductory chapter has done no more than sketch the very broad parameters of change in the context of which more detailed answers to these questions will have to be developed. In many respects it is an unsettling prospect. On the one hand there is a powerful push towards greater segregation, or diversity, within higher education systems and greater differentiation within higher education institutions. This push dominates not only national policy making but also institutional management. If the key responsibility of university and college leaders is to manage change, it is generally assumed to be in the direction of increased segregation and differentiation. We are all niche institutions now – or so it seems. On the other hand the evolution of the social and knowledge systems is in a different direction – towards the erosion of the great categorizations of modernity, such as the state and the market, the economy and culture. If, in a knowledge society, knowledge systems become pervasive and transgressive (and, therefore, no longer clearly demarcated from other systems), the capacity of knowledge institutions like universities to occupy distinctive niches becomes problematic. Institutional leaders who resist reductionist and mechanistic interpretations of the 'management of change', choosing instead to keep their options – and their frontiers – open and preferring softer (and malleable) visioning to hard-edged (and inflexible) planning, may be resonating these larger uncertainties.

2

The Role of the Vice-Chancellor: Theoretical and Historical Perspectives

In Chapter 1 the wider context in which leadership and management in higher education are exercised was discussed. The argument, briefly, was that in a knowledge society the demarcation between specialized knowledge production systems, in which higher education plays a leading role, and social systems more broadly is becoming much weaker. The production of knowledge, or 'research', and the development of knowledgeability, or 'teaching', are both becoming more widely distributed across a range of types of institution and environments – of which higher education is only one. However, the dynamics of national policy making in higher education continue to be dominated by a push towards segregation, or diversity. The rationale for this segregation is to protect research-oriented institutions from the pressures of massification, and wider-access institutions from the temptations of so-called 'academic drift'. Institutions, too, are seeking to become more differentiated internally as they struggle to accommodate an accumulation of new roles and functions, and to secure niches in the academic market place which has been created by the (feigned?) retreat of the state. It is against this confused background that the organizational culture(s) of higher education is developing, characterized on the one side by the persistence of traditional forms of collegiality (to service the academic core) and on the other by new managerial forms of leadership (to develop the entrepreneurial periphery).

This chapter covers two broad topics. First, different models of leadership are discussed. Although most general models of leadership have been developed in the context of private-sector, rather than public-service, management, leadership styles in higher education have been increasingly influenced by these models. There are two main reasons for this. The first, and more trivial, reason is the persistence of the post-Thatcherite fetish about the virtues of both the private sector and managers. It was – and is – casually assumed that only by adopting the culture of the private sector and the cult of management can public institutions like universities develop much-needed habits of enterprise and innovation. The second reason, of course, reflects the coalescence of the political, social, economic, cultural and scientific (or, more broadly, educational) systems which was sketched in Chapter 1. If it is true that the boundaries between these once separate systems are becoming more permeable, it is likely that organizational patterns, and so management challenges, are also converging. In short, running a university is now much more like running a company: not because universities have become more like companies or even that universities, like large companies, are now complex organizations; but because both universities and companies are evolving towards some new hybrid form of organization.

The second topic is the evolution of the office of vice-chancellor in the UK since 1945. Five main phases are identified. The first ran up to about 1960; vice-chancellors presided over rather than managed their universities, which were 'administered' by registrars and bursars. The second covered the 1960s; in this period vice-chancellors were institution-builders – literally so in most cases and in a symbolic, or visionary, sense in many cases, especially in the new campus universities founded during that decade. The third phase was bisected by the Jarratt Report on university efficiency; partly inspired (or coerced?) by that report vice-chancellors became involved in more detailed management processes and gradually evolved towards a role not dissimilar from that of the chief executive in the private sector. The fourth phase was dominated by a number of external challenges from the newly elected Thatcher government which cut deep into university budgets and by the emergence of the polytechnics (not yet universities) as significant rivals; during this period the role of the vice-chancellor was politicized (it had been partially politicized 15 years before during the period of student revolt) and they became preoccupied, even overwhelmed, by the demands of crisis management. The fifth, and final, phase extends from the watershed of the early 1990s, when the university sector was extended to include the polytechnics and expansionary and budgetary turbulence was superseded by so-called 'consolidation', until the present. Vice-chancellors are now faced with an accumulation of challenges: continuing crisis-management, budgetary austerity and politicization; but now also the fundamental re-engineering, repositioning and even re-enchanting of their institutions.

Models of leadership

Vice-chancellors as leaders

University vice-chancellors have figured only at the margins of the academic literature about leadership. The heads of other higher education institutions barely figure at all. There has only been one major study of leadership in British higher education (Middlehurst, 1993). The remainder of the literature consists of attempts to apply theories of leadership to universities (Adair, 1981), empirical studies of the social origins of vice-chancellors (see below), micro-studies of academic leadership (McNeish, 1997) and general accounts of university management and administration in which the particular role of vice-chancellors is rarely highlighted. The bulk of the academic literature refers to American higher education, which is an exceptional system because of its size (14 million students, a fifth of the global total), its extent (it has taken over the further, or technical, education sectors which are still prominent in Europe), its diversity ('systems' with hundreds of thousands of students masquerading as multi-campus universities on the one hand; on the other small liberal arts colleges) and its political economy (by European standards both politicized and privatized). In this system the university or college president has a different role, which makes direct comparison with the role of the vice-chancellor difficult (Rosenzweig, 1998).

There are two main reasons for this marginality. First, until as late as the 1970s universities were not seen as institutions that had to be managed – still less as managerial institutions. The second, and perhaps more significant, reason is that the very limited studies of vice-chancellors that had been undertaken were firmly situated in wider accounts of the formation and development of elites. As a result their origins and connections received much more attention than their roles and functions (Collison and Millen, 1969). Of consuming interest was whether they had been educated in grammar schools or at Oxford or Cambridge (In both cases the broad answer was yes – vice-chancellors in the mid-twentieth century had often been 'scholarship boys'). The non-academic literature displayed the same bias. Personal memoirs tended to concentrate on 'position', in every sense: social, political and academic. Such memoirs are reasonably informative about the committees on which vice-chancellors served, their wider connections and their views on issues of the day; they convey almost no information about the detailed management tasks undertaken by vice-chancellors.

This marginality makes it difficult to assimilate vice-chancellors into the main body of literature about organizational leadership. All that will be attempted here is a brief survey of general models of leadership and of management and their possible application to the evolving role of the vice-chancellor. The first task is to distinguish between 'leadership' and 'management'. Vice-chancellors have always been 'leaders', although perhaps of an archaic variety. Only recently have they also been seen, or come to see themselves, as 'managers'. However, in this respect vice-chancellors are not exceptional. Similar patterns can be observed in other organizations. In large international corporations, for example, presidents/chairmen certainly and chief executive officers arguably also act as 'leaders', concerned largely with developing high-level strategy, because detailed managerial responsibilities are devolved to manufacturing units and sales and service organizations (often subsidiary companies and sometimes distributed worldwide). There may be an interesting parallel between devolution in large corporations – now also increasingly popular in not-so-large organizations in both private and public sectors – and the relationship in universities between the vice-chancellor and the senior management team/central administration on the one hand and the faculties, departments and research centres on the other.

There is a further complication: in higher education 'academic' is the adjective that attaches itself most readily to 'leadership', while 'management' is often twinned with 'administration'. As a result they may refer to two distinct domains: on one hand the so-called 'public life' of higher education represented by the evolution of systems and the development of institutions; and on the other the 'private life' of teaching and learning, research and scholarship (which, of course, is really more 'public' than the 'public life' because it directly engages the 'users' of higher education). These two domains are no longer as distinct as they were two decades ago when Martin Trow first coined the contrast. Within institutions the growth of credit systems, a greater emphasis on curriculum renewal and the clearer articulation of academic planning have made it necessary to develop institutional policies and processes; the private world of exchanges between students and teachers has been invaded. At the same time, external regulation, quality assurance, subject benchmarking and the like have compromised both academic freedom and institutional autonomy; national policies are no longer concerned only with the allocation of resources and the structure of the system. However, the distinction in universities between 'academic' leadership and management/administration remains as an additional complication.

The distinction between leadership and management is easy enough to describe in generic, or conceptual, terms: leaders create the vision and generate the strategy for their organisations while managers operate systems, monitor progress and assess performance. But even these generic statements are not always illuminating. Is vision different from strategy? If it is, is vision to be understood as an expression of fundamental corporate values (as it may have been in companies like Marks & Spencer), or, more trivially, as mere marketing and public relations (as in the now ubiquitous customer 'charters', industrial kite-marks and mission or vision statements)? In an operational context the distinction between leadership and management is less clear-cut. Empirical studies suggest that 'leaders' actually spend rather little time on vision and strategy; mostly they are coping with crises and engaging in comparatively routine managerial tasks. Indeed, vision and strategy often emerge from these apparently unvisionary and unstrategic tasks through a process of accretion. Similarly, 'managers', by their gradual but persistent maintenance or re-engineering of corporate systems, help to create organizational cultures which, in turn, shape vision and strategy. In practice, therefore, leadership and management are inextricably embroiled. The fact that leaders now devote more time and energy to 'visioning' may reflect the superficial relationship between vision and marketing rather than deeper links with corporate values. If higher education institutions fail to draw a clear distinction between leadership and management, they are not alone.

Theoretical perspectives: from traits to situational styles

Despite, or perhaps because of, such ambiguities, modern society remains fixated upon leading individuals. Reinforced by the news reporting of the contemporary media, there remains a strong focus on the talented and successful leaders (or, in contrast, the cataclysmic failures) in all walks of public life. Companies and organizations (universities increasingly are no exception) go to extraordinary lengths to appoint and retain leaders associated with strong performance, effectiveness being closely linked in mind, if not in fact, with the qualities of the person at the top (Engwall, 1999). Describing successful (and by implication, unsuccessful) leaders in terms of their personal qualities, or attributes, was one of the earliest approaches to theorizing leadership, although reviews of such research by Stodgill (1948) and Mann (1959) showed only inconsistent evidence of differences in the characteristics of leaders and followers. Nonetheless, the personality traits associated with leadership continue to fascinate, both in popular imaginations of successful leaders and in more modern works on the clusters of traits required of leaders in particular situations (see, for example, Miner, 1993).

In higher education, interest in the qualities brought to bear on academic leadership – interpersonal abilities such as being open, empathetic and compassionate to name but a few – remains evident, particularly in studies on the selection and training of leaders (Kaplowitz, 1986). Indeed, the importance of such elements in the understanding of leadership approach or style has been reinforced in more recent times by the emergence of gender as a perceived major influence on the way the leader's job is interpreted, although assertions about the importance of gendered leadership have to contend with the problem of isolating the impact of inherited gender traits from socially and culturally determined traits (Middlehurst, 1997).

From early trait theories of leadership, attention shifted to how leaders attempt to influence individuals and groups to pursue organizational goals. In this genre of the literature, various theorists have sought to identify those aspects of behaviour associated with effective leadership. Hence, in the 1950s and 1960s, there emerged a number of 'universal' theories which in effect postulated a 'one best way' approach to how the effective leader should operate. This school of thought probably reached its culmination in the 'managerial grid' created by Blake and Mouton (1969), with its four basic styles of management: team management, country club management, task management and impoverished management. These styles were mediated by two broad, but critical, dimensions: a concern for people and a concern for production. Although the managerial grid concept was further refined (see, for example, Blake and McCanse, 1991), the problem with such theories was the assumption that it is possible to associate certain leadership behaviours with effective leadership, whatever the situation. The failure to find such consistent relationships led to another strand of leadership theory in which researchers sought to identify the different situations in which leaders could be successful. This led to a massive proliferation of a sub-species of situational style theories of leadership. Two of the most influential have been Fiedler's (1967) least preferred co-worker (LPC) model and House's (1971) path–goal theory. These theories were essentially concerned with the quest to establish a satisfactory explanation of the (complex) relationship between situational variables, leadership behaviour and effectiveness.

In Fiedler's contingency model, for instance, leadership style is held to be related to the extent to which the situation enables the leader to exert influence over group members. Such influence is held to be dependent on three conditions: the leader–follower relationship; the task structure; and the leader's formal position of power. Depending on the situation (described by Fiedler as octants), leaders should opt for a relationship-oriented or task-oriented style of leadership. In House's path-goal theory, on the other hand, the motivational functions of the leader and making the personal pay-offs to workers for goal achievement are central. In one version of this theory (as developed by House and Mitchell, 1974), four behavioural styles are postulated: directive leadership, supportive leadership, participative leadership and achievement-oriented leadership. The leader's adoption of the most effective style is dependent on two broad sets of situational variables. These include, first, the environmental pressures and demands under which organizational members operate, and, second, the subordinates' personal characteristics (including their own perceptions of abilities and their relative autonomy in the workplace).

Such situational theories have been influential, focusing attention on the clusters of factors (not neglecting luck) which can make the difference between a leader's success (effectiveness) and failure (ineffectiveness). The problem has been the failure to demonstrate, through either tests or empirical observation, any clear or consistent relationship between leadership styles and situational variables, on the one hand, and leadership success and effectiveness, on the other. Such a quest is ambitious in the extreme, since inevitably leadership behaviours and situations at anything less than the abstract level are complicated by the complex interplay of structures, organizations, consciousness and action. Organizations are essentially open systems, influenced at least as much by what happens outside as inside the organization. Since situational style theories concentrate on leaders' actions in particular circumstances or contingencies, they have been heavily criticized because they assume that the leader merely reacts to events. The underlying assumption, in the extreme form of situational style theories at least, is that the leader is affected by the contingencies but can do relatively little to change them. The reality is, of course, that the contingencies of any organizational situation shift and change under a whirl of structural, institutional and cultural influences, yet situational style leadership theories concentrate on only one main dimension: the leader–follower relationship.

Transformational and transactional styles of leadership

Contextual approaches to leadership extend the insights provided by situational theories and emphasize that individual leaders' traits and leader–follower relationships will be heavily influenced by the nature of the organizational context. In contextual approaches the focus is less on leaders' behaviours than on how they adapt their styles and approaches to the circumstances facing the organization. However, what evidence is there that chief executives are able to modify their leadership style or approach in order to ensure appropriateness to the organizational context? Some indication is derived from those theorists who, building on Weber's original conception of charismatic leadership, have developed the concepts of transformational and transactional styles of leadership. These basic types were identified by Burns (1978) on the basis of a study of political leaders. Transactional leaders operate through a process essentially of exchange with their followers, whereas transformational leaders appeal to different instincts via more inspirational exhortations for effort and performance.

The two basic models identified by Burns were further developed by Bass and his research associates (Bass, 1985; Bass and Avolio, 1994). In the Bass versions, transactional and transformational approaches remain conceptually distinct, but are likely to be deployed by the same leader in different degrees according to the situation. In these schemata, transformational approaches embrace three related but distinct categorizations. The first, charisma, entails the capacity of the leader to inspire in subordinates various combinations of enthusiasm, belief, trust, loyalty, respect etc., which, importantly, are related to the leader's vision and mission. The second, individualized consideration, relates to the leader's capacity to see subordinates as individuals and to treat them in line with their particular capabilities and needs. The third element, intellectual stimulation, concerns the ability to focus attention on problem solving in line with the sets of beliefs, vision, etc. encapsulated in the leader's approach. The transactional approach, on the other hand, appeals to different instincts. In the Bass models it comprises at least two elements: contingent reward and management-by-exception. Contingent reward concerns the leader's expectations of the standard of work of subordinates and the rewards they can expect provided they meet the performance required. Management-by-exception is the expectation that subordinates perform to the expected and are left to get on with the task. Intervention by the leader is confined to taking action only when things go wrong, essentially by providing negative feedback.

It is evident that neither transformational nor transactional styles of leadership can be interpreted without reference to elements derived from previous theorizations of leadership, whether derived from the personal characteristics (traits) of the leader, the situation or the leader–follower relationship. However, it has been postulated that the two broad leadership styles – transformational and transactional – can be matched to the two broad organizational states – divergent and convergent (Burnes, 1996). When the organizational context is divergent, making existing goals and structures increasingly inappropriate, the leader's task is to challenge the status quo, encourage innovation and change: in short to adopt a transformational style of leadership. Conversely, when the context is convergent and the organization is broadly in line with the environment, the leader needs to optimize performance within existing structures and norms. In the convergent state a transactional approach to leadership is required. In these circumstances a transformational approach would be counter-productive, just as a transactional approach would be ineffective when the organizational state is divergent. We explore these ideas further in Chapter 7.

From context to organizational culture

Alongside these contrasting styles of leadership must be set differences in organizational cultures. From the cultural perspective the organization is not portrayed as though it exists in a value-free world. Instead, it is argued that organizations have cultures which incorporate particular combinations of values, norms, customs and practices (ways of behaving) which influence the way work is arranged and performed. The assumption is that cultures change over time and that they can be purposively managed and changed. This assumption has led to a whole swathe of literature describing and advocating cultural change and how to achieve it, most famously perhaps in Peters and Waterman's (1982) seven steps to excellence. In reality, of course, there is little agreement about the nature of culture and whether so-called 'strong' cultures are appropriate in all organizational contexts. Organizational goals are not always clear or uncontested (especially in universities), although implicit in much of the literature of corporate culturalism is an acceptance of instrumental compliance by employees with corporate values (Willmott, 1993: 541).

However, one argument in favour of incorporating a cultural perspective into the study of leadership is that it provides a better chance of unpacking the ways in which leaders' styles might be influenced by the nature of organizational culture and politics. Of course, in the setting of the university, there is nothing new about drawing attention to the organization as political bureaucracy (Baldridge, 1971) and few with any experience of working in universities would argue with the view that contest and competition, rather than collegiality and cooperation, mark much of the internal life of the academy. Indeed, in the path-breaking treatise on American university presidents by Cohen and March (1974), there is a persuasive rehearsal of precisely this argument. For Cohen and March, it is only through identifying and evaluating the ways in which university governance (management) operates that one can begin to understand the implications for leadership styles. In their metaphors of leadership (competitive market, administrative, collective bargaining, democratic, consensus, anarchy or some such combination) lies the general point that the particular model of the organization's characteristics dictates a presidential (leadership) style. And, conversely, as they express it: 'the appropriateness of the style . . . is determined by the adequacy of the model' (Cohen and March, 1974: 37). That is to say, the overall organizational context needs to be understood if we are to advance a convincing account of chief executives' leadership styles.

From theory towards practice

If this is so, then organizational scale is clearly important. Smaller organizations are unable to afford as sophisticated a division of managerial labour as large organizations; strategists must also be systems people. For example, in universities heads of department typically must combine academic and managerial roles in ways which vice-chancellors (who, in effect, have abandoned their own personal academic careers) do not. However, 'scale' cannot be assessed purely in quantitative terms. There are large organizations with 'small' – or personal and intimate – cultures. Universities, despite their rapid growth, may fall into this category. The few senior civil servants, management consultants and industrialists who have become vice-chancellors are struck by the lack of 'back-up', not only within their own offices but more widely in universities. Similarly, there are small-scale organizations which nevertheless have impersonal and bureaucratic organizational cultures.

History – or, better perhaps, maturity – is also important. Recently formed organizations are likely to exhibit transformational, symbolic and charismatic styles of leadership because their transactional and bureaucratic systems are immature. In contrast, organizations with strongly embedded systems and well established corporate memories are unlikely to respond well to these styles of leadership. But, of course, many organizations go through cycles of growth, stability, decline – and, possibly, renewal. This is certainly true of diurnal institutions such as universities. Their organizational cultures, and consequently styles of leadership and management, have to evolve. The leadership style appropriate for steady-state conditions would be much less effective in circumstances where radical re-engineering was required. Yet long-lasting organizations, which because of their longevity have the greatest need to evolve, tend to have developed embedded organizational cultures despite, in the case of higher education institutions, the persistence of personalized styles of leadership. The combination of bureaucratic management and personal leadership may help to explain why universities are so deeply affected by crises which would not greatly trouble similarly sized organizations.

General theories of leadership, therefore, cannot easily be applied to higher education, not least because these theories must now be radically adapted to reflect the new organizational environments which are emerging, and because higher education itself is passing through a period of profound transformation. It has become a truism to emphasize the (comparative) decline of large bureaucratic organizations, whether in the public or private sector (Drucker, 1993; Handy, 1994). Some caution must be exercised here. Delayering, out-sourcing and devolution of responsibilities have not necessarily led to a dilution of corporate power. Yet important changes are under way which cannot be discounted. Perhaps the most important is the erosion of 'bureaucratic' careers. Not only have large-scale management cadres been slimmed down; managers themselves must now follow non-sequential career paths. These changes appear to place greater emphasis on strategic and charismatic leadership styles. They also appear to endorse the weak management cultures which characterize many higher education institutions. However, again, caution must be exercised. Although it is tempting to draw parallels between the traditional patterns of university management and the more flexible and less hierarchical forms of management that are emerging in the new (post-industrial and post-modern?) economy, the similarity may be superficial. Perhaps a safer conclusion is that once-monolithic and rule-bound corporate cultures are dissolving into more open and intuitive organizational cultures. If this is so, functionalist and instrumentalist analyses of leadership are likely to be less effective than cultural, even phenomenological, accounts.

The evolution of the role of the vice-chancellor

The office of vice-chancellor, as the title suggests, began as a substitute for the chancellor. As such it was imbued from the start with both symbolic and procedural power – but power exercised in a substitute role. These two fundamental characteristics still remain in the age of chief executive vice-chancellors. First, the role has charismatic potential: internally because the vice-chancellorship is a high-status role and, therefore, vice-chancellors possess (and always have possessed) great symbolic power; and externally because they are the personal embodiment of their institutions. Second, the role is postulated on collective decision making, because vice-chancellors still take many decisions as substitutes, 'acting' no longer for the chancellor but as chairs of the senate or academic board, rather than in their executive capacity as heads of university administrations (and these 'acting' decisions often address more significant – and strategic – issues than 'executive' decisions which are more likely to be concerned with procedural matters).

Before Robbins

The first of the five stages in the post-war evolution of the role of the vice-chancellor covers the period from 1945 to 1963, the year in which the Robbins Report was published. It is now conventional to regard the 1950s as a decade of conservatism, sandwiched between the welfare-state reforms of the 1940s and the renewed radicalism of the 1960s. Whether or not this stereotype is a fair description of national life generally, it is certainly not true of higher education. First, these 18 years were a time of great development. In the immediate post-war years there was much discussion about the need to expand, and to reform, higher education, although this was overshadowed by more urgent efforts to develop a universal system of secondary education. The scale of pre-Robbins expansion was substantial. In the civic universities student numbers doubled and large-scale development of their estates was undertaken. All the pre-war red brick university colleges finally became fully fledged universities. The new green-field universities, conventionally (but misleadingly) associated with the Robbins expansion, were already planned.

Second, the idea that universities were part of a public system of education came to be firmly accepted, beginning with the rewriting of the University Grants Committee's (UGC's) terms of reference to include a duty to serve the needs of the country in 1946 and culminating with the creation of the Department for Education and Science to which responsibility for universities was transferred from the Treasury in 1963. Third, the foundations of the future binary system were laid. The need to enhance higher technological education was emphasized in the post-war Percy and Barlow reports, and eight technical colleges were designated as colleges of advanced technology (CATs) and directly funded by the Ministry of Education following the 1956 White Paper. Finally, the hearts-and-minds battle for expansion, to be achieved following Robbins, was largely won in the 1950s. The fury of the 'more means worse' brigade was evidence not of their influence but of their defensiveness.

Against this background of rapid change the role of the vice-chancellor was far from static – or passive. The title of the Rede Lecture given at Cambridge in 1963 by Sir Douglas Logan, for many years Principal (then, effectively, vice-chancellor) of the University of London, was 'Universities: the years of challenge' (Logan, 1963). It is true that many post-war vice-chancellors did not undertake the managerial tasks which fill the days of their successors two generations later. The word itself – management – was rarely used. The contemporary term was 'administration', in which the key figures were not the vice-chancellor but the bursar, who looked after the money, and the registrar, who looked after almost everything else. The one area of administration which many vice-chancellors reserved to themselves was staff appointments, particularly of senior staff and especially of professors. The habits of this post-war period lingered on into later decades. One of the authors recalls visiting the university of the then chairman of the Committee of Vice-Chancellors and Principals in 1971 as a member of the team that had produced the first issue of *The Times Higher Education Supplement*, only to be told by the vice-chancellor that this new newspaper was 'something for the registry'.

Nevertheless, vice-chancellors were powerful figures in the terms outlined at the beginning of this section on the evolution of the role. They exercised a charismatic authority not unlike that of headmasters of public schools; indeed, it was far from unusual for public school headmasters to become vice-chancellors and vice versa, a transfer market that is inconceivable today. They exercised this authority through their status within the institution, presiding on ceremonial and other 'dignified' occasions, and outside it through elite local connections and national networks. Their influence over the (admittedly, much simpler) academic business of the university was assured by chairing the senate and other key committees. If they paid little attention to managerial tasks, it was because such tasks were essentially procedural, even trivial. Public funding had removed the uncertainties of the past when universities depended on student fees and corporate and civic sponsorship, but the autonomy of the universities still went unchallenged. As a result, the 'internal' management of people, property and money was uncomplicated and the management of 'external' relationships was still embryonic. The vice-chancellors of this period were certainly authoritative figures and even visionaries, although in a typically understated English way. They sometimes pre-figured (as in the case of the Morris brothers at Leeds and Bristol) the institution-builders of the next decade (Hetherington, 1954; Shimmin, 1954; Duff, 1959).

Institution-builders

The second period, the short decade from the Robbins report in 1963 to the onset of student revolt in 1967–8, saw an intensification, and culmination, of the trends of the 1960s. Three were particularly significant. The first was the establishment of the new universities. Although, as has already been pointed out, they had been planned before Robbins and before Sussex had actually admitted its first students, they have become indelibly associated with the 1960s. The spatial, as well as academic, landscape of British higher education was transformed by their growth. The traditional intimacy of the college, to which many universities had clung through the 1940s and 1950s despite the expansion of student numbers, was superseded by a new future-oriented sense of community, the campus. Nor was this development confined to the new universities actually founded during the 1960s; several of the former colleges of advanced technology (CATs), redesignated as technological universities following Robbins, also moved to new-build campuses and many of the civic and red brick universities accelerated and enlarged the building programmes of the 1950s, creating new university precincts in our Victorian cities. This physical transformation was accompanied by – indeed, represented – academic innovation. New maps of learning, and interdisciplinary structures, were designed (Beloff, 1968; Perkin, 1969).

The second, of course, was the much increased rate of expansion. Conventionally this has been attributed to Robbins. More accurately, it reflected the sea-change that came over British society during the 1960s. The famous

Robbins principle simply codified an emergent social principle, that higher education should be available to the able and the willing regardless of class (and, increasingly, gender too). The result of the Robbins principle was that the British system crossed a crucial threshold not so much between elite and mass higher education, which did not really happen until the 1980s, but between exclusivity and openness. The third was the articulation of an explicit binary system and the designation of the polytechnics. The idea that higher education was divided into universities and the 'other' was hardly new; what was new was the emergence of a dynamic structure within which a critical mass of rival institutions was able to develop. So, during the 1960s, British higher education underwent a process of both quantitative change, the establishment of new institutions and expansion of student numbers, which was immediately obvious, and qualitative change in terms of social positioning and academic orientation, the full consequences of which only emerged much later.

For vice-chancellors the dominant motifs were institution-building and managerial complexity. For the first time for many decades, perhaps ever, a significant number of vice-chancellors were able to play a key role in designing new institutions or, in the case of the ex-CATs, virtually new institutions. What had previously been an isolated experience, as with the foundation of Keele in the 1940s, now became general. And it happened almost instantly. In the past new university foundations had often had to survive decades of precarious life before they had been able to overcome their marginality; the new universities of the 1960s were built according to master plans which were largely completed in a few years, and their place in the mainstream of higher education was not only acknowledged but celebrated. The second motif, growing managerial complexity, was more muted. In the short run it was registrars, not vice-chancellors, who mobilized rapidly professionalizing administrations to manage the new roles which universities acquired as a result of expansion. Vice-chancellors typically devoted their energies to the normative and conceptual challenges of institution-building, leaving the messy details to be addressed by others. Some reflected at book length on these challenges (Sloman, 1963; Caine, 1969; Carter, 1980); others in essays and lectures (Bowden, 1966; Mansfield Cooper, 1966; Ashby, 1968; Stewart, 1968; Dainton, 1981).

The third motif of the 1960s, no larger than a man's hand in that decade, was that the vice-chancellors' estate had been enlarged. Although few vice-chancellors contemplated that the directors of the newly established polytechnics would one day join their ranks, their potential impact was very significant – in three senses. First, the polytechnics had a critical mass which previous non-university institutions such as the CATs had never acquired. This meant that, if and when a unified university was created, the polytechnic directors could not simply be co-opted as cadet members of the vice-chancellors' club. They were too numerous. Second, the polytechnics had been established as alternative institutions which were designed consciously to develop novel forms of higher education. Although the temptations of 'academic drift' were, are and always will be strong, the circumstances in which the polytechnics were established made it inevitable that rivalrous relationships would persist. Finally, as local authority institutions, the polytechnics brought into higher education different traditions of leadership and management. Briefly, polytechnic directors were more likely to see their role as that of an old-fashioned college principal with subordinate staff rather than as an academic *primus inter pares*, and as a hands-on manager who headed the institution's administration (largely because their institutions were subject to a range of external controls which did not apply to traditional universities but which had to be managed). Equally, as local authority employees they lacked the social charisma and elite connections traditionally enjoyed by vice-chancellors.

The end of innocence

The third period in the evolution of the role of vice-chancellor stretched from the late 1960s, when the bright and confident dreams of the first half of that decade were shattered first by student revolt and then by the first onset of austerity, to 1979 when the election of a Conservative government under Margaret Thatcher heralded a new iron age. The key event was the financial retrenchment of the mid-1970s following the oil shock, the two miners' strikes, escalating inflation and eventually the intervention of the International Monetary Fund to restore the economy's equilibrium. 'The party's over', in the famous phrase of Anthony Crosland, ironically the prophet of welfare-state social democracy as well as the architect of the polytechnics. For universities it had two immediate effects. The first was the direct loss of funding. Not only was the developmental momentum of the previous decade brought to a halt, but many of British higher education's future flaws can also be traced back to the mid-1970s: the failure to articulate and evaluate options, the difficulty in explaining, justifying and accounting for its activities and achievements, the weaknesses in control systems. The second was that retrenchment simultaneously fuelled demands for greater external accountability (it was now essential to achieve the best possible value from limited resources) and eroded the universities' limited capacity for planning (planning-for-scarcity succeeded planning-for-plenty).

However, the 1970s were not only a decade of crisis. They were also the time when the polytechnics became firmly established (while retrenchment ruled out any early move into the university sector). The peculiar binary structure of British higher education, half-hierarchical and half-rivalrous, first emerged in the 1970s. That was also the decade when the research council system became established not simply as a source of project funding but as a different kind of alternative to the UGC system. Both characteristics have not only persisted but strengthened over the subsequent quarter-century. The 'diversity' of modern British higher education is a direct descendant of that binary structure, despite the formal establishment of a unified university system; and the emphasis on separately steered research can also be dated back to the 1970s. There were also moments of light, the most famous of which was the survival against all the odds of Britain's most distinctive higher education institution, The Open University.

Thatcherism

In higher education, as in most areas of national life, the Thatcher period (1979–90) has taken on a mythic quality – retrospectively. Depending on political tastes, it was either the time when higher education was dragged kicking and screaming into the modern world or the time when universities came under sustained ideological assault (Kogan and Kogan, 1983). However, expediency characterized the new government's approach to higher education as much as ideology (Scott, 1989). In its first years its approach was tentative. The only significant changes were the intensification of the policy of charging overseas students differential fees (which had been begun by a Labour government in the 1960s), by moving towards so-called 'full-cost' fees, and the regularisation of the polytechnics' role as an alternative sector (again, of course, initially a Labour policy), by establishing the National Advisory Body (NAB) for local authority – and, later, public sector – higher education. Only two years later, after Margaret Thatcher had overborne the objections of her one-nation Tory Cabinet colleagues (the so-called 'wets'), was she able to begin to make the large-scale cuts in public expenditure demanded by the monetarist economic policies now being pursued by her government.

For the universities the decisive break came in 1981 when the UGC was required to impose substantial cuts in their budgets. Although the '1981 cuts' have subsequently acquired great symbolic significance, amounting almost to an expulsion from Eden, they were driven by expenditure, not educational policies. Indeed, the assault on the welfare state that developed in the later Thatcher period was caused as much by the pragmatic need to force the public sector to cut its cloth to match its reduced income as by the unfolding of an inexorable ideological project. There were, of course, episodes of pure ideology: on the government's side the ultimately unsuccessful attempt to abolish the Social Science Research Council (now the Economic and Social Research Council) *pour encourager* the social scientists; and on higher education's side the University of Oxford's very public refusal to award the Prime Minister an honorary degree. But these were also exceptional episodes. The important structural changes, such as first the 'turning' of the UGC into a state planning agency and its eventual abolition and the incorporation of the polytechnics as free-standing institutions, were brought about by the need to make pragmatic adjustments to the system.

The importance of these changes can also easily be exaggerated. The transformation of the UGC from a buffer between universities and the state into a planning agency had been begun by Labour in 1946 when the committee's terms of reference were modified, advanced by a Conservative government's decision to make the committee responsible to the newly established Department of Education and Science in the early 1960s, given a further twist later in that decade when, under a re-elected Labour government, the committee first offered formal 'guidance' to the universities, and intensified by the growth in student numbers and funding turbulence during the 1970s. Similarly, the 'nationalization' of the polytechnics had been a long drawn out policy, dating back arguably before the birth of the polytechnics to the decision to establish the CATs as national institutions in 1956. The decision to create the polytechnics as quasi-national institutions, of course, had been taken by Anthony Crosland. The process that led to the establishment of the NAB and later to the incorporation of the polytechnics in 1987 had been begun in the dying days of the previous Labour government. So a strong case can be made that both these fundamental structural changes were, in effect, bi-partisan policies which owed much more to the *longue durée* of bureaucratic adjustment to higher education's changing position in society than to political preferences or ideological projects. This case is made more convincing by the fact that the greatest change of all during the Thatcher period, which reached its climax under her successor John Major, the more than doubling of student numbers and the belated creation of a mass system of higher education, happened by stealth, even by default.

Nevertheless the evolution of the role of the vice-chancellors was rapid during the Thatcher period. First, vice-chancellors had to become skilled in crisis management. As a result of the UGC's decision to be highly selective in its distribution of the much reduced grant in 1981, several universities were faced with the need for fundamental restructuring. The 'headline' example was Salford University under the leadership of its recently appointed vice-chancellor John Ashworth, but other hard-hit universities engaged in even more radical restructuring. Interestingly, in the light of the widely held prejudice that universities were unmanageable and vice-chancellors indecisive, only one institution, the then University College Cardiff, came close to floundering despite the scale of the disinvestment in higher education during this period. Second, vice-chancellors had to take on more politicized roles. Although a robust fight-back against the Thatcher government's higher education policies failed to develop, vice-chancellors did come to recognize that the battle for hearts and minds was increasingly important. The essentially defensive public relations strategies first developed in the late 1960s and early 1970s to limit the damage caused by student revolt were brushed off and given a much more positive spin. The contemporary emphasis on 'marketing' in higher education can be traced by the belief first engendered in the Thatcher period that universities could no longer rely on their elite connections. However, vice-chancellors proved to be less successful as political street-fighters than institutional managers (again, contrary to standard perceptions).

Third, vice-chancellors had to learn new skills to cope with an increasingly intrusive policy environment. The trickle of letters from the UGC in the 1960s, and the municipal routines of administration in the non-university sector, became a flood as first the UGC and NAB and later their successors, the Universities Funding Council (UFC) and Polytechnics and Colleges Funding Council (PCFC), developed new selective initiatives, devised new funding methodologies and demanded new information. The first research assessment (RAE) was undertaken by the UGC in its dying days. The seeds of teaching quality assessment, now subject reviews, were also sown when the Committee of Vice-Chancellors and Principals (CVCP) established its Academic Audit Unit, which later became the Higher Education Quality Council (HEQC) and then the Quality Assurance Agency (QAA). A 'returns' culture developed. Vice-chancellors began to spend more and more of their time making 'returns' to various agencies – responding to consultation exercises, providing data, making bids. Fourth, vice-chancellors in the Thatcher period first had to engage seriously with the heterogeneity of the system. The success of the polytechnics, which was reflected in faster student growth and rewarded by their liberation from local government (and the establishment of parallel national agencies in the shape of the NAB and PCFC), created a dynamic and rivalrous two-sector system. Furthermore, the overall expansion of higher education had transformed, and diversified, its social base. Increasing selectivity also contributed to the heterogeneity of the system. The pressure grew for a fundamental re-evaluation of the roles and purposes of higher education, which led a decade later to the Dearing Report. But, on the whole, vice-chancellors proved to be much more adept at managing the 'returns' culture than at fundamental rethinking.

The Jarratt effect

The 1980s were also bisected by the only post-war policy episode which directly touched the role of the vice-chancellor, the Jarratt Report on university efficiency. In many respects Jarratt built on the evolutionary changes of the 1970s rather than the revolutionary events of the 1980s luridly associated with Thatcherism (although the report was one in a line of 'efficiency reviews' conducted by Lord Rayner, then chairman of Marks & Spencer). The many other recommendations made by Jarratt – for example, for joint council/senate planning committees – are now largely forgotten, implemented or unimplemented. All that has endured is the report's central assertion that vice-chancellors should be regarded as the chief executives of their institutions. In one sense this was a trite assertion; most vice-chancellors had always been described as 'chief academic and administrative officers'. In another sense (and this is why it is remembered, not without controversy, even today), it aimed to produce a profound shift in the organizational culture of universities. To registrars (and the few surviving independent bursars) the Jarratt message was that vice-chancellors were in charge; any idea that the vice-chancellor should be regarded as the (admittedly executive) chairman and the registrar as the chief executive officer was firmly squashed. This was significant because a small group of registrars had been moving in that direction since the late 1960s, assisted by the fact that their vice-chancellors had failed to recognize the potential for accumulating bureaucratic power by managing the increasingly complex processes of university administration. This movement was now curtailed, or almost, because the dualism between 'dignified' vice-chancellor and 'efficient' behind-the-scenes manager (now more likely to be the finance director than the registrar) has never been completely suppressed.

To senior academics who guarded the 'donnish dominion' the message of Jarratt was that, in future, the authority of vice-chancellors should be rooted in managerial competence rather than collegial charisma. Vice-chancellors should wield power directly as chief executives rather than indirectly in substitute roles – for example, on behalf of the senate representing the academic community. It is this aspect of Jarratt that has caused the most enduring controversy and been castigated as 'managerialism'. However, the former aspect was perhaps more important. The repositioning of the vice-chancellor at the centre of institutional management has gone largely uncontested. But its evident correctness today should not disguise its novelty 30 years ago. This repositioning of the vice-chancellor has led to the emergence of senior management teams and the re-engineering of institutional administrations. In contrast, the ability of the vice-chancellor to prevail by sheer managerial will over the objections of the academic community, without resorting to older forms of charismatic and symbolic authority, has remained constrained. When 'managerial' power (in this second sense) has been exercised, it has rarely been for long or effectively. Sometimes it has contained the seeds of its own (self) destruction; often it has been negated by non-compliance which is difficult to punish in a low (or non-) sanctions institution like a university.

The key drivers behind the Jarratt revolution in university management are easy to identify. The first was expansion, the second complexity and the third austerity. All three were tightly articulated. The expansion of higher education meant that universities were now much larger (and expenditure on higher education has grown, if not in step, substantially). The academic, financial and personnel systems which had once been able to cope, because in smaller institutions there was more scope for personalized solutions and interventions, were now exposed as inadequate. Universities had also become more complex institutions; a key element of this complexity was the growth in externally funded research. Again administrative systems that relied crucially on tacit knowledge and convention were no longer suitable. But the elaboration of management was costly – and at a time when the free-and-easy growth in university budgets characteristic of the 1960s was coming to an end and even being reversed. However, tighter management was also needed to make the operation of universities more efficient – in order to secure the maximum academic advantage from the available resources and also to reassure sceptical funders about their competence. The Jarratt solution was to import the best business practice into higher education. More specifically, the solution to the pressures of growth, complexity and austerity was to transform vice-chancellors into chief executives.

The 1990s

The fifth and final period began with the creation of a unified university system in 1992, when the binary policy was finally abandoned and the polytechnics became universities, and has continued up to the present. The decision to break with the binary structure was both a shock, because the decision itself appears to have been off-hand, and inevitable, because it was consistent with the longer-term trajectory of the polytechnics. But the effects of this move towards a more unified (and, therefore, more diverse) higher education system were almost immediately muffled by the onset of 'consolidation', the decision to end the period of uncontrolled growth in student numbers that had characterized the late 1980s and early 1990s. For the first time since 1945, certainly since 1960, serious questions were asked about the desirability of further growth in higher education. Instead institutions were faced with a new set of policy constraints, all with their own acronyms such as MASNs (maximum aggregate student numbers).

As a result, the long-term consequences of the (irreversible) abandonment of the binary system and the (temporary?) abandonment of a growth culture remain unclear. Has the hegemony of the university as the only valid model for mature institution of higher education been confirmed, or have universities been irreversibly dumbed down? National policy has oscillated confusingly between these two possibilities. At times the attention has shifted to further education as the focus for future growth, while higher education has been (tentatively and implicitly) allocated a more conservative role; at other times policies such as the RAE and the selective relaxation of MASNs (disguised as successful bids for additional student numbers) appear to have been based on the belief that dumbing down was a real threat. The increasing emphasis on 'quality' also tends to support this thesis. The implications of the end of growth, too, have yet to be properly digested. Is it a pause, or the start of a larger transformation of the higher education system in which universities have a privileged position into a lifelong-learning culture characterized by shifting alliances among a heterogeneous set of 'knowledge' institutions? The failure of the Dearing Report to ignite the debate about the future of higher education reflected these continuing uncertainties.

The 1990s were dominated by two important developments. The first has already been mentioned: the rise of the quality assurance 'industry'. Universities are now preoccupied by their 'scores' in teaching quality assessment (TQA) and subject reviews and their success in achieving formal academic recognition, professional accreditation and corporate kitemarks.

The reasons for this shift from autonomy to accountability are complex. Part of the reason certainly is fear of dumbing down, or, more positively, the desire to maintain traditional high academic standards; part is the more intense interaction between 'producers' and 'users' in an age when both skills and knowledge are becoming highly contextualized; part is the growth of the 'audit society', in which trust is conditional rather than blind (the two latter reasons were discussed in Chapter 1). The second development is the reimposition of tuition fees by the newly elected Labour government in the wake of the Dearing Report. There were two main reasons for this change. First, 'free' higher education had come to be seen as a relic of the welfare state, an anachronism in the new age of enterprise and also in a mass higher education system. Second, it seemed to be the only way to solve the recurrent funding crises that had beset higher education for more than two decades.

The impact of these uncertainties and developments on the role of the vice-chancellor has been curious. Of course, the intensity of the bureaucratic interactions between universities and what are now called stakeholders has increased once again – in two areas in particular. The first is quality management, which has now become one of the key corporate responsibilities of higher education institutions. This renewed emphasis on academic affairs, admittedly within a highly bureaucratic framework, has led to a significant rebalancing of the role of the vice-chancellors (and may also help to explain the reversion to more 'academic' vice-chancellors). The second is what has been called initiativitis, the burgeoning 'bidding' culture that has been produced, specifically, by the proliferation of special programmes and, more generally, by a recasting of the relationship between state and higher education into a customer–contractor mould. Financial management, of course, remain a dominant preoccupation – but less so perhaps in the more stable funding environment produced by 'consolidation'. It is perhaps significant that the (ostensible) causes of the most recent higher education 'crisis', the Thames Valley University affair, were academic rather than financial.

However, there is another dimension in the evolution of the role of the vice-chancellor which has received much less attention. Uncertainties, whether about funding or about fundamental purposes, are no longer regarded as aberrations, anomalies that must be rectified. Instead they are now accepted. In a curious sense universities are now much freer to develop their own institutional profiles – and even institutional personalities. Here vice-chancellors play a key role, confusingly composed of traditional forms of symbolic power and innovative forms of marketing skill. The growing emphasis on mission and vision statements, therefore, is not simply further evidence of the pressure on higher education to mimic alien corporate practices. Instead, it reflects the larger uncertainties – which are also opportunities – that are the condition of modern universities, and also the growing significance attached to symbolic acts in a sound-bite political economy and postmodern culture.

Conclusions

This chapter has reviewed the applicability of general theories about leadership to the evolution of the role of the vice-chancellor. Our conclusion is that, although interesting and even intriguing, these theories can only be illuminating if they are firmly situated in the context of higher education. They suffer from two weaknesses. The first, which can only be remedied by future research, is they have been developed with other environments in mind (especially the business sector and, within that sector, large rather than small companies). With a few highly creditable exceptions the literature of leadership does not address higher education. However, our argument is not that higher education is an exceptional arena in which the general rules do not apply; it is that generalized accounts must be sensitive to the particular contexts to which they are applied. This leads on to the second weakness. Most theories of leadership are conceptual frameworks which are not well grounded in empirical research. So all are true – and simultaneously misleading. All vice-chancellors have to transact as they struggle to transform; all, whether they like it or not, possess symbolic power and charisma, while at the same time being deeply embroiled in routine bureaucratic tasks. But, more seriously, our research suggests that serious mismatches exist between self-perceptions of roles (as reported in interview data) and objective descriptions of these roles (as recorded in observing what vice-chancellors actually do). The most common is that vice-chancellors define their role as predominantly strategic while spending most of their time on routine management.

The second part of this chapter has attempted to review the development of the role of vice-chancellor not in theoretical but in historical terms. A historical account does succeed in identifying broad trajectories, such as the growing involvement of the vice-chancellor in managing (and often taking very personal responsibility for) the intense interaction between higher education and its stakeholders. But such an account also exposes the continuities and regressions, ambiguities and uncertainties which still characterize the role. This is equally, arguably more, important. However great the weight of analysis and/or research that is applied to the role, it remains highly individualistic, even idiosyncratic. There are many ways of succeeding (and failing) and little point in attempting to determine, in a non-specific sense, their relative importance. The determining factor remains a complex articulation between the person, the institution, the detailed tasks, the particular situation and the enveloping environment. A historical account is perhaps able to illuminate these subtleties in ways which purely theoretical accounts cannot.

3

Career Paths: Patterns of Continuity and Change

The historical account of university leadership developed in the previous chapter identified close ties between the development of higher education and expectations about the role of vice-chancellors. The argument was that during the post-war period their role underwent progressive transformation. Before the 1960s vice-chancellors, as today, were responsible for the activities of their individual institutions, but they played a largely symbolic or presiding role postulated on collective decision making. Over successive decades, however, vice-chancellors became much more involved in the core management/administrative functions of the university, no longer merely 'substitutes' for the chancellor or even leading academics acting in their capacity as chairs of senate/academic board, but chief executives performing a role not dissimilar to that of their counterparts in the private sector. Reflecting these changes, universities now go to great lengths to appoint and retain the executive leader. Whereas in the 1970s it was still not unusual for the successor to an outgoing vice-chancellor to be appointed without even advertising publicly, universities will now routinely engage executive recruitment consultants to assist in the preparation of elaborate job and person specifications and act as 'headhunters' dedicated to scouring the global market for suitably qualified and experienced candidates. As an article in *The Times Higher Education Supplement* explained, headhunting has 'exploded' in higher education and a £35,000 retainer to the recruitment consultants 'gets you a new v-c' (*THES*, 30 July 1999).

Over the past few decades, then, both expectations of the role and the processes of selection of vice-chancellors have changed substantially. We explore and assess the actual practice of leadership in the light of the shift towards the chief executive model of leadership in subsequent chapters. In this chapter, however, we are more concerned with changing patterns in the characteristics of the individuals who actually occupy the top posts in university leadership. We focus specifically on vice-chancellors' career paths and ask a series of questions about the attributes of those who become the vice-chancellors. If expectations of the role of the vice-chancellor have changed, what evidence is there that there have been any corresponding changes in career preparation and professional development during the period since 1960? Are universities now managed by an emerging cadre of professional executive leaders whose career paths are more diverse than in previous generations? From which recruitment grounds are vice-chancellors typically drawn? And what evidence is there to suggest that the recruitment patterns of those heading old (pre-1992) universities are different from the leaders of new institutions?

To answer these questions we explore extensive data on the educational, career and other related attributes of vice-chancellors appointed to university leadership since the 1960s. Briefly, these comprise 341 separate 'cases' arranged in two separate but linked databases containing biographical information on all vice-chancellors appointed (details of our methodology are included in the appendix). These data provide a comprehensive longitudinal view of the typical 'avenues of mobility' to the top university job. The focus on individuals enables us to investigate in some detail a key dimension of the broader hypothesis explored in this book: that a new model of executive leader has emerged in post-war British higher education. If this is so, then it is reasonable to expect evidence of some major changes in the make-up and career experiences of the leaders of Britain's increasingly diverse collection of universities and academic communities. The assumption behind this facet of our study and those of previous generations of vice-chancellors and their overseas equivalents is that some clues to the nature of the university and the role of the executive leader can be derived from an understanding of vice-chancellors' careers (Cohen and March, 1974).

Benchmarks: earlier generations of vice-chancellors

'The leaders of science and learning', as Guttsman once referred to vice-chancellors, have traditionally been treated by sociologists and social historians as one of the key occupational elites in British society (Guttsman, 1963; see also Halsey and Trow, 1971; Giddens, 1974; Wakeford and Wakeford, 1974; Perkin, 1978–9). This literature provides some important benchmarks about the personal characteristics and career routes of vice-chancellors of the Robbins era. These were 'mature family men', typically in their mid- to late-fifties, drawn from white, middle-class backgrounds, whose ascent to the top of the university hierarchy was built on success in the meritocratic and competitive milieu of compulsory and post-compulsory education (Szreter, 1968). As a group they were more diverse in terms of backgrounds than members of comparable organizational elites (Rubinstein, 1987), but insofar as vice-chancellors were privileged by any form of social advantage it was through educational and/or career experience at Oxford or Cambridge. Estimates of 'Oxbridge' influence on subsequent career progression and appointment as vice-chancellor vary slightly according to the categorizations of experience employed and the method of classifying universities. Szreter's snapshot study of members of the CVCP in 1966–7 indicates that if one includes all vice-chancellors who at some point in their careers had 'sojourned' there, then 66 per cent had previous Oxbridge experience. This increased to 76 per cent if the heads of the then technological universities were excluded.

Szreter's estimates concur broadly with the findings of Collison and Millen's (1969) study. They found that in the 1960s Oxbridge remained the 'principal source of vice-chancellors', with 59 per cent of the 1967 cohort having been undergraduates at one of these two institutions. This proportion had declined only slightly from the pre-war era. Using 1935 as a baseline, the same authors found that 66 per cent of vice-chancellors in post in that year (a much smaller group of course) had previously been undergraduates at Oxbridge. Most of these men – even in the 1960s the appointment of women as vice-chancellors was still a long way off – were predominantly graduates in the arts. Although arts backgrounds had declined slightly in importance since the 1930s, mounting post-war concern with the nation's science and technology was reflected in an increase in vice-chancellors with science backgrounds from 19 per cent in 1935 to 41 per cent by 1967 (Collison and Millen, 1969). Even so, whether from arts or science backgrounds, the vast majority of vice-chancellors of the 1960s, like their pre-war forbears, had risen to the post after successive promotions in academia. The dominant career line was academic teaching and/or research. Non-academic routes, measured by non-university experience, were conspicuous by their absence.

Szreter reminds us that those from purely academic routes may, nevertheless, have gained some familiarity with the administrative problems of the university along the way. Most vice-chancellors had previously held professorships or senior Oxbridge posts (especially deputy vice-chancellorships) and would not have been totally immune from such concerns. Some also had wartime experiences which would have increased the chances of a broader social experience than those arriving in the vice-chancellorship by the purely academic route. But, taken as a whole, vice-chancellors of the 1960s had arrived in their posts after a series of similar, mainly academic, experiences and career filters. Vice-chancellorships were essentially the pinnacles of successful academic careers involving a series of academic promotions and long-term socialization as undergraduate, postgraduate and professional scholar in the practices and ways of thinking associated with the academy. Scholarly attributes rather than formal university 'administrative' experience, even less non-university experience, were those most valued across a system still imbued with a faith in the dominion of the don.

By the end of the 1960s, the changes associated with the post-Robbins period were beginning to gather momentum – the creation of the polytechnics, the technological universities and the new universities, as well as the general expansion of student numbers were all unleashed during this period. Yet for the most part universities still operated within traditional academic paradigms. As a consequence, selection procedures continued to reproduce what was familiar and safe: vice-chancellors as custodians not just of established institutional ethos, but of a more broadly defined set of academic values derived from long socialization in a traditional academic milieu. In a caveat to this essentially conservative portrait of typical routes to the vice-chancellorship, Szreter speculated that the appointment in 1967–8 of a distinguished career diplomat to the leadership of a large red brick university, in a reversal of its established tradition, might be the portent of a more extensive challenge to the donnish dominion in future years (Szreter, 1968: 40). It is to this question and an assessment of the broader impact of subsequent changes in the structure and politics of British higher education on the careers and experiences of those appointed to the vice-chancellorships that we now turn. The aim is to establish whether there have been any fundamental changes since the 1960s to what Giddens terms the dominant 'channels' through which recruitment to the vice-chancellorship takes place.

Age and period of appointment

The broader historical thesis about the shift towards a chief executive model of leadership in higher education has implications for the age and period of appointment at the top of the higher education hierarchy. Instead of being seen primarily as a prestigious 'end-of-career' post – the pinnacle of career progression – it would not be unreasonable to expect the chief executive model to attract somewhat younger candidates appointed because of their managerial and/or leadership expertise and experience. Recruitment specialists argue, not unreasonably, that as organizations universities are in different stages of development and their leadership requirements vary according to stage and circumstances. The theory is that appointments should be tailored to particular briefs. These can be extreme, as in the crisis-torn examples of Huddersfield, Southampton and Thames Valley, when for a variety of reasons the institution has been navigated into deeply troubled waters (*THES*, 30 July 1999). Even in less extreme circumstances, analysis of recent job advertisements for vice-chancellors reveals a quest by appointing committees to find a candidate able to match highly specified attributes rather than just a generalized experience acquired by virtue of a long academic career. Two recent examples, both for vice-chancellorships in prestigious old universities, illustrate the point:

> Candidates must be able to demonstrate successful experience of leadership and management of organisational change. In this regard it is vital that the next Vice-Chancellor and Warden possesses the capacity to innovate and to think imaginatively in strategic terms whilst at the same time demonstrating a clear commitment to the ethos of the University.
>
> (University of Durham, 1997)

Figure 3.1   Age at appointment by type of institution by decade

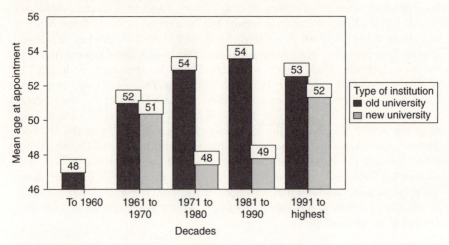

In seeking its next Vice-Chancellor the University is seeking to appoint an individual of exceptional calibre to provide academic and executive leadership . . . The University is a complex organisation . . . It therefore requires a first class Chief Executive with skills in financial management and in income generation, able to guide the organisation in an uncertain environment.

(University of East Anglia, 1997)

This specificity of job and person requirements has been reflected in pay and pensions packages. One survey reported that by 1993 six-figure packages were becoming commonplace among UK vice-chancellors, with 28 universities declaring remuneration of more than £100,000 and a further 15 more than £90,000. Although these figures were lower than comparable private-sector rewards, various commentators noted that the trend was upward (*THES*, 9 February 1996).

Despite these trends, there is no substantial evidence in our historical survey of a shift away from the long-established pattern of prestigious end-of-career appointments towards the recruitment of significantly younger candidates. Certainly our data did not reveal any distinct longitudinal trend in age of appointment decreasing over time. The average age at appointment for those in our study was 52 years (with a range of 27 years, the youngest being 38 and the oldest 65). Vice-chancellors of 'old' universities tend to be older on appointment than their 'new' university counterparts (an average age of 53 in the old compared to 50 in the new). Figure 3.1 shows the consistency over these decades together with the differences between types of institution.

However, average age at appointment does not reflect accurately recruitment patterns in the two sub-sectors of higher education over the decades.

Table 3.1 Longitudinal recruitment patterns of age at appointment by type of institution

	1950s	1960s		1970s		1980s		1990s	
Age	*OU*	*OU*	*NU*	*OU*	*NU*	*OU*	*NU*	*OU*	*NU*
50 or under (%)	67	38	42	25	79	19	63	22	30
51–55 (%)	28	39	35	42	21	34	29	52	55
56–65 (%)	6	23	23	34	0	48	9	26	15
Total (*n*)	18	56	26	53	19	65	35	46	20

Key: OU, old universities; NU, new universities.

To obtain greater insight, we have examined recruitment ages per decade by institutional categories. Table 3.1 reveals that, far from decreasing, the age of appointment in old universities has actually been higher in the 1970s, 1980s and 1990s than the 1950s and 1960s. In the new universities age at recruitment did decline in the 1970s and 1980s, but unexpectedly subsequently rose again in the 1990s. For this sub-sector, the lowest age range (50 or under) accounts for the greatest proportion of vice-chancellors in every decade apart from the 1990s.

What evidence, then, is there to support the notion that higher education has copied the private-sector practice of relatively short-term chief executive style appointments associated with highly specified briefs? If this has indeed been the case we might expect to find evidence of long-term decline in the length of tenure associated with the top leadership job. Taking the period since 1960, vice-chancellors stayed at the helm for an average of 9 years in both the old and new university sectors (9.1 years for old universities and 8.9 years for new). Before the 1960s, old university vice-chancellors typically held office between 11 and 16 years. Over subsequent decades the average period in office declined gradually, from 16 years in the 1950s to 11 years in the 1960s, eight years in the 1970s and seven years in the Thatcher era of the 1980s. By the 1990s average period in office was less than five years (although this figure may be misleading because it includes many still serving vice-chancellors).

A similar decrease in period of office has occurred in the new university sub-sector. From ten years in the 1960s and 1970s, the average period in office declined to seven and four years respectively in the 1980s and 1990s. The evidence on this is quite clear: periods in office are getting shorter in both old and new sectors. There is some support in these statistics, then, for a shift towards the more modern business practice of appointing chief executives for shorter (sometimes fixed) terms, typically of five years (Sarch, 1997: 31). Paradoxically, evidence from recruitment specialists dealing in the vice-chancellor labour 'market' is less clear. Those interviewed claimed that despite the increasing specificity of task allocated to incoming vice-chancellors, few universities had followed private-sector practice and appointed on fixed-term contracts. This largely anecdotal view, however, does not preclude the expectation that performance review might result in rather earlier departures than anticipated. Certainly there is some (again anecdotal) evidence that in recent years some vice-chancellors have departed earlier than planned because of mounting dissatisfaction, acted upon by council/governing bodies, that leadership functioning had drifted seriously and remedial action was not likely to be forthcoming from the existing vice-chancellor.

Educational backgrounds

While age at appointment has remained fairly constant across the decades, duration of period in office has shown a noticeable long-term decline. What evidence is there that this decline is associated with other changes in the backgrounds of vice-chancellors? To test this, we examined our data on educational backgrounds initially for evidence of change in two of the most enduring elements in the pre-1960s characteristics of university leaders: experience of Oxford or Cambridge and specialization in arts rather than sciences. In both cases we hypothesized that the substantial shifts in the size, configuration and organizational characteristics of higher education since the 1960s might betoken a decline in the salience of Oxbridge influence as well as a shift towards science (including social science) and technology rather than the arts as a training ground for future vice-chancellors.

Oxbridge influence

Undoubtedly there has been a long-term secular decline in the importance of undergraduate attendance at either Oxford or Cambridge in the backgrounds of those who have made it to the top leadership post. Taking the cohort appointed since 1960 as a whole, just over a third (34 per cent) had been Oxbridge undergraduates. Of these, 18 per cent had been to Cambridge and 16 per cent Oxford. These 'Oxbridge' undergraduates have been widely dispersed across the sector (with the exception of the new Welsh universities), accounting for 37 per cent of old, 22 per cent of new, 41 per cent of London principals and all of The Open University vice-chancellors.

After 'Oxbridge', the next largest group of vice-chancellors (31 per cent) first tasted the life of the academy as undergraduates at English old universities (including, of course the various sub-categories of civics, red bricks, 'plate-glass' institutions etc.). Table 3.2 provides a comprehensive breakdown of the proportions of vice-chancellors attending different types of institution as undergraduates. It should be stressed that these data are not directly comparable with Collison and Millen's (1969) study of educational backgrounds, but they do afford some measure of comparison. Collison and Millen found that by the 1960s Oxbridge was still accounting for two-thirds of vice-chancellors' educational backgrounds. However, in their study the

Table 3.2 Undergraduate university attended by vice-chancellors appointed since 1960

Institution	Undergraduate university													Oxbridge experience		
	Old	Poly	Camb.	Oxf.	Lond. coll.	Scot. old	Wales coll.	For.	Eire old	CT	NI old	Eire CT	Total	UG (%)	PG/T (%)	% diff
Old	36 (26.5)	1 (0.7)	31 (22.8)	21 (15.4)	15 (11.0)	15 (11.0)	7 (5.1)	8 (5.9)	1 (0.7)		1 (0.7)		136 (40)	38.2	51.5	+13.3
New	50 (53.8)	3 (3.2)	10 (10.8)	10 (10.8)	9 (9.7)	3 (3.2)	4 (4.3)	1 (1.1)		3 (3.2)			93 (27.4)	21.6	23.7	+2.1
Camb.	2 (20)		6 (60)	2 (20)									10 (2.9)	80	100	+20
Oxf.			1 (12.5)	6 (75)	1 (12.5)								8 (2.4)	87.5	100	+12.5
Lond. coll.	4 (23.5)		6 (35.3)	1 (5.9)	2 (11.8)	2 (11.8)	1 (5.9)	1 (5.9)					17 (5.0)	41.2	50	+8.8
Scot. old	3 (8.3)		2 (5.6)	6 (16.7)	1 (2.8)	22 (61.1)	1 (2.8)	1 (2.8)					36 (10.6)	22.3	43.2	+20.9
Wales coll.	2 (14.3)			5 (35.7)	1 (7.1)		6 (42.9)						14 (4.1)	35.7	57.1	+21.4
The Open U.			1 (50.0)	1 (50.0)									2 (0.6)	100	0	−100
NI old	2 (25.0)		2 (25.0)	1 (12.5)		1 (12.5)		1 (12.5)	1 (12.5)				8 (2.4)	37.5	50	+12.5
Scot. new	2 (40.0)		1 (20.0)			1 (20.0)						1 (20.0)	5 (1.5)	20	0	−20
Welsh new	2 (50.0)						2 (50.0)						4 (1.2)	0	0	0
London U.	1 (14.3)		2 (28.6)	1 (14.3)	1 (14.3)	2 (28.6)							7 (2.1)	42.9	85.7	+42.8
Total 1960–97	104 (30.6)	4 (1.2)	62 (18.2)	54 (15.9)	30 (8.8)	46 (13.5)	21 (6.2)	12 (3.5)	2 (0.6)	3 (0.9)	1 (0.3)	1 (0.3)	340	34.1	45	+10.9
Total pre-1981	52 (27.1)	1 (0.5)	39 (20.7)	33 (17.6)	16 (8.5)	24 (12.8)	13 (6.9)	5 (2.7)	1 (0.5)	3 (1.6)	1 (0.5)		188	38.3	49.7	+11.4
Total post-1981	52 (34.2)	3 (2.0)	23 (15.1)	21 (13.8)	14 (9.2)	22 (14.5)	8 (5.3)	7 (4.6)	1 (0.7)			1 (0.7)	152	28.9	39.1	+10.2

Note: Figures in parentheses are percentages.
Key: Old, old universities; Poly, polytechnics; Camb, Cambridge; Oxf, Oxford; Lond. coll., University of London colleges; Scot. old, Scottish old universities; Wales coll., University of Wales colleges; For., foreign; Eire old, Eire old universities; CT, colleges of technology; NI old, Northern Ireland old universities; Eire CT, Eire colleges of technology; UG, Oxbridge experience at undergraduate level; PG/T, Oxbridge experience at postgraduate and/or teaching level.

Oxbridge colleges were over-represented at 61 per cent of the sample, compared to just 5.3 per cent of our overall sample. When these divergence in sampling are taken into account, the difference between the findings on Oxbridge influence declines somewhat. It can no longer be argued that in terms of undergraduate experience these two institutions are the 'principal source of vice-chancellors'. Nevertheless, Oxbridge continues to exert a disproportionate influence when measured against the numbers of other institutional types.

However, the force of this finding needs to be qualified by the caveat identified by Szreter concerning the proportion of vice-chancellors who have sojourned at Oxbridge at other times in their careers. When post-graduate and/or employment experiences are taken into account, then Oxbridge influence increases considerably. Nearly half (45 per cent) of vice-chancellors appointed since 1960 could include such experience at one of the Oxbridge colleges in their curriculum vitaes. Table 3.2 provides a more comprehensive picture of the extent of Oxbridge backgrounds in recent generations of vice-chancellors. It demonstrates with some force that using a wider definition than merely undergraduate attendance, an Oxbridge connection is far more prevalent in the educational and career backgrounds of vice-chancellors than previously indicated. This is true of the Scottish old universities and the Welsh colleges in particular, but also the old universities in England and Northern Ireland as well. For vice-chancellors of London University, over 50 per cent of these leaders had an Oxbridge connection when postgraduate and academic experience are taken into account.

Nor has the prevalence of Oxbridge connections declined markedly over time. We have divided the period since 1960 rather crudely by using 1981 as a dividing line. Before (and including) 1981, the proportion of vice-chancellors with Oxbridge undergraduate experience was 40 per cent of all those appointed, while almost 50 per cent had Oxbridge postgraduate or teaching experience. After 1981 there was a 10 per cent fall in the proportions of vice-chancellors appointed with both forms of Oxbridge connection, to 30 and 40 per cent respectively. Figure 3.2 indicates these temporal variations in Oxbridge influences. Certainly we can identify a steady decline in the proportion of vice-chancellors with Oxbridge undergraduate experience since the early 1980s. Postgraduate experiences replicate this pattern, although in somewhat greater extremes. Yet, in some contrast, old universities have turned to Oxbridge as an indicator of some sort of pedigree in their vice-chancellors in greater numbers over the same period.

It is not unreasonable to conclude, therefore, that any decline in the salience of an Oxbridge connection in the recruitment of vice-chancellors has declined only gradually over the period as a whole. Whatever the significance attached to possession of an Oxbridge connection, as an attribute for the aspiring vice-chancellor it can be a critical factor in successful ascent of the career hierarchy. Certainly it remains disproportionately represented among vice-chancellors appointed throughout the period since 1960. Confirmation of its importance comes from a separate study by Farnham and

Figure 3.2 Undergraduate institution by decade and Oxbridge postgraduate and teaching experience

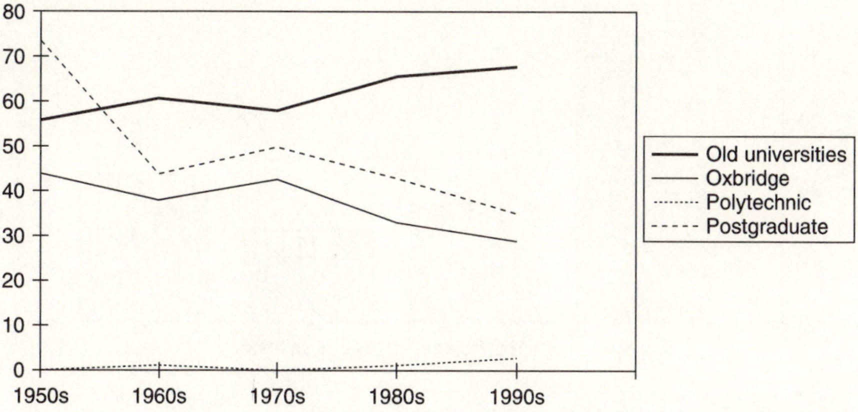

Jones (1998), which found Oxbridge strongly represented in the backgrounds of vice-chancellors, particularly those heading the ancient institutions, civic universities and 'other' university institutions.

What sort of qualifications?

Despite the continued strong representation of Oxbridge connections in recent generations of vice-chancellors, our data do suggest that there have been a number of other changes in their academic backgrounds. It will be recalled that earlier (pre-1960) generations of vice-chancellors were essentially children of the arts rather than the sciences. Using information on first degree obtained (based on reclassifying into an amended HESA based coding of disciplines into science, technology, social science and arts) we were able to compare changes against the earlier study by Collison and Millen. Figure 3.3 presents the results of this exercise. It shows that those with a science degree account for nearly a half of all vice-chancellors appointed since 1960. Of the remaining vice-chancellors, first degrees in the arts, technology and social science were distributed fairly evenly.

The proportions of vice-chancellors with science background are similar in both old and new universities (49 per cent old and 42 per cent new). However, arts backgrounds are unevenly distributed. In the old universities, a quarter had arts backgrounds, the second largest category. In the new sector, those with arts degrees were the minority (15 per cent), while those with technology backgrounds (22 per cent) and science (21 per cent) formed the second and third largest groups respectively. Social science lagged considerably behind this figure in the old universities (11 per cent). Undergraduate degree of the vice-chancellor serves as a fairly accurate proxy,

Figure 3.3   Academic discipline (first degree) of vice-chancellors

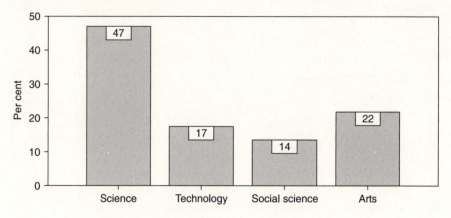

Figure 3.4   Academic background by university sector

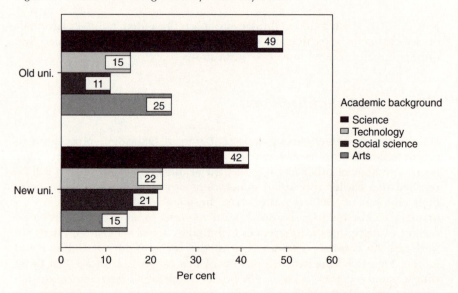

therefore, for the diverse origins and academic missions associated with the former binary divide. These differences are captured in Figure 3.4.

The timing of changes in academic backgrounds is shown in Figure 3.5. The rise in science from the 1950s is clear, its ascent checked only by the emergence of technology and social science degrees represented in the vice-chancellors appointed (mainly to new universities) in the 1980s and 1990s.

Information on first degrees is probably the most consistent indicator of disciplinary backgrounds of vice-chancellors, since possession of postgraduate qualifications is not universal. In fact, 40 per cent of the population in our survey did not possess a masters degree, while 36 per cent were not

Figure 3.5 Academic background by decade

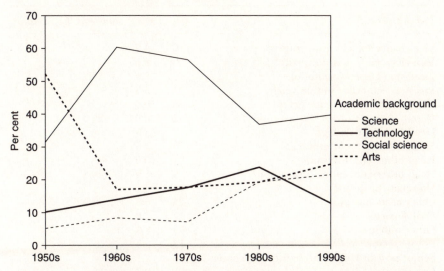

holders of a doctorate. However, there are important differences between the two sub-sectors. Masters of arts remain more strongly represented among old university vice-chancellors than new (55 and 38 per cent respectively). Conversely, twice as many new university vice-chancellors as old were holders of a science masters (17 cent and 8 per cent respectively). In the case of doctorates there were no major differences between types of university. However, since the 1970s the numbers holding a doctorate have increased sharply to over two-thirds of the cohort.

The evidence from our data indicates that, in terms of credentialization, it is traditional academic learning that counts as a career preparation. Possession of professional qualifications is limited to small numbers in the main professional areas of study: engineering, law and medicine. Only 10 per cent of the vice-chancellors in our study held a professional qualification in management. Academic honours are much more prevalent than professional qualifications. Nearly two-thirds (60 per cent) had been awarded UK honorary degrees, while a quarter had non-UK honorary degrees. The most prestigious honours, such as Fellows of the British Academy or the Royal Society, were held by small numbers of vice-chancellors (5 and 14 per cent respectively).

Recruiting grounds

The reservoir of individuals, or recruitment stratum as Giddens (1974) refers to it, out of which vice-chancellors are drawn is made up almost exclusively of those in senior university positions. This reservoir is depicted in Table 3.3. A quarter of vice-chancellors were either pro-vice-chancellors or

Table 3.3   Vice-chancellors' immediate previous position

Previous position	No.	%	Sub-total %	Total %
Vice-chancellor old university	16	4.7		
Vice-chancellor new university	9	2.6		
Head non-UK HE institution	10	2.9	10.2	
Pro vice-chancellor old university	47	13.8		
Deputy director new university	36	10.6		
Deputy director other HE institution	2	0.6	25.0	
Head Oxbridge college	17	5.0		
Head college of old university	6	1.8		
Head other HE institution	34	10.0		
Head other educational institution	5	1.5	18.3	53.5
University professor	89	26.1		
Other academic post	23	6.8	32.9	86.4
Civil Service	17	5.0		
Other public service	10	2.9		
Private sector	12	3.5		
Senior post in HE research/funding council	7	2.1		
Other	1	0.3	13.8	100
Total	341			

deputy directors immediately prior to promotion to the vice-chancellorship. Another quarter were university professors. But of those who were professors, almost a half were dual post-holders, i.e. a dean, head of department or other administrative post such as bursar, registrar or director of research. Most of the remaining vice-chancellors not in these positions prior to appointment present only a minor variation on the logic of academic hierarchy. About 10 per cent were tempted from existing posts as vice-chancellors in another institution. Another 17 per cent had been heads of one of the Oxbridge colleges, an old university college, or another higher education institution. Overall, therefore, almost 80 per cent of vice-chancellors were previously professors and/or higher managerial post-holders and over half were either head or deputy (or their equivalents) in other higher education institutions. Although horizontal moves clearly take place, these are invariably conditioned by perceptions of status and prestige in the pecking order of universities, in that movement is generally seen as upward, rather than down or even sideways. The important point is that the recruitment stratum is well defined (a conclusion drawn by Cohen and March (1974) about the American presidency) as overwhelmingly academic, and exceptions to it are confined largely to experience in the civil service or some form of public service.

These results demonstrate considerable continuity in the career paths of earlier generations of vice-chancellors. Almost all appointed since 1960, over 90 per cent, were previously career academics who, typically, have successfully clambered the academic hierarchy through a series of promotions. This almost universal selection from a single occupational environment has remained consistent since at least the 1930s (Collison and Millen, 1969). Only in the 1960s did the proportion of career academics drop slightly, from 90 to 88 per cent, a figure consistent with Collison and Millen's 1967 figure. However, the construction of vice-chancellors' previous careers has a number of features not necessarily captured in the data above. Although academia is the dominant career path, along the way we found some significant variations in patterns of experiences.

Other experiences

In our cohort of vice-chancellors, a third (34 per cent) had previous experience in the public sector (broadly defined to include the civil service), 20 per cent in salaried employment in the private sector (including the holding of a non-executive directorship post) and 16 per cent in both the public and private sectors. Nearly a third (30 per cent) had made no earlier deviations from the academic straight and narrow. However, given that most vice-chancellors are recruited overwhelmingly from a single occupational group, the fact that a majority could lay claim to broader occupational experiences seemed worthy of further exploration.

Our analysis of the data revealed some important differences in the backgrounds of old and new university vice-chancellors if narrower definitions of private-sector experience are employed. If we include only the holding of a salaried post to be a meaningful indicator of non-academic experience, then vice-chancellors of polytechnics/new universities were nearly twice as likely to have such experience as their counterparts in old universities. This feature of the data did not vary over time, although those in post during the 1950s and 1960s were more likely to have some experience of the civil service than in later decades. The distribution of non-executive directorships during incumbency of the vice-chancellorship provides an interesting variation on access to non-academic experience, however. If polytechnic/new university vice-chancellors proved more likely to have held salaried positions in the private sector, their counterparts in old universities prove more likely to hold directorships. No fewer than one in three vice-chancellors of old universities have been, or remain, non-executive directors in private companies. Among polytechnic/new university vice-chancellors the figure is just one in eight. These directorships include companies in information technology, petro-chemicals, power generation, banking and insurance, as well as a wide range of media organizations. Of course, some of these directorships are directly related to academic 'enterprise', since many vice-chancellors may be ex-officio members of the boards of university spin-off companies.

We found that the period from the 1950s to the 1980s was the most vibrant as far as such links with industry were concerned, with a fourfold increase (from 11 to 40 per cent) in the proportion of vice-chancellors holding directorships. Those in office during the 1990s displayed rather less propensity to link themselves so directly with the activities of business, despite the much vaunted need for closer university–industry links. Only a quarter of those appointed in the present decade hold such director-ships (though this proportion may yet increase). Interestingly, those vice-chancellors engaged in such activity exhibit a growing tendency to link themselves with a range of enterprises. Those holding multiple director-ships rose from only 6 per cent in the 1960s to 22 per cent in the 1980s.

The apparent reluctance of 1990s vice-chancellors to engage simultan-eously in the direction of business enterprises does not extend to other activities. Involvement in academic/professional bodies is recorded for nearly half the vice-chancellors and may be taken as further corroboration of the notion of involvement in academic leadership broadly defined. But the most conspicuous facet of external involvement is the rise in engage-ment with local/regional health organizations. During the 1990s the num-bers of vice-chancellors involved in this activity increased twofold over any of the previous decades examined. A substantial minority are also members of one of the funding bodies/agencies (21 per cent) and research councils (33 per cent).

The proportions involved in funding body/agency membership have risen slightly over the period since 1960, from a sixth before the 1970s to around a quarter in each decade since. Meanwhile, membership of the research councils has risen by a similar margin. Further evidence of engagement with the governance structures of the state is provided by membership of government advisory bodies and appointment as ministerial/departmental advisor. Despite the apparent rise in importance attached to 'expert' know-ledge, the proportion of the former declined from around a third in the 1960s to only 13 per cent in the 1990s. The proportion of those in the latter category remained constant at around 18 per cent.

Selection and socialization

Our final set of data reveal the interplay between selection and socialization processes. So far we have represented the predominantly academic career path as a single recruitment stratum. However, if we examine patterns of careers and appointments the picture emerges of a more complex and stratified recruitment strata. Despite the extensive national and interna-tional searches associated with the activities of the headhunters, the reality is much more structured and predictable recruitment pattern. The main division, consistent across the decades since the 1960s, is between the poly-technic/new university and old university sub-sectors.

The polytechnic/new sub-sector is characterized by a high proportion of appointments from its own recruitment stratum. Nearly 80 per cent of its vice-chancellors were appointed from previous posts (not necessarily in the same institution) in the same sub-sector. There is, therefore, a small but important movement from old to new universities, with around one in five of the vice-chancellors of polytechnics/new universities having come from old university posts. In complete contrast, there is virtually no movement whatsoever from the new to old sector. Only one (0.5 per cent) old university vice-chancellor in our data-set had been recruited from a previous post in the new sub-sector. This was a rather stark finding. It does not close off the possibility of cross sub-sector movement earlier in academic careers. But it suggests that appointment panels, particularly in the old sub-sector, act in highly conservative ways, choosing the candidates most likely to reflect the experiences and values associated with existing academic and operational cultures. The main determinant appears to be a desire to find candidates most likely to be acceptable to the main internal (and external) constituencies over which leadership is likely to be exercised.

Independent, if anecdotal, evidence in support of this contention is provided by the perceptions of recruitment specialists. Even new universities shy away from breaking with established reliance on the academic recruitment ground. Reflecting on the reasons why, one recruitment specialist observed:

> We've been asked by universities to approach such people [i.e. from outside the academic tradition], but at the short-list phase they've always chickened out on the grounds the troops wouldn't buy it . . . We've had them on long lists and short lists, and the clients have always said, we can't, the troops would just . . . be on the barricades.

The appointment process itself, in both sub-sectors, provides another powerful reason for the selection of 'people like us'. There is, we were told, a culture in many institutions of fairly widespread 'ownership' of the appointments process through the operation of a so-called 'immersion process'. This involves the last few short-listed candidates giving public lectures, advertised widely, before appointing panels move to a decision. More typically, the last three candidates still in the race meet with pro-vice-chancellors, deans and other university representatives, whose views are collated through a structured questionnaire and fed back to the appointing committee. Recruitment specialists argue that such processes damage the strength of short lists and condition the type of candidate appointed. At the opposite end of the spectrum, therefore, are the small, but increasing, number of appointments handled in complete confidentiality. One informant described this in glowing terms:

> We say [to appointing committees], if you want to get the best out of our fee, you will have an appointment committee who, if necessary, will interview off-campus in a hotel . . . in an anonymous railway hotel with waiting rooms so that nobody sees each other. None of this nonsense of having dinner together or sherry parties together. None of that nonsense. They come, they go, they're met at train stations in cars.

Then you'll have a strong short list. If you want to traipse them round, fine, but you're only going to get people who [are at] deputy vice-chancellor level.

If there is a widespread shift in the future to this style of recruitment then the prevailing power of conventional experience, acquired inside the same sub-sector as the vacant post, may begin to decline. However, the historical data suggest that many institutions end up with vice-chancellors who have some sort of connection, often with the sub-sector and sometimes with the particular institution. A third of vice-chancellors appointed since 1960 fall into the latter category, being appointed from within the ranks of the same institution. This is a model similar to European practice, although without the election process associated with the rectorship. Around a quarter of UK internal appointments are accounted for by Oxbridge college heads taking up their rotational vice-chancellorship or heads of higher educational institutions being in post when their institutions acquired polytechnic status. However, three-quarters of the appointments captured in our data were previously pro-vice-chancellors, deputy directors or other academic post-holders. Internal promotion to the top job has been more prevalent in the new sector (43 per cent) than the old (32 per cent). Horizontal moves from one vice-chancellorship to another are rare and when they happen they tend to remain within the sub-sector. Only 1 out of 15 old university vice-chancellors moved to the new sub-sector; in the new, only 1 out of 8 crossed to the old. The reason advanced by those involved in recruitment for this limited sideways movement was the problem of confidentiality, or the lack of it, described above. Existing vice-chancellors, it seems, are often tempted by the idea of a move, particularly to a more prestigious institution. Invariably they are put off by the prospect of their interest becoming public, thereby jeopardizing their credibility in their present posts.

Taken together, these data suggest the existence of two largely separate recruitment strata. One is located in the polytechnic/new university sub-sector and serves almost exclusively the appointment of vice-chancellors in that part of the sector. The other is located in the old sub-sector and exists to serve the needs of appointment of old university vice-chancellors, although occasionally it will be used by new universities anxious to widen their recruitment net. Certainly there is virtually no cross-sectoral movement, either sideways or vertically, from the new sub-sector into the top job in the old (with the caveat that the data refer solely to respondents' immediate preceding post). Given that earlier studies, particularly in the American context (see Cohen and March, 1974), have arrived at similar conclusions about socialization and selection processes, this finding itself may not be very surprising. Nevertheless, it is stark in the sense of its consistency across all the career levels immediately prior to appointment. The binary divide may have been formally abolished, but in terms of patterns of recruitment the gap between old universities and the former polytechnics remains wide and significant.

Conclusions

These findings indicate considerable continuity, even conservatism, in the recruitment of British vice-chancellors. The academic hierarchy has remained overwhelmingly the main source of recruitment and continues to serve as the main ladder or 'avenue of mobility' to the top university post. As a consequence, as an occupational group vice-chancellors continue to display some remarkably enduring characteristics across the generations. In the period since 1960 they have remained overwhelmingly male, white and typically in their fifties, taking on the vice-chancellorship as the capstone of an academic career. Most were recruited from previous posts as professors, pro-vice-chancellors or deputy directors in new universities. Only a small proportion were recruited from industry or the civil service.

There have been few changes to this established pattern. Average age at appointment has remained largely unchanged, many (around a third) have no history of previous employment outside higher education and the proportions of those vice-chancellors with career experiences outside higher education have not changed in any major way over time. Only in length of time in office has there been any significant movement, with average duration declining over time. While vice-chancellors in the polytechnic/new university sub-sector are nearly twice as likely to have experience of employment in the private sector as their old university counterparts, it would not be unreasonable to conclude that for a significant minority of those in the top university posts wider experience of modern business practices and management processes has remained limited.

In a sense we should not be surprised by the entrenchment of the vice-chancellorship in the careers of the academy. Our analysis of selection and socialization processes suggests that these wider experiences, while not unwelcome, can be no substitute for academic experience and expertise. Universities on the whole seek to identify candidates who embody pre-existing cultures and values – whatever else they may be able to offer they have to be acceptable and credible to the rank and file academics. There are exceptions to this rule, but the evidence on patterns of recruitment provides a clear picture of the power and potency of successful academic careers.

There is clear evidence of the existence of two parallel, largely separate, recruitment strata within academia. Those in the key recruitment stratum posts in the former polytechnic/new university sub-sector are very unlikely to be recruited to serve as vice-chancellors at Oxford or Cambridge or any of the other 'ancient' universities, and they are even likely to be excluded from all the old universities. It is one of the starkest conclusions from our data that over the period since 1960 there has been almost no movement from new to old universities. Conversely, it is possible to achieve promotion from the recruitment stratum in the old universities to a vice-chancellorship in a polytechnic/new university. But movement across the binary divide, both before and after its formal abolition in 1992, was limited, with only one in five vice-chancellors being recruited from the recruitment stratum in the old sector.

The turbulence and rapidity of policy developments associated with the transition from an elite towards a mass version of higher education in Britain, still unfolding of course, merely highlights the traditional features and evolutionary character of vice-chancellors' careers. It remains the case that experience of an Oxbridge education/training tilts the balance of chances of being appointed to a vice-chancellorship markedly. Although there is little doubt that Oxbridge influence has declined since the 1960s, it remains disproportionately prominent. Nearly a third of vice-chancellors appointed since 1981 had previously been Oxbridge undergraduates. Take postgraduate and academic/teaching experience into account and Oxbridge influence increases still further, to nearly 40 per cent.

There is no evidence from our research that the shift towards more executive interpretations of the post of vice-chancellor has produced major changes in the career preparation and professional profiles of those appointed to the top leadership post. On the contrary, there is remarkable continuity across the decades. Vice-chancellors' careers, even those appointed in the 1990s, are seemingly more in step with leadership expectations of previous eras than the present. What continues to count in terms of recruitment success is demonstrable evidence of shared educational and academic career experiences, a similarity of outlook or 'life-space'. It is clear, too, that certain institutions function as 'switchboards' in the distribution of individuals into these leadership posts. Oxford and Cambridge pre-eminently, old universities close behind, appear to offer the kind of socialization and formation of social contacts most valued by a majority of academics and, perhaps more surprisingly, lay governors directly responsible for the appointment of vice-chancellors. In this respect at least, the vice-chancellorship may be no different in the post-Dearing world of mass education from how it was on the threshold of the Robbins enquiry of the early 1960s.

4

Corporate Leader:
Vision and Strategy

Over the past twenty years the management literature has stressed two themes
as central to the success or failure of organizations. The first approach has
concentrated on operational issues, the day-to-day pursuit of operational
excellence, how to create a well run organization. The second has concentrated on strategic dimensions, the importance of vision, mission and strategy to organizational success. This chapter explores the extent to which
vice-chancellors have engaged with the task of providing strategic direction
and leadership, a task increasingly associated with modern corporate leadership. Subsequent chapters explore vice-chancellors' interaction with organizational management and involvement with day-to-day operational issues.

Chief executives across a wide range of organizations have become increasingly preoccupied with strategic management and planning – or so the
management literature suggests. There are numerous definitions of what
this entails, but broadly speaking most writers suggest it is about defining
and agreeing the nature of the business. As one contribution suggests, it is
'the framework which guides those choices that determine the nature and
direction of the organization. It is what an organization wants to be' (Tregoe,
1989). Other writers (e.g. Drucker, 1974), have emphasized the importance
of mission and the need for managers to pay greater attention to this aspect
of their role. Most writings about mission follow one of two views: one
approach sees mission in terms of corporate strategy while the other ex-
presses it in terms of philosophy or values. The first approach sees mission
and strategy as completely intertwined. In contrast, the second approach
focuses on organizational culture, the norms and values that influence how
people behave. It amounts to an organizational or business philosophy that
helps to generate a common approach among those who work for the same
organization. Inevitably recent management analysts have attempted to bring
these approaches together and develop a multidimensional approach. One
such model (Campbell *et al.*, 1990: 27) identifies four strands or elements:
purpose, strategy, behaviour standards and values. 'A strong mission exists
when the four elements link tightly together, resonating and reinforcing

each other.' What then develops, the authors argue, is a *sense* of mission, an emotional commitment to the organization which acts as an immensely strong and powerful motivator.

An extensive literature now exists differentiating vision from mission and how mission relates to strategy. All three are seen as central concerns of senior managers and specifically the chief executive. But this literature primarily derives from studies of industrial and commercial organizations, which have, in many cases, more opportunity to define or redefine the nature of their business. At one extreme a director of Hanson, a conglomerate, is quoted as saying: 'All of our businesses are for sale all of the time. If anyone is prepared to pay more than we think they are worth, we will sell. We have no attachment to any individual business' (Campbell *et al.*, 1990: 63). Other organizations take a different view, attaching not only financial value to businesses and organizations. To use current terminology, they see themselves as having commitments to multiple stakeholders, and not just to maximizing profits for shareholders, as in the Hanson example. The question is whether such analyses are useful to an understanding of the role of the vice-chancellor or whether, despite post-Jarratt emphases on greater efficiency and managerial expertise, the university remains a special case.

One reason for uncertainty lies in university traditions and history. Universities, certainly on the European model, have been collegiate organizations with a rector or vice-chancellor chairing a senate to take strategic decisions about the academic development of the university. The administration, headed by the registrar, manages the non-academic areas. The latter is a permanent career post. The former, whether appointed as in the UK, or elected as in much of continental Europe, is generally of shorter duration. One retired vice-chancellor (Price, 1994) has argued that the concept of a vice-chancellor as chief executive, linked as it is the market-oriented culture that has been introduced into British public services, runs against the grain of university development.

The introduction of quasi-market principles to strengthen patterns of public accountability, using government agencies such as funding councils with chief officers accountable to the National Audit Office, has required in turn chief accounting officers in each university or college. This is one strand in the role of chief executive. The other complementary strand derives from the recommendations in the Jarratt Report (1985), which urged the relevance of industrial and commercial models of planning and organization and the importance of the head of the institution taking greater responsibility for its strategic direction. Paradoxically, strategic plans were first required of polytechnics and colleges in 1989, but from 1992, following the demise of the binary system and the creation of unified higher education funding councils in England, Scotland and Wales, strategic plans were formally required from all higher education institutions (HEFCE, 1993). Institutions were advised that the plan should be set in the context of the mission statement and cover academic aims and objectives, student numbers, staffing, physical and learning resources, finance and quality. Since then both the system and individual institutions have been in a state of transition, with the emphasis from the funding councils being on trying to encourage institutions to use their strategic plans for the purposes of internal monitoring and review. This chapter seeks to establish how far the process of strategic planning has developed, whether vice-chancellors view this activity as important to their role or it remains largely a task for the administrative services, and how far vice-chancellors have adopted the role of chief executive in practice, rather than in title only.

What do vice-chancellors do?

When the role was explored in an open-ended way with vice-chancellors themselves, and with chairs of university councils, the views expressed showed high levels of agreement. Both groups cited strategic leadership, and developing and articulating the university mission, as being centrally important. Vice-chancellors used terms such as 'developing the strategy', 'having a vision of where the university is going' and 'offering leadership and charting a course for the university in the medium to long term' more or less interchangeably when describing their role. This is consistent with data we collected from America and Europe (discussed in Chapter 8), where university presidents/rectors cited strategic planning as the most important area of university policy for which they had responsibility. A UK study by Bargh *et al.* (1996) suggests that governors consider their strategic role to be the most significant, when asked to rank their various roles and responsibilities. This is perhaps not surprising, as it is the crucial arena in which the roles and responsibilities of council or board of governors intersect with those of the vice-chancellor. It is therefore not only important, but potentially highly sensitive.

One reason for such sensitivity may be that confusion about the role of the vice-chancellor is matched by equal uncertainty about the role and function of the governors. Or, to put it slightly differently, the way in which university management and governance operates in practice does not always match the formal definitions of responsibility, as set out in the new universities in the instruments and articles of government, and in the old universities in the university statutes. Broadly, these specify that vice-chancellors are responsible for the day-to-day management of the university, determining academic activities in conjunction with academic board or senate, and managing the budget and resources and the proper use of funds from the funding council(s). In the old universities the main responsibility of the council lies in control of finance, personnel and estates, leaving academic issues broadly to senate. In the new universities, however, greater oversight, if not control, of teaching and research was intended and incorporated into the articles of government. It is obvious there is a considerable overlay of formal responsibilities between the various bodies and individuals, and since many of them are exercised via the committee structures of the institution, this adds a further layer of operational complexity.

The Bargh *et al.* study of university governance concluded that, in practice, the role of council/governing bodies in strategic planning is largely reactive (Bargh *et al.*, 1996). They receive policy proposals already at a fairly advanced stage of development, which are largely the work of the executive group led by the vice-chancellor. The latter may well informally consult the chair of council, and of other council committees, but the initiative rests with the vice-chancellor's office. Formally, then, this is an area of shared responsibility but one in which the vice-chancellor takes the initiative in presenting, both to the council and to the rest of the academic community, a view of the university and how it should develop. This view of where the initiative resides is, by and large, a shared one between chairs and vice-chancellors, with the former arguing that the vice-chancellor has got to 'lead the academic view' because 'he understands the academic life'. This perception is interesting, because it clearly locates strategy in the academic arena, a view also accepted by chairs in both old and new universities.

Clearly there is strong consensus on the importance of strategic leadership, and setting/developing the university mission is seen as central to that process. However, many vice-chancellors, particularly in old universities, see strategic planning, in the sense of developing a mission or direction for the university, as a new task. Many describe the ending of the binary system as a critical watershed. As one put it, 'before 1992 I think we had the feeling we were all heading in much the same direction, essentially'. The change in the size and scale of the system changed what had often been seen as a largely administrative task – producing a mission statement and strategic plan as part of public accountability to the funding council – into a task raising more fundamental issues and values for the whole academic community.

By contrast, the new universities with their different traditions are more familiar with this problem. Having successfully developed the polytechnic image and ethos, which was both modelled on and simultaneously contrasted with, the traditional university (a different kind of higher education offering more vocational, part-time and sub-degree opportunities to students with a more diverse range of entry qualifications), they now have to decide the equally difficult task of what kind of universities they will become. The existence of self-consciously different kinds of institutions within the university system, albeit not as diverse as in countries such as the USA, raises questions about mission and values for the entire system. Hence the heightened awareness of 'mission as values'.

The requirement of the funding councils for institutions to produce a strategic plan also has a clear operational message. Since the early eighties, with the government reduction in recurrent grant for universities and the subsequent UGC selectivity exercise in the distribution of grant to individual institutions, universities have lived with the requirement for detailed planning in many aspects of their affairs. When Sir Peter Swinnerton-Dyer succeeded Sir Edward Parkes as chairman of the UGC in 1983 the university system as a whole was becoming increasingly centrally driven, if not planned, with the UGC consulting universities at the instigation of government about resources, student numbers to 1995, capital costs, the balance of subjects, research and so on. The recommendations of the Jarratt Committee (1985) added to the pressures to see commercial or industrial planning models as relevant, and strategic planning was very much part of the ethos of 'new realism' which pervaded universities at that time. Increased managerialism is an acknowledgement that a university is not only a community of scholars, but also a public enterprise which needs to demonstrate efficiency and effectiveness in its use of resources.

Harvey-Jones (1988) has argued that the pace and range of activities associated with the role of the modern vice-chancellor is comparable to strategic leadership in other contexts. However, strategic planning has many different dimensions and there is a need to examine what vice-chancellors actually do as part of the strategic planning process. Moreover, in view of our argument developed in Chapter 2 about the important differences which exist between higher education institutions and other types of organizations, there is a need for closer examination of the executive leaders' role in the strategy process. Part of this examination concerns the broader context of university operation. Is there still unanimity about the nature of 'the business' in higher education, or are financial and other pressures causing a reassessment of the objectives of universities? To what extent do vice-chancellors consciously tap into the industrial or commercial experience of strategic planning offered by some members of council/governing bodies, and how relevant is such experience to managing a university? These questions are explored through the various dimensions of strategic planning as it is now interpreted in higher education settings.

Developing the mission

Given that strategic planning is seen as a central task, how exactly does it happen and how is the sense of ownership, which vice-chancellors and chairmen see as essential, engendered in practice? First, many old universities feel that key aspects of their mission, such as research, are simply 'given', part of what being a university is about. External circumstances may have enhanced its importance in financial terms, but the interconnection of teaching and research is generally seen as a core value throughout the system as a whole which even the new universities are obliged to acknowledge. Increasingly institutions are collaborating to help to define and market their institutional niche. The establishment of sub-groups within the CVCP shows how much this has become embedded in the system, with the Russell (research) group being matched by the modern (new) universities group. As one vice-chancellor from the Russell group put it, 'just being there [at meetings] is very important. If we weren't there it would raise all sorts of issues.' Part of strategic planning is therefore about positioning the institution by joining the right 'clubs' and networks. This in turn sends powerful signals both externally to the wider community and internally to the academic networks within the institution.

The internal process of strategic planning is formal, involving appropriate committees (council, senate, strategic planning committees), with less formal meetings of senior management groups, and frequently informal meetings with staff to spread the message and initiate discussion more widely in the institution. Vice-chancellors referred to 'a messy networking process', 'an iterative process designed to engage all staff in the debate', 'a series of structured meetings to discuss draft statements of mission and values' when describing their institutional procedures. The process sometimes starts with a draft plan prepared by the senior management team, or a less formal paper written by the vice-chancellor to initiate discussions. At this stage it may resemble a series of short points embodying key values and objectives on the basis of which the more formal and developed strategic plan will be produced. For many in the institution it is phrases such as 'academic excellence', 'a research-led institution', 'strong access mission' and 'commitment to regional regeneration' which are the keynote points. Finding those key phrases, which resonate in the right way but still point the institution towards critical areas of development, is a central task.

The extent to which strategic planning is now part of the 'routine' of university management was confirmed by the observational data collected during our research. Our periods in universities with vice-chancellors afforded several opportunities to observe the chief executive and senior colleagues engaging in strategic planning. Sometimes this was part of the weekly cycle of senior management meetings; at others the less frequent but regular strategy 'away-days' held off campus. The latter, variously described as 'wild times', projecting 'beyond the millennium' and 'thinking the unthinkable', usually focus on the medium- to long-term direction of the institution. The following example is taken from the annual executive board seminar at one post-1992 university, held a few months prior to the publication of the Dearing Report. This meeting, attended by all the senior managers together with deans of faculty, was introduced by the chief executive with a personal view of the present and future state of higher education. The university of the future would be accountable for the development of society's key skills. However, there were dangers: from the Harris report on research funding and from the Russell group of 'ivy-leaguers'. Questioned by a dean who thought there was a strong incentive to become elite, share traditional values and opt out of the 'twenty-first century NVQ brigade', the chief executive was unequivocal: 'There's no time to grow the ivy'. He continued:

> I think we should produce graduates who are skilled learners, people who are a comfortable part of the learning society and learning organizations ... This is not the Thatcherite view of the enterprising graduate ... We're searching for a definition of a graduate which is clear,

flexible and tuned to the professional, community and business needs of the twenty-first century.

These perceptions prompted a short but vigorous debate about what words adequately describe the graduates that the university was already producing. 'Vocational' was seen by the chief executive as dangerously downmarket, and henceforth contributions from around the table focused on employability, knowledge and learning skills. Alignment with sophisticated knowledge-based companies located in the local community was advocated by several. Later the chief executive summarized the debate by observing that while the university was expert at what it did, the problem was how to communicate it. What he wanted to see from his colleagues was a commitment to develop an institution with the 'public self-confidence which will communicate with various markets'. The contrast and, paradoxically, the goal was Oxbridge, where things were done with an air of 'effortless superiority'. The search was for quality.

Having postulated a vision, the chief executive gently steered the debate into a discussion of how they could (to use the jargon) 'lift the vision'. Two problems were identified from around the table. One was the local authority inheritance of being 'hang-dog' ex-polytechnic. The other was the 'wrong image' associated with the university's vocational and access mission. There was no dissent, articulated at least from around the table, to the view that the university needed to manage its image better and create a strong association with quality. The chief executive argued the need for a search for greater quality in two areas: improving the university's research rating to attract better quality students and attracting better academic staff. Both, he said, would project quality, but there remained a need to 'find distinctiveness and celebrate it. There will be no new slogan – it is not a verbal problem – it is a problem of behaviour, a set of values and attitudes.'

A single board meeting is unlikely to produce a definitive, uncontested view shared by all the actors present. Certainly some wild ideas – thinking the unthinkable – were cast into the debate. The vice-chancellor had brought to the seminar thoughts on strategy and positioning developed by the strategy steering group, headed by the deputy vice-chancellor and a small core of other senior managers. This group had in turn consulted widely, undertaking what were called 'presidential tours' to explain to staff the university's corporate objectives and the problems faced. The vision presented to the seminar, therefore, carried with it tacit steering group and grass roots endorsement. The invitation to think the unthinkable did not lead to any major change in the vision. As one of the pro vice-chancellors later observed during interview: 'I don't think we've identified anything that makes us significantly different from any other universities. I still don't think we've hit on something that we all want to agree will characterize us.' What is perhaps significant is that such events have now become almost a routine part of university life, probably differing only from one institution to another in the range of people invited to participate. Overall the process is diffuse and multi-layered, with the importance of values (one vice-chancellor called the mission statement 'an ethical document') strongly underlined.

Academic leadership

What is obvious from the example above is that the key strategic issues are seen as academic. The question of what kind of university an institution aspires to become involves considering the kind of teaching and research in which the institution wishes to be involved, the types of students it seeks to recruit – and how to achieve these objectives. This in turn influences the priorities vice-chancellors accord to different aspects of their role, and most of them emphasize the importance of academic leadership. In many cases they found it difficult to separate these different strands of their activities, and academic leadership and strategic management often appear, during interviews, to be interchangeable categories. One was quite clear that 'the vice-chancellor is responsible most importantly for the academic leadership of the institution'. Another preferred to see himself as 'the principal academic officer. What is that? It's about providing them [academics] with the facilities they need for their teaching and research.' A third suggested that 'the aim has to be to create an environment in which the prime purpose of the university can be accomplished by the academic staff'.

These overarching statements translate in practice into a wide range of daily activities, some of which involve detailed and time-consuming bits of administration or mundane meetings that appear decidedly non-strategic when viewed in isolation. Illustrating his hands-on role, one vice-chancellor said 'I was talking to the head of department about the deal we were going to do for this [newly appointed] chap. I know how you sort out space and I was able to tell him to get on to estates and to let me know if they're dragging their heels and I'll just walk across there and sort it out.' Another was convinced that his 'senior colleagues regard it as a weakness that I humour my academic board and I will defer and postpone things while I work to build a consensus rather than ram things through'. On such occasions the vice-chancellor will need to embark on a series of informal meetings with the key people to secure the necessary consensus, and this can prove both time-consuming and demanding.

Consensus about the importance of academic issues does translate into rather different perspectives in the area of research, which in old universities is central to the academic mission and has resulted in many vice-chancellors being set quite specific objectives. One vice-chancellor confirmed he was told at interview that the university's target was to become one of the top twelve UK research universities. Another with a slightly less specific target, but of a similar kind, said 'they aspire to be a serious university of the traditional kind. We're sort of clinging on by our fingernails and my job is to make sure we get at least a handhold.'

Of course, the resources which are at stake in achieving a high rating in the research assessment exercise means this is also a critical financial issue which it would be pointless to ignore. Equally, however, it would be foolish to deny the powerful symbolic image evoked by references to a research or Russell group university. Terms such as 'traditional', 'serious' and 'old-fashioned' are some of the euphemisms used by vice-chancellors and chairs to describe universities with a strong emphasis on a research mission. It shapes the view councils have of the kind of person who would make a suitable vice-chancellor and has consequences for the way vice-chancellors in these universities perceive their role and prioritize their tasks.

Given this mission, a primary concern is to conserve and strengthen the intellectual resources of the university. Consequently, they invest a considerable amount of time in identifying and appointing suitable people to professorships. Most vice-chancellors said they chaired all appointment committees at that level, and several alluded to considerable additional time spent in following up suitable contacts, having dinner or informal meetings with candidates and ensuring appropriate arrangements are made for new and valued professors. Some said they chaired panels because they were tougher about *not* making an appointment if candidates were unlikely to make an impact in the desired way. As one vice-chancellor put it, 'individuals really make a difference in universities. You can turn round entire departments within a period of two years.' The importance of individual 'stars' whose influence is manifested in a kind of personal following is also evident in comments from vice-chancellors across research universities. 'Building up the research image, the expertise, bringing in the big names', was how one saw his role. Some suggested this was ultimately how vice-chancellors came to be judged, and their successful appointments often outlasted them. It is good professors who make a difference in institutions. Here is interesting confirmation of Middlehurst's (1993) view that although transformational leadership is normally associated with institutional heads, in an academic context there is scope for transformational leadership at several levels. It is clear this is what many vice-chancellors are seeking from the people they appoint to professorships.

A somewhat different perspective emerges from some of the new universities. One vice-chancellor was convinced that he was now less involved with academic issues but even he, at a later point in the interview, drew a distinction between academic and educational leadership and saw his role very much as an educational leader: 'the regional university initiative is very much mine; the academic I see as a more internal matter.' Other views suggest that developing strategy in academic areas is a complex affair in a modern university, with the vice-chancellor managing the interface between the governors and senior academic colleagues, taking important but different soundings from each as the overall strategic direction is set and/or constantly fine-tuned in the light of new developments.

Within the institution, academic leadership is a partnership between the deans [of faculty] and the vice-chancellor. They are if you like mini vice-chancellors and I look to them, in a two-way process, as to where the university ought to be going in each faculty. They have much more subject expertise than I have. But I expect their thinking to be constrained by what we've said corporately about the nature of the university.

Mission as values

The comments also reveal strong continuities in the value system with the emphasis on academic standing and ethos. It illustrates what Green (1997) has called the paradox in higher education, namely the tension between the mission to conserve values such as scholarly enquiry and transmission of knowledge, and the equally pressing need to adapt and change. Managing this tension is a key strategic task of the vice-chancellor. This combination of academic and symbolic leadership with managerial expertise is what creates the possibly unique features of the role.

The environments of the past two decades have been particularly stressful, necessitating extensive change. Polytechnics, for example, first made the transition to independent corporate institutions in the late 1980s and then achieved university status in 1992, acquiring significant additional responsibilities in the process. A period of significant and concentrated expansion took place in the late 1980s and early 1990s and all universities now face greater monitoring and regulation for quality in both teaching and research, together with continued financial constraint. Some suggest the modern university has consequently to be both entrepreneurial and adaptive (Davies, 1987; Clark, 1998). These organizational characteristics are said to reflect an explicit university mission and a focused portfolio of activities. In addition to academic disciplines organized in traditional departments and faculties, there are typically a series of satellite units established for the purpose of multidisciplinary research and for exploiting the commercial potential of academic expertise through closer client links. The university itself, suggests Davies, is more of a holding company for its decentralized units than an integrated bureaucracy. Originally, according to Middlehurst (1993: 63), such a model seemed more applicable to the USA than to Europe; however, 'six or seven years later, the image has considerable application in the British context as the former polytechnics are added to the university sector and as the old universities become more diversified in their mission and funding sources.'

This, however, can mistakenly ascribe some of the developments associated with globalization to the ending of the binary divide and the accession of the polytechnics to university status. Universitas 21, a recent development creating 'an elite global network of research-intensive universities which is to be registered in Britain as a legally incorporated business organisation with the aim of attracting corporate clients' (Izbicki, 1999), makes it clear that the entrepreneurial model could be seen as equally applicable to universities with a wide diversity of missions. The Davies model also conveyed overtones of moral disapproval at the direction in which universities are developing. It is a good example of the way in which organizational developments often stand proxy for the value systems underpinning academic life and attitudes to such developments reflect the conflicting value systems which currently exist.

Green has also suggested that in the new universities the academic chief executive officer may function more like a corporate executive. Without a long tradition of faculty self-governance, she argues, such institutions are perhaps freer to take top-down decisions and to behave more like businesses. If these arguments genuinely reflect new trends in university development there are obviously significant implications for the role of the vice-chancellor and the concept and practice of strategic planning and leadership. It is therefore important to consider whether evidence exists of change in the mission of universities and the role of vice-chancellors. Some vice-chancellors argue that universities have already changed significantly and so has their role – in the example quoted above, that they are less involved with academic developments. Others suggest that priorities for some are beginning to change. One vice-chancellor (Bull, 1994: 83), writing about managing change in a new university and reflecting on the experiences of the past decade, has described some of the developments which have engendered strong antipathies on the part of many academics.

> In 1989 the vocabulary of the then polytechnics underwent a remarkable transformation. Students became 'clients', or 'customers', heads of department 'managers'; the language of finance – cash-flow, profit centres, full-cost pricing, liquidity ratios – became commonplace.

This rather crude illustration of the effects of marketization, also a reflection of the period following the polytechnics' assumption of corporate status, which caused many to embrace business language with excessive enthusiasm, has now been tempered by the move to university status. It is interesting to reflect whether such a move has also had a normative effect, subtly influencing not only the perception of those people considered suitable for appointment to the post of vice-chancellor (rather than polytechnic director) but also the appropriate conduct of management and governance. At this stage firm conclusions would be premature, but evidence of a one-way flow in appointments to the vice-chancellor post is beginning to emerge and the strength of collegial values does not appear to be diminishing. At a minimum, the polytechnics are unlikely to prove the Trojan horse that many feared.

Management styles and culture

> The vice-chancellor is responsible for generating the style and culture of the organization. Now style and culture is a multifaceted thing. It's how the university relates to its academic mission, the setting of that mission and the way that mission will be delivered.

This view, expressed by a chair of governors, is endorsed by many vice-chancellors, who emphasize the importance of culture as compared to structure. As one put it, 'creating the right informal atmosphere of teamwork, co-operation and purpose is immensely more important than the formal structural framework' (Price, 1994: 37). Motivating people is critical and this requires an appropriate style of management. Most vice-chancellors and chairmen agree these are not the kind of organizations where you can sack people because they don't agree with the chief executive. It is also part of what one chair was referring to when he said that 'universities are people organizations'. It clearly has affinities with the strategy associated with Hewlett-Packard, described by Peters and Waterman (1982) and known as 'management by wandering around' (MBWA). For Hewlett-Packard's strategy to succeed it needed to attract and retain high-quality individuals – in their case engineers and product managers – in order to dominate high-value niches of the electronics industry. In turn this required an appropriate management style which recognized individual creativity and did not depend on close control or hierarchical systems. MBWA was the result. If an important part of developing a strategy is to establish 'the style and culture of the organization', then this approach to management is clearly intended to send important messages to the rest of the university about values and standards and behaviours. A high proportion of vice-chancellors either explicitly or indirectly see themselves as adopting this style or approach to managing the organization. This requires the vice-chancellor to be seen as accessible, either by being perceived as personally approachable or by doing many things which could just as easily be undertaken by other parts of the administrative machinery. A vice-chancellor of a new university put it slightly differently but nonetheless reflected a similar approach: 'I'm deeply suspicious of people who abdicate on the grounds that their role is to be strategic and float above everything thinking deeply . . . I spend time on all sorts of unimportant things . . . It helps you keep in touch with the mundane things people care about.'

The interconnection of style and mission can be seen from one new university that found itself in a difficult position, needing to expand numbers very rapidly both to generate sufficient income and to develop greater critical mass to support the required diversity of academic programmes. The vice-chancellor was adamant that:

> the only way we can cope with this growth is by having very firm central control. So we restructured and a major factor was the need to break the baronies. They were just blocking the way I wanted to drive the university. When I talk about the baronies they were trying to hold out against what was an agreed culture, agreed by the governing council and supported by the academic board.

This anecdote is interesting for several reasons. First, it shows that universities are capable of being run, at least for periods, in a much more centralized way, and in this way significant change can be driven through. The vice-chancellor clearly has enormous leverage as and when he or she chooses to use it, and one way of reading this account is to note how very similar this is to an industrial or commercial enterprise. However, the vice-chancellor had clearly felt the need to align the council and academic board with the policy so it could be presented as individuals holding out against 'an agreed culture'. Moreover, the vice-chancellor was at pains to emphasize that the restructuring exercise was not just imposed by him. 'We had a big consultation exercise and I appointed three wise men and they went round and talked to everybody and we had mass meetings and so on.' In the driving through of a strategic plan great attention had clearly been paid to the institutional culture of widespread consultation and formal agreement from the key committees.

Symbolizing the mission

There is still an important sense in which the vice-chancellor must be seen to symbolize or embody the mission of the university. Trow (1985) suggests that symbolic leadership is 'the ability to express, to project, indeed to seem to embody the character of the institution, its central goals and values in a powerful way'. The intensity of this symbolic attachment varies but it is nonetheless widespread. Chairs in particular expressed these views when asked about the qualities they looked for when appointing vice-chancellors. There were near unanimous views about the need for vice-chancellors to be academics, to have a strong academic background rather than to be people with business or commercial experience. Most chairs agreed with the view expressed by one that 'universities are not like a business, they've just got to behave in a business-like way'. They acknowledge there is something paradoxical at the heart of the vice-chancellor's role as a consequence. 'I think being a distinguished scholar and a good runner of a university is very difficult. In other walks of life these things rarely come together. I mean, woe betide having an airline pilot run an airline.'

Nonetheless this chair saw having an academic as essential 'because universities are about standards – academic standards. That has to be the top man's priority.' This emphasis on understanding the business from the inside was endorsed by the chair of a new university. In contrast to other kinds of business organizations, in which 'accountants can be drafted in to run BT or something like that', he 'wouldn't like to draft in an accountant to run a university'. Others suggested an academic was particularly important for certain kinds of universities. One could not envisage 'a university like this one, a research "Russell group" university, appointing a businessman'. In an interesting echo of the view quoted above, this chair argued:

> Universities are still different. It's not just that they are big and complicated. Authority, presence, standing, they're all part of the picture. This is why vice-chancellors probably need to be academics. This may

go with a particular kind of leadership which is still, perhaps, more personal and less systematic than in organizations of a similar size.

This more personal leadership also means it is crucially important that other academics have respect for the vice-chancellor, who therefore needs to be of good academic standing. For one chair this also implies that a vice-chancellor should 'have a field of professional expertise'. In some cases the precise area of expertise was also be seen as symbolically important. 'The complaint was that [the person chosen] was an engineer. So they all, the physicists in particular, banged on about it. So after a bit I said you don't know how lucky you are. You're getting both a scientist and an engineer in the same person.' In other cases it is a question of academic standing being reflected in academic titles. Being a Fellow of the Royal Society was seen as an essential prerequisite for appointment in one university. One chairman recollected the questions raised at a recent appointment. 'Why is he a mister, people asked – you know just an MA; the short answer is that in his field there are not many PhDs. Then they said, why did he become a bursar – implying a failed academic.'

Some vice-chancellors also identify themselves as academics, in spirit if no longer in day-to-day practice. Academic values are seen as the bedrock, the foundation stone, of the system and the vice-chancellor must both guard and reflect them in order to be successful. This does not imply an uncritical acceptance, but rather an ability to identify with staff in the institution and for the staff, in turn, to perceive this. Vice-chancellors often cultivate symbolic policies for this purpose. Several made a point of publicly identifying with their staff, particularly *vis-à-vis* monitoring agencies or other external bodies. 'I would hope I'm fairly notorious for reminding bodies of what people at the coal-face think', was one view. Another said, 'I see myself as an academic who was sitting exactly where they were not long ago', and in consequence tried to ensure that he identified himself with anti-bureaucratic populist measures which 'go down well in senate'.

Mission and structure

Over a quarter of a century ago commentators were beginning to stress the effects of the post-Robbins expansion, and the consequent increase in university size, on the ability of a vice-chancellor to maintain a traditional span of control with existing management structures and forms of government (Moodie and Eustace, 1974). Three trends were identified as possible ways to overcome the managerial dilemmas facing a vice-chancellor: one by increased managerial posts leading to a more formal managerial hierarchy, interestingly identified as the American presidential solution; the second by stronger planning committees involving key deans and pro vice-chancellors in forms of cabinet government; and the third by devolving many decisions to deans and faculties. All of these possibilities have been tried in varying combinations and most universities exhibit an eclectic mix which seems to fit the particular institution. Strategic planning, however, often remains the 'messy networking process' described by one vice-chancellor. In contrast to industrial and commercial organizations, there are no elaborate planning departments in universities modelling options for the future. While Jarratt has certainly strengthened the use of performance indicators and planning parameters, strategic decisions remain, at an important level, intuitive.

The vice-chancellor of a large civic university (Wilson, 1994) has described how a search for organizational structures to underpin his strategy led him to Mintzberg's analysis of different kinds of organization and specifically the notion of the professional bureaucracy and adhocracy (Mintzberg, 1973). The first is characterized by the front-line staff being high-grade professionals, such as university teachers, who want to keep some measure of control over strategic development. Hence the typical array of university committees through which they can have their say. According to Mintzberg these are good at delivering particular products to a high standard. Where flexibility is required then adhocracy is preferable, with fluid project groups, less hierarchy and good lateral communication. This latter organizational form is, according to Wilson, a more appropriate way to deal with activities such as research. Clearly there are strong similarities between this account and the organizational description given by Davies cited above. Both suggest that a more turbulent environment has placed significant pressures on traditional organizational patterns, requiring those leading and managing institutions to devise new strategies for organizational delivery.

The extent to which traditional university structures can be transformed in the light of strategic needs is shown in the earlier account of a university with an urgent financial and academic need to grow. Most vice-chancellors reject the Davies model, the majority preferring a 'flat' system to remove hierarchies. One described taking out a layer by abandoning faculties and moving to a two-tier system, with strongly devolved powers to large departments. But this does not imply an absence of central control. Rather, there is a constant tension between the demand for central accountability and the flat devolved systems that many senior managers now believe encourage academic creativity and entrepreneurial developments to flourish. Some have attempted to streamline the committee structure, which is often seen as synonymous with university organization. One vice-chancellor suggested that to give a responsibility to a committee should be an exception, as in most academic institutions responsibilities are very fuzzy as a consequence of their location in the committee structure.

> I see late twentieth-century collegiality based on a recognition that the world outside has changed. The pace of change has increased and one cannot sit around waiting for everyone to agree. Once you've discussed something a decision has to be made. So it's a different sort of collegiality but it's still important.

While many might share these sentiments few have changed the committee culture and, as earlier examples demonstrate, many prefer to seek consensus in respect of controversial decisions and will defer decisions until they believe consensus is secured.

Conclusions

As these accounts make clear, the vice-chancellor not only engages in strategic planning but sees it as a key part of the role. Although this is formally a shared responsibility with council or governors, in practice it is the vice-chancellor, together with the senior management team, who initiates the process and carries responsibility for leading and managing the discussions and any consequent changes throughout the institution. Clearly there are parallels here with role of chief executive in other organizations, leading some to conclude that the heightened emphasis on the strategic planning role is a direct concomitant of the decision, following Jarratt, to acknowledge the vice-chancellor as chief executive of the university. This view sees strategic planning as part of the new managerialist culture, externally driven by the demands of the funding councils and the growth of a market culture in higher education.

Historically, however, it is also possible to see elements of the current focus on mission statements and vision as directly descended from the attempts by many foundation vice-chancellors of the new universities in the sixties (Sloman, 1963) to articulate a distinctive philosophy (the term they preferred to vision) for their university and sometimes, by extension, for the wider system, at a time of significant change in higher education. On a somewhat less grand note, Lord Fulton suggested to the Franks Commission that 'somebody has got to lie awake at night feeling responsible, not for inventing the shape, but for seeing that there is one' (Moodie and Eustace, 1974: 146). Viewed from this perspective, while the present format and language deployed in strategic planning very much reflect the ideological perspectives of the late twentieth century, the activity itself is one that vice-chancellors of earlier generations might have recognized and shared.

It is not, however, just a question of language and style. External factors have sharpened the emphasis on strategic planning. This is not only the formal requirements of the funding council(s) but also the increased size and diversity of the university system as a consequence of the end of the binary divide. One vice-chancellor suggested that prior to 1992 universities generally had the feeling they were all heading in much the same direction, whereas 'now there's a much greater diversity and this has created pressures for each institution to decide where in the range of activities it wishes to be placed'. Earlier such diversity (though never perhaps in reality that different) was centrally constructed, the result of government policy towards the two sectors of higher education. Now it is open to each institution to find a new place in the higher education system, although clearly radical repositioning is far from easy. Indeed, current institutional insecurities combined with somewhat limited opportunities for manoeuvre may well result in·an exaggerated emphasis on comparatively limited differences. Several commentators have suggested there remains a strong resistance to the idea of diversity in English higher education and culture (Trow, 1989), which constrains the ability of institutions to develop radically different visions of their future. There is still a tension between markets and central control being played out in higher education.

It is clear from the research that strategic planning is seen by vice-chancellors and chairs as a complex process involving more than the development of a vision and mission. There are two dimensions that are often intertwined in their accounts of strategic management and leadership. One identifies the formal processes that enable the institution to meet the requirements of external accountability. These include the preparation of strategic plans and mission statements so that the core activities of the university can be evaluated and assessed in an appropriate and self-defined context. The emphasis on this dimension has been accentuated by the present regime of declining resources, in which hard choices and bidding for additional funding are a daily reality. As Britain moves from an elite and binary system to a mass post-binary future, there is a second more difficult and complex task, of constructing a vision of the university which is rooted in current practice, but has normative force, particularly for academic staff. This second dimension must engage with the fundamental values and ethos which underpins the operation of universities, which are now threatened by the wider transformation to a mass system. The first dimension stresses control, structure and organization; the second culture, values and intellectual renewal. A modern vice-chancellor, to be successful, must engage with both dimensions.

The Jarratt view of a chief executive was rooted in the desire to promote greater managerial efficiency. Strategic planning was conceived largely as safeguarding the resources of the institution by promoting more rational and informed decision making in the context of a clear planning framework. Hence the emphasis on the importance of council. It sought to move the university once and for all from an 'amateur' and collegial system to a professional and executive decision-making process – the world of strategic choices. But these were still envisaged as choices within controlled limits and were primarily about resources and organizational structures and improved managerial systems. Arguably, however, the present focus on strategic planning is really a manifestation of the wider failure to resolve the intellectual and cultural dilemmas posed by the transformations affecting the university sector in the late twentieth century. Mass higher education poses intellectual as much as managerial and organizational challenges, and so far the university world remains racked with ambivalence about its future(s). In that sense strategic planning can be seen as part of a debate about the core values which underpin higher education. The task of defining and agreeing the nature of the business, a key objective of strategic planning in industrial contexts, is here bound up with this wider debate and uncertainty about the role of universities in the twenty-first century.

Hence the inability to pin down the process, still less to devolve it neatly to planning departments. The vice-chancellor must reflect and contain the optimism/pessimism, approval/disapproval – the mood swings – that affect the modern university, while continuing to manage the organization. Above all there is a need to reassure academics that something recognizably a university will continue to survive and flourish; no easy task in a postmodern world.

5

The Pattern of Days: Internal
Roles and Relationships

The foregoing chapters have addressed two separate, but related questions: who are the vice-chancellors; and what do they think they do as university leaders? The first of these sought to establish and interpret the changing patterns of promotion to the top job. The second explored vice-chancellors' own perceptions of their role in providing visionary and strategic leadership. Our analyses suggested two contrasting themes. The first is the importance of continuity and tradition. This was most apparent in the selection of those who make it to the apex of the higher education job hierarchy. Despite the sea changes which have occurred in recent years in the size, structure and diversity of higher education, the typical avenues of mobility have remained largely unchanged since the 1960s. Elements of continuity, conservatism even, were also evident in the competing demands of living in a turbulent environment while simultaneously trying to maintain and (re)define notions of collegiality and professional autonomy handed down from previous eras.

In contrast, the second theme stresses the unfamiliar and unpredictable. In creating a coherent vision for their organization, in setting a future destination and how to arrive there, vice-chancellors are implicitly, some explicitly, thinking about how to create and manage change, how to influence events and people. It was not difficult to track through the interview data the discourses associated with the grand visions: the impacts of economic and cultural globalization on higher education, the shifting frontiers of the state and the region, public and private, teaching and research, industry and employment, etc. While the mindsets and language of the vice-chancellors were reasonably clear and consistent, we could not say much about the mindsets in operation. Our account was necessarily decoupled from the daily practice of leadership, the very processes by which aspects of vision and mission are moulded and interpreted by the values, ethos and culture of the organizations; how chief executives try to influence events inside the institution. This chapter turns the spotlight on the day-to-day interactions between vice-chancellors and their organizational domains, both the professional/academic and the managerial/administrative. It is concerned with the daily detail of managerial and administrative activity and the contours of their activities.

Switching the focus of attention from leaders as persons and perceptions to leadership as process and action (Hosking, 1988: 147) enables us to explore in greater detail the ambiguities of leadership and management. Universities are at the cutting edge of new knowledge production and distribution. They are creative, 'networked', organizations with many different levels of interaction and interconnectedness. What does this creativity and connectivity mean for practical day-to-day leadership? Vice-chancellors are clear that developing grand visions and translating them into strategies and policies are key parts of the leadership role. But how is this actually done on a day-to-day basis? Is it a solitary task or does it involve others? What are the processes of trying to implement their policies and plans? How closely do they become involved in internal management as leader-managers? Can we identify any patterns in the sort of tasks they get involved in? Who are the key members of the internal senior management team, other academics and members of the governing body or council with whom they interact? What sort of relationships are involved and how are they conducted?

This chapter explores these questions in two parts. In the first, attention is focused on the broader contours of the landscapes of vice-chancellors' days. It tries to recreate a sense of the range of activities and issues, the ebb and flow of ideas and information, which connect the levels of transformation with transaction in the daily working lives of vice-chancellors. In the second, attention is switched from the contours to details in the landscape. It analyses vignettes of action as exemplars of the connectivity between the grand vision and plans and what one writer has termed the 'incremental nature of policy making' at the level of day-to-day management (Thody, 1997: 77–80). The vignettes relate to both the academic and managerial domains of vice-chancellors' roles and represent an initial tracing of the ways in which organizational contexts and cultures can impinge on the work of vice-chancellors.

Landscapes of days

The literature of management and leadership outside education settings had provided a number of important insights into how the landscape of executive leaders' days might be studied. Carlson's pioneering study of Swedish managing directors provided the first systematic investigation of how senior managers spend their time, a task which, he observed, had already been extensively tackled in time and motion studies of manual jobs but not of executive work (Carlson, 1951). Much of the subsequent literature has concentrated on behavioural frequencies and the time consumed by different managerial tasks (Stewart, 1967; Mintzberg, 1973; Kotter, 1982; Luthans *et al.*, 1988). The preoccupation with the measurement of activities and comparison of managerial 'events' is not unproblematic, however. For example, structured observation approaches (see Mintzberg, 1973; Bussom *et al.*, 1981; Martinko and Gardner, 1990) need extensive pre-conceived written protocols to enable observers to construct minute-by-minute narratives which are subsequently classified into elaborate schemes of managerial events, purposes and forms of initiation. The diary survey method, used in the seminal American study of university presidents by Cohen and March (1974), likewise depends on the understanding of the respondents themselves about the range and purposes of tasks involved. In a recent study of Australian vice-chancellors based on the diary survey method, the author noted the unease expressed by two respondents about the limitations of the diary as the sole methodological approach (Sloper, 1996: 207).

As we discussed in Chapter 2, these critiques have informed our own research design, guiding us towards the sort of questions we sought to ask about executive leadership in higher education and the research instruments deployed to assemble the data with which to answer them. We were not concerned with being able to quantify with detailed precision the amount of time chief executives spend on each category of activity. Nor did we wish to get bogged down in arcane discussions about the categorization necessary to construct accurate indices of what they did, hour-by-hour, day-by-day. The danger of such accounts is that they lead to a reductionist and deterministic approach to understanding the actions of chief executives and other managers. Universities are not simple bureaucratic structures easily understood in the 'organization as machine' metaphor (Morgan, 1986). To collapse the task of explaining the role of the vice-chancellor into component parts in this way would, in our view, risk missing the essential dynamics of leading creative organizations in complex environments.

Our approach to understanding the broader landscape of daily events and actions draws extensively on our unstructured non-participant observation of vice-chancellors, supplemented by interviews with key members of senior management teams, academic staff, governors and vice-chancellors themselves. This combination, we believe, is comparatively rare in observational studies of leadership (Yukl, 1989: 278). Its great strength is that it allows us to begin to make sense of how longer-term vision and shorter-term strategies relate to the daily round of activities. As Thody has observed, through such an approach it is possible to follow the progress, albeit necessarily fragmented and incomplete, of a sample of policy lines as they make their way 'through the interstices of daily activities' (Thody, 1997: 60). In order to ensure that as far as possible we have understood the broader context of these policy lines we have further supplemented our data, wherever possible, with documentary investigation designed to provide a more rounded picture of their appearance in daily activities.

The framework of meetings

Although no attempt has been made to quantify the particular patterns of work of vice-chancellors, there are broad similarities on the ground. Their working days are framed by pre-arranged schedules of meetings. These comprise four distinctive types. First are the regular series of meetings, formal and semi-formal, either with other leading members of the university's senior management or with the key sub-committees of council/governing body. Meetings of the executive management team are usually held weekly, with other regular, but less frequent, meetings or 'away-days' also taking place with a wider constituency of university managers to address specific issues such as strategy and planning. The vice-chancellor and other senior members of corporate management also meet with management teams more broadly defined. These meetings include members of the executive, the deans or other heads of operating units and heads of the major service divisions. Again, these are regular and generally take place either weekly or fortnightly. Additional meetings may be convened to cover specific issues. The second 'collegial' category of meetings arises out of the university calendar of larger 'representative' committees, part of the administrative 'cycle' in which the vice-chancellor participates and usually chairs. These, like the first, are an unavoidable component of the job and include formal meetings with senates, academic boards, councils, governing bodies and various other committees.

The third category of meetings is the more informal. Some of these are with other key members of the university's leadership, such as the chair of council or governing body, the pro vice-chancellors and/or deputy vice-chancellors and the directors of the various administrative divisions. Although they are outside the formal committee structure of the university, such meetings play a vital role in information gathering or imparting which will feed into the development of personal agendas. In particular, vice-chancellors spend lengthy periods with chairs of council or governors and other key lay members. The relationship with the chair of council or governors in particular is a vital, though often opaque, element in the leadership of the institution conducted behind the scenes in the spaces between the formal rounds of meetings (Bargh *et al.*, 1996). Our observation periods afforded glimpses of this relationship and other informal contacts between the chief executive and senior managers, and these are discussed in more detail in Chapter 7. Other one-to-one meetings, mostly on personnel type issues, are arranged in a more reactive manner and serve to bring the vice-chancellor into contact with individuals at various levels of the organization. Such meetings can serve similar informational functions. These less formal meetings, some regular and semi-constitutional, others more *ad hoc* and sporadic, are part of the custom and practice of executive management in each institution. Nominally they form part of the landscape of most chief executives' days, but the uses to which they are put and the degree of reliance on them in the practice of management varies from individual to individual. They arise largely because the vice-chancellor has agreed to their arrangement and may involve regular meetings with representatives of various interest groups inside and even outside the university.

Externally focused meetings form a fourth category. They are a frequent occurrence in the chief executive's working diaries. Most of these arise from the vice-chancellor's membership of a particular committee or group. They may be formal, perhaps part of the cycle of management meetings, or informal, arising on an *ad hoc* basis as occasion or events require. Meetings with high-profile individuals, from the local and regional to the national and international, are an important part of this latter cycle of meetings. They are partly network building and partly letting people and their organizations know that the university thinks they are important, and so building goodwill. Sometimes they are also intended to identify people who might serve on university committees and bodies including governors whose names go on to shortlists. Information flows, both internal and external, are a central feature of all such meetings. Their importance is illustrated by the range of personal interest meetings which many chief executives attend. Examples include urban education and economic regeneration groups, local, regional and national arts committees, vocational education and women's network groups. The boundaries between these private interests and the public domain of the university are difficult to disentangle. Chief executives justify their involvement on the grounds that they fed into the university indirectly by forming a nucleus of 'interested' and well disposed people, particularly in locally important organizations.

Between scheduled meetings, the working days of chief executives are punctuated by periods of interactions with personal assistants (PAs) and other members of the office. These are occasions when diary dates are fixed, messages received, telephone calls and out-of-course meetings arranged, and incoming and outgoing correspondence processed. Although these meetings thread through the day, the first session is particularly important. Each day's schedule is discussed, including forthcoming days if the vice-chancellor is not going to be in the office. The week's appointments for all the executive are also involved and checks are made to ensure that there is always someone on campus or within easy phone reach. Phone calls received and to be made are discussed and those to be made pre-booked: 'Tell X I'll ring between 2 and 2.30 p.m. on Thursday.' Appointments are rarely made without clearance from the chief executive.

These sessions were important in two respects. First, the functioning of the chief executive's office depends on the ability and sensitivity of key administrative staff, especially the PA. They interpret and field information and are an essential conduit between the office and other key areas of the organization. Second, the observations suggest that the PAs and other immediate assistants can fulfil important roles almost as confidantes. Ideas and plans might be discussed openly and perceptions of other senior managers and academics compared. Advice is sometimes sought: 'How urgent did it sound?' or 'Do you think X can deal with that?' It was not unusual, therefore, for sessions with PAs to contain a curious mixture of topics, ranging from the most confidential details of high policy down to personal events and even the health of domestic pets.

Finally, although we are dealing with the internal domain of the chief executive, it is worth noting that most regularly spend one or two days per week on average outside the university. Meetings of the CVCP in London form a major commitment in this respect, particularly if there is any participation in the various committees of the organization. Participation in other activities, part of the round of personal interest meetings described above, may also exert a significant toll on time and demand periods away. Such external foci are an explicit and expected part of the role of a vice-chancellor, even if the incumbents have a fairly high degree of discretion in developing this role. Thus there were some differences in emphasis. Some chief executives interpret their role primarily in a national and international context, acting as an 'ambassador' within the UK, EU and overseas as well as networking on behalf of the university in Westminster, Whitehall and the research and funding councils. Membership of top London clubs for residential and dining purposes is an accepted facet of this role, although the heavy overtones of elitism and exclusion of women has been observed by a number of serving chief executives (Gee, 1997).

Others may interpret their organizational role in more local and regional contexts. Although chief executives in this mould tend to spend rather less time out of the university, some continue to maintain the tradition of membership of a London club. Our observations of table talk between chief executives and trusted colleagues during moments of relaxation over lunch or drinks record animated discussions of the importance and relative merits of membership of alternative London clubs. Other views exist, of course. One chief executive eschewed and lamented the draw of London clubs, preferring instead to retain a much sharper focus on the local and the regional through a series of 'networking' breakfasts with entrepreneurs and other key players across the community.

Time and the problem of fragmentation

The advantage of non-participant observational research is that it results in data-rich information – an average of 20 pages of detailed and closely written field notes per day of observation. These data allow construction of summaries of 'typical' days on campus. They are not reflective, however, of the time spent off-campus on university business, often of an evening or weekend, or periods of work at home. Nevertheless, they do convey a sense of the landscape of the vice-chancellor's working day. Three features stand out.

The first is the protracted length and diversity of the typical working day. When off-campus events and time spent at home reading and preparing are taken into account, the vice-chancellors in our study regularly worked between 14 and 15 hours a day, not unusual by chief executive standards in whatever field, but long days all the same. Such days include 'eating for the university' – a range of meals taken as working breakfasts, lunches or dinners or as quasi-social occasions when the vice-chancellor engages in an official university role with the external community. When the round of meetings and other business had ended, there would frequently be an evening engagement of some sort. Such is the diary scheduling that time alone, on campus at least, for contemplation or reflection was rare. Driving or, for the richer universities, being chauffeured, and the first-class seat on the train or plane, often provide invaluable interludes for reflection and thought. Taking the lower of these calculations produces a commitment of 70 hours to the job during a five-day week. This figure is consistent with Sloper's (1996) calculation of an average 68.7 hours in the working week of Australian vice-chancellors, but suggests they work longer hours than American university presidents (based on Cohen and March's 1974 estimate of 50–55 hours). These figures, of course, exclude weekend hours spent on university business.

The second aspect concerns the fragmentation of the job and the sheer volume of the day's informational traffic. Research in other business and organizational settings has tended to confirm the view that managerial work tends to be 'brief, varied, fragmented, spontaneous and highly interpersonal' (Martinko and Gardner, 1990: 344) and in this the contours of vice-chancellors' days would appear to be no exception. Typically, a full working day when the chief executive was on campus would incorporate between five and ten meetings, sometimes more and occasionally less. However, the range of topics covered in these meetings is immense. For some meetings, extensive preparation and briefing from support staff is essential. Preparation time between meetings may be extremely limited, requiring the chief executive to spend time routinely reading and preparing papers at home each evening or in moments of space between, or travelling to, meetings. On the other hand, some of the issues arising in meetings require very little pre-planning or briefing. Some chief executives engage (interfere, according to some of their immediate colleagues) in the details of apparently trivial, banal even, policy matters – car parking and gardens, for example. Others avoid the detail wherever possible and will even send substitutes to perform the ritual and ceremony associated with academic awards. Achieving a balance is not easy. Our research concurs with the findings of Cohen and March, in the American context, that in many cases the chief executive has difficulty saying 'no' not just because he or she does not really want to, but because of 'the frequent reminders of the fact that one *is* the [chief executive], the attention to the minor things one *can* do' (Cohen and March, 1974: 150, original emphasis).

The third feature, paradoxically, is lack of control, or 'order', over the contours of days. Perhaps this is both a reflection and a cause of their involvement in detail. Even the most determinably 'hands-off' chief executives have to engage occasionally with substantive issues which might be only loosely aligned, at best, with the core business of the university. On more than one occasion we observed the executive leader in long meetings which were subsequently described as 'a waste of time'. Involvement in 'executive' concerns such as broad strategy, planning, human resources or finance was invariably punctuated by a diverse range of other concerns and distractions requiring an immediate response or action, or just a sympathetic ear. The background noise to the job and the flow of ideas into and out of the chief executive's office can be immense. In coping with the reality of busy schedules, the pressure of what Gladstone once called the rigorous prosecution of government business, issues were rarely compartmentalized with neat boundaries. Control was sought by vice-chancellors, but it seemed rarely achieved.

Dealing with this multifarious activity can easily create the impression of fragmentation and dissonance and, to be sure, our observations captured periods when such descriptions were apt. But the problem with the observational technique (which we recognize) is that over periods measured in days and even weeks the coda to events and activities is rarely seen. Piecing our data together and searching for elements of order and predictability in the patterns of the day reveals a rather different interpretation. By this we mean that the work of chief executives might be better understood in terms of the metaphors of complex, dynamic systems. The landscapes of their days exhibit elements of 'order', 'chaos' and 'complexity'. Order in this sense refers to the organization of the day and its activities: the striving for some degree of predictability. Order can, therefore, represent a set of familiar routines in which the leader grinds his or her way through a set of well rehearsed and so predictable responses in a quest for some stability. Chaos, on the other hand, represents the opposite extreme: a lack of pattern and order of any sort where work and meetings seem endless, apparently aimless and ultimately fruitless. In between these states is the so-called zone of complexity. For theoreticians of complex dynamic systems, it is here, in the zone referred to as the 'edge of chaos', that creativity, whether individually or in teams, is most likely to come into being and where behaviours display elements of *both* order and disorder (Lewin, 1992; Kauffman, 1995).

The landscapes of days constructed from our observations can be interpreted through such metaphors. The diaries have certain core similarities: the framework of meetings, personal contacts, the dense traffic of information flowing into and out of the chief executive's office. Here are elements of order and chaos. Certain events and activities were predictable, run of the mill affairs, where the leader adopted behaviour stereotypical of slow moving and unresponsive organizations. Other parts of the days' events descended into chaotic behaviour, when long-running problems and internal divisions surfaced and resurfaced without apparent resolution. In between were the complex or edge of chaos interludes when the chief executive engaged in seemingly more creative dialogues with various constituent groups inside and outside the organization. These metaphors help to make sense of the traffic of the day, the processes of prioritizing and deprioritizing, of ensuring the general coherence of the broader vision and strategy when sudden and unexpected events demanded attention and threatened to spiral out of control. How chief executives respond to and operate within their particular landscapes is the subject of the next section.

Working days: vignettes of action

Three broad categories of leadership actions can be discerned from the plethora of activities described above. The first is the corporate leader. In this role the expectation is that chief executives are able to translate the grand vision and strategies into suitable organizational behaviour. Actions in this role focus attention on the ways in which chief executives attempt to reconcile the internal operation and strategies of the institution with the external, often turbulent, market place. In line with resource dependence theory, the behaviours of chief executives and others responsible for the corporate well-being of the institution need to be understood by reference to the external agents – policy makers and policies – that set many of the key parameters of institutions and their actors in higher education (Slaughter and Leslie, 1997: 66). Above all, it is about ensuring that organizational behaviour is commensurate with the constraints and opportunities of funding and other resources.

The second category concerns the interpersonal dimension: the ways in which chief executives relate to and motivate their immediate colleagues; how the task of team building and commitment to the corporate vision is approached. This dimension incorporates dealing in a qualitative sense with the extensive flow of information. Monitoring the institution from the perspectives of key members of the senior management team is one aspect of this role. Another is the dissemination of information internally. The grouping of activities into two broad categories – corporate and interpersonal – is intended to provide a heuristic tool with which to make sense of the observation period. It builds on the work of various analysts who have developed similar frameworks within which to understand the content of managerial work (see, for example, Mintzberg, 1973, 1975; Kotter, 1982; Stewart, 1982).

Corporate leader

Strategy and a funding crisis

The first vignette illustrates one vice-chancellor's attempt to pursue the development of strategic direction, while simultaneously managing a worsening funding deficit. The researcher was able to track the progress of these issues as they arose in various meetings over a ten-day period. The first session was a midweek meeting of the university management team (UMT), a broad group including the deans of faculty and senior managers. The main agenda item was developing a new 'corporate' approach to funding schools. The background to the funding problem was a history of inconsistent funding across the university's schools which had provoked resistance to the implementation of new cuts made necessary by a further reduction in government funding. The subject was led by one of the deputy vice-chancellors, the chief executive intervening on only two occasions: once

.ɔ support the deputy when one of the deans attempted to reopen a policy issue already resolved and, second, to respond to a challenge from another dean who argued that 'cuts like these can't be managed'. 'Is this reasonable or not?', the chief executive asked. The intervention produced a string of suggestions. At the end of the debate the chief executive reminded the group that they must arrive at a collective decision on how to use the available funding and that the deans must produce plans of action detailing the strategies at school level. The group must think in terms of joint purpose, not simply winners and losers.

The budget problem resurfaced the following week at a meeting of the university's small executive group. The meeting commenced with attempts by several present to put items on the agenda for their next executive 'away-day'. The chief executive resisted, reminding colleagues that the executive's job is to create a strategic agenda: this was the only opportunity for long-term thinking and it should not be spurned. Each member of the executive then reported on his or her area of responsibility. It was agreed that head-hunters should be engaged to fill the post of head of human resources, instead of the usual practice of relying on responses to public advertise-ments. The names of new student residences were discussed from a list of possibles: discussion centred on the need to convey the right sort of corpor-ate image for the university.

The funding problem was next on the agenda and the meeting was joined by the head of finance to present the draft budget. This led to in-depth discussions about various financial problems, with particular reference to overspending schools, the question of how they got into their present par-lous position and how the problems could be overcome. It was clear that some schools had simply spent in anticipation of income which, for a vari-ety of reasons, had never materialized; others were simply overstaffed relat-ive to others. How to present each case to the governors was discussed at length: there were fears that the poor state of school finances would reflect badly on the ability of the executive to manage effectively. A range of 'creative' presentations of the figures were examined. It was agreed that some of the deans would need to attend the next executive meeting to underline the seriousness of the situation. Finally, attention was turned to the subject of possible merger with a local college. After agreeing tactics and who would accompany the chief executive in forthcoming talks, the executive dispersed.

We next pick up these issues the following day at a regular bi-monthly meeting of the UMT held at a local hotel. These sessions 'off the premises' supplement the usual weekly cycle of meetings of the executive and UMT and are intended to focus on forward thinking and planning. This session was led by two external management consultants, together with the univer-sity's head of staff development. Nominally two items were on the agenda: to examine new approaches to teaching and learning and to develop a vision and strategy for implementing organizational change. However, the head of finance was also present in order to deliver a budget presentation.

Although the meeting was chaired by one of the deputy vice-chancellors, the chief executive articulated the essential tasks facing the university. The key point was the assertion that 'Not to change is not an option.' The core business was student learning. To protect this in the face of yet more resource reductions by squeezing a little bit more from here and there was simply no longer an option. Change, therefore, must involve some fundamental rethinking. After setting the tone and key theme, the vice-chancellor subsequently intervened in discussions on three brief occasions. The consultants took over, giving examples from elsewhere of what has been tried, what is working and what has failed. Some institution-specific issues emerged. For example, there was a consensus that too many modules were being offered, imposing resource strains on assessment. Staff needed to reorientate their teaching and learning approaches, to move away from 'teaching' as currently conceived.

Later in the day, the chief executive and the rest of the executive left the away-day to travel to a meeting with the chair and vice-chair of governors. Here penetrating questions about the budgetary situation were asked. 'Do schools have knowledge of each other's budgets? What are the explanations for the overspending in some schools? What is the rationale for the presentation of certain details?' Various alternatives were suggested by the board representatives, together with requests for further breakdowns of particular figures. The lay members were very much in the driving seat, the executive in effect in the dock. The governors argued that they wanted to make the university's (and the board's) position 'bomb-proof'.

Although the meeting with governors was not the end of the chief executive's working day, the budgetary issues were raised again the next day during informal talks over breakfast prior to the resumption of the UMT away-day. The session commenced with a presentation by the consultants, attempting to summarize the thrust of thinking. From the floor, reservations were expressed about whether there was substantive progress towards real change. The discussion became desultory and dispirited. At this point the chief executive intervened, suggesting that the meeting allowed itself a 'wild time': for example, why not aim for a 50 per cent reduction in all assessment with effect from the next academic session? The intervention produced a flood of ideas, including annual elections of the chief executive.

When the wild session closed, ideas were gathered. It was agreed that something radical and symbolic needed to be done if staff were to be convinced of the seriousness of the problems. The consensus was that assessment should be significantly reduced across the university. One of the deans opposed on the grounds that the implications of such a radical measure had not been sufficiently thought through. At the morning coffee break, this dean wandered off alone into the courtyard. The vice-chancellor intervened to ensure no one followed, adding, 'He needs to learn he's on his own.' The remainder of the session was devoted to summation, various groups working out the first practical stages of implementing change and developing a vision for their own schools. The chief executive was not directly involved in any of these sessions but remained as a participant. It was agreed that all the schools would be able to draw on external consultants paid for by the centre to assist the design and implementation of change.

A new graduate programme

This vignette illustrates the vice-chancellor's engagement in academic development in a setting outside the formal collegial environment of senate or academic board. As in the previous case, the task facing the vice-chancellor was to assess an unexpected opportunity to develop a new graduate programme within a broader capital funding and estates perspective. In order to understand the vice-chancellor's role in this meeting, some background is necessary.

One of the university's sites had for some years been shared with other tenants, including a large media-based organization. Although central, the site was not popular among staff or students. For a variety of reasons, an opportunity had arisen to acquire use of the whole building. However, the deal was contingent on the successful outcome of negotiations with the media organization about the hire of its now-redundant facilities for use by students recruited to a new graduate programme in the media. Based in the building, the programme would recruit full-fees students, primarily from overseas. Market research by the dean of faculty and relevant head of department had been favourable, and they were strong advocates of pushing the estates deal through.

This was the prelude to a meeting involving the vice-chancellor, the finance director, the estates director, the dean and the head of department. The dean opened the meeting with a short statement on the positive picture suggested by market research and his personal view that use of the building's facilities would give the university a unique selling point in the international market. The director of estates concurred, observing that the major element to the deal was the property itself. Taking the facilities 'off-the-peg' represented a major financial advantage over creating from new, since the savings could run to several million pounds. It was, he said, 'a heaven sent opportunity'. However, according to insider sources the corporate owner expected the university to 'put up or shut up within the next two to three months'. The director of estates would supply a full brief to the vice-chancellor about the property and rent issues. He realized that it needed to be looked at within the context of the estates strategy and that the chairman of governors would look at it very critically. To the vice-chancellor he concluded, 'We're looking at gaining your support.'

The vice-chancellor's initial question sought information as to why the timetable had suddenly become so tight. As far as he knew the possibility had been on the cards for some two years. The response was that the crucial issue was the upturn in the regional economy and the corporation's desire to restructure its operations. The vice-chancellor was worried by the sudden rush, fearing that the estates advisory panel, the committee through which the proposal would be channelled, would be suspicious of a proposal that appeared to come from nowhere. 'It's a pity', he reflected, 'we didn't put a marker on it earlier.'

With the vice-chancellor clearly concerned about an adverse reaction from board members, particularly in view of the financial stringency of the moment, the director of finance joined the debate. He emphasized that the figures regarding students and income from recruitment to such a course were 'realistic'. He was supported by the director of estates, who also stressed that consultants in the proposed field of study had stressed that qualified students would be highly employable. He claimed that all the testing of the market had confirmed what they wanted to hear.

At this point the vice-chancellor turned to 'bottom-line' figures, asking if the figures would be break-even or surplus. The director of finance said he projected net surpluses. They would not be very great, but 'the bottom line is producing a net surplus'. Despite an interjection from the dean of faculty to say that the figures were very conservative, the vice-chancellor continued with his line of questioning: 'I don't want to pore over the figures, but . . . there won't be a major capital cost at any time?' The director of finance confirmed: 'It fits with the strategic plan . . . It is all about new fields, international leadership.'

Having listened to the advocacy of all those around him, the vice-chancellor acknowledged the commitment and enthusiasm of colleagues. In view of this and the financial assessments he agreed to support the idea and take it to the governors. The problem was one of timing. The board, as ever, was sensitive to the present financial circumstances of the institution and would need to be reassured about the commitments involved. However, because he was personally enthusiastic about the opportunity he would use emergency procedures if necessary. As a first step he promised to open discussions with the chair of the governing body that evening, when they were due to meet at a local business function. After the meeting, the dean of faculty was clearly elated by the vice-chancellor's support, but acknowledged that the next phase would depend critically on the vice-chancellor's ability to take the chair (and so the board) with him.

Interpersonal roles: key relationships in action

The approaches of chief executives to the problems described above confirm the importance of the leader's interpersonal roles with key senior management and academic players. According to Chemers (1993), three underlying processes to these roles can be identified: first, image management, which concerns the perception of the leader by others; second, relationship development, which focuses on the exchange with subordinates, i.e. how they are motivated; third, resource utilization, which concerns the ability of the leader to make use of personal talents and energies of subordinates. There is a strong contrast here with the individualistic elements of leadership. Instead, the focus is on the dynamics of interactive leadership at executive level, and how team members interact or distance themselves from each other, how power is shared in decision making and how language is used to give meaning to interactions (Bensimon and Neumann, 1993). According to Mintzberg (1973), these interpersonal roles are important in two respects. First, the formal authority of the leader/manager's role confers status on the leader, which in turn allows the development of interpersonal contacts. These contacts yield access to privileged information, which then enables the leader to make effective decisions. Second, interpersonal roles are used to empower other people to make decisions, who in turn provide new flows of information. The final pair of vignettes illustrate some of the key relationships between chief executive and other senior staff and how these are used in practice to build a leadership team and to develop corporate commitment.

The finance director

The first vignette is drawn from interchanges between one of the chief executives and the university's director of finance during one of their formal weekly meetings. The chief executive had already alerted the researcher to the key role played by the finance director in the management task. This particular finance director had previously been employed outside the higher education sector and was still finding his way in the life of academe. The chief executive particularly valued his ability to think creatively. The meeting took place against a background of intensifying financial pressures, imposed mainly by the then government's continued policy of holding student numbers at steady state (consolidation). The chief executive had requested prepared budgets ready for a forthcoming meeting of the board of governors. Specific information was requested about the financial implications of an early retirement scheme, the commitments arising from promoting research activity prior to the RAE, the budgetary positions of the various faculties, the IT budget and strategy (particularly capital demands of IT), a windfall from the Higher Education Funding Council and two items raised by the audit committee.

After listening to the finance director's immediate thoughts on each area, the chief executive responded with instructions and/or questions. For example, on the early retirement scheme the finance director said that he knew the numbers involved but the financial implications would not be available until next week. The chief executive responded: 'That's a priority. Do they involve long-term commitments? People [on the board] will want to know.' In considering possible over-commitments arising from research spending in anticipation of the RAE, the finance director confirmed that one school had been particularly active bringing in new research 'stars' and the financial commitments were considerable. 'How did we get into that position?', the chief executive asked. The finance director responded: 'The previous dean made assumptions of funding following student recruitment and gambling with research ratings.' In his view the best approach would be to provide the school with lifeline funding from central budget: 'So what

are we going to do? . . . Your recommendation is we put £X thousand in?'
'Yes, [the dean] is managing it but he needs a baseline.' With the various
items having been run through in similar fashion, the meeting drew to a
close after an hour. The finance director recapitulated: 'Overall, it's looking quite good – we're going to balance the budget.' The chief executive,
clearly more relaxed, summarized the position and tactics: 'That's terrific
. . . I'm quite happy to go with this . . . It's really good – we're meeting pay
awards, strategic objectives and funding blips . . . So we can say to the board
that we are clearly on line to reduce the baseline.'

After the meeting the chief executive confirmed to the researcher that
this was a clear example of day-to-day 'hands-on' management. The creative
thinking emanated from the director of finance's office, but the interchange
reveals how the chief executive empowered the director to make effective
budgetary advice. With financial stringency the watchword of consolidation,
the chief executive required the director of finance to run a sound financial
ship and keep the faculties in check. In this connection, it was also significant that the chief executive had recently decided to become personally
involved with the interim appraisal of the deans. In previous years he had
delegated the task to the deputy vice-chancellor. Now, in an atmosphere of
'unprecedented financial and political pressures', the need to be more
'domestic' and 'hands-on' was evident.

The deputy vice-chancellor

The second vignette is drawn from the weekly meetings of the same chief
executive with the deputy vice-chancellor. Like the roles of all the senior
managers in the case study institution, the deputy's role is negotiated annually. The basic job description and accountabilities provide a framework to
guide these negotiations, but once settled the parties sign up to new objectives and performance is reviewed against the objectives agreed. Hitherto
the deputy had taken major responsibility for international activities, on the
grounds that they had become vital as a source of income, yet fraught with
'quality' and adverse publicity dangers. The deputy's own description of his
role was a 'change agent', someone 'to get things done' and 'remove block-
ages'. Despite the international dimension, as we have seen he had also led
the steering group on strategic planning and remained closely involved
with the general academic life of the university: 'I enjoy getting things done
– I know all the course leaders and they know me. I deal with 80 per cent of
the core business of the university.'

The relationship with the chief executive was described as akin to friends
who think alike. Their weekly meetings, informal and convivial, were used
to discuss a range of issues. In order to make sense of the informational
sharing which occurred, it is necessary to allude to a meeting between
vice-chancellor and deputy earlier in the day. This occurred prior to a
meeting with a local further education college principal over the terms of
the university–college collaborative agreement. Negotiations, conducted on
the university's behalf by the deputy, had reached an impasse. The deputy

brought the chief executive up to speed with the negotiations and advised taking a hard line, even if it meant terminating the collaboration.

The chief executive concluded that it was worth listening to find out whether the college wanted a deal, at which point the deputy exited by the side door. The principal was invited in by the main door. The researcher was excluded from the first fifteen and most confidential minutes of the meeting, but was admitted thereafter. The atmosphere was cordial. The chief executive remarked that it was all 'very interesting ... There are nuances to it that I hadn't been aware of.' The principal confirmed that approaches from other institutions had been made. The chief executive remained poker-faced as the names of various competitors were raised. After listening intently, the chief executive asked, somewhat rhetorically: 'I take it from all this background that we're still your preferred partner?' The principal affirmed and then, almost as a casual aside, offered an olive branch of a variation of the terms being asked.

After the principal's departure the chief executive informed the researcher that he thought there was more to the affair than he had first thought. It would be worth asking around – talking to government office about plans for the sub-region, as well as to contacts on the county council, some industrialists and the chair of governors. The important point was to weigh the opportunities and threats.

Over lunch, the deputy and chief executive reviewed this and other pressing matters. The latest statistics on student repeats across faculties were discussed and problems in one area raised as a priority for action. On the subject of the local college, the chief executive said the conversation had centred on the threat from the competition and confirmed that a local university had started to exhibit decidedly predatory inclinations. The deputy expressed some surprise that this particular institution was 'sniffing round', and that this intelligence changed the situation somewhat. The fear was that the rival was reacting specifically to the policy of trying to tie up 'exclusive agreements' with local colleges and, fearing the outcome of the Dearing Review, was trying to move in before it was too late. Conversation then changed to other matters and the meeting ended with a reminder that they were both attending a local authority reception later in the evening when they would talk further about arrangements with the college. 'Can we afford it?', the deputy asked. 'Can we afford not to?', came the reply.

Conclusions

This chapter has focused on the daily activities and processes of the vice-chancellorship. Adopting the case for problematizing and illuminating the social practice of leadership, we then began to trace the outlines of chief executives' days. The need to think of leadership in terms of the language and metaphors of complex political systems, rather than engineering and simple linear models of command and control, was emphasized and then related to the context of an increasingly marketized and massified system of higher education, itself no longer immune to broader technological and global trends.

Despite the differences in the historical and organizational backgrounds of the case study universities, the landscapes of days of the chief executives bear some major similarities. The layout of their work, in the operational sense, is embedded in a meetings 'culture'. Diaries are tightly scheduled, given shape by a combination of formal meetings arising out of the committee and managerial structures of the institution and informal meetings with key groups and individuals involved in its governance and management. In the operational sense, it is primarily through these forums that the exercise of academic and executive leadership can be observed. It is also in the pattern of meetings with external constituencies that we can see how chief executives attempt to engage with their ambassadorial and representational roles, although these are explored more fully in Chapter 6.

These meetings and the use of the spaces between them afford some insight into certain common characteristics in patterns of behaviours. All work long hours, spend most of their time with others, engage in a broad spectrum of topics, many of which do not necessarily connect directly with the core business of the organization, and will rarely be seen issuing orders or making big decisions. In the same way, the ideas, imagination, ability to think strategically or manage change successfully, all of which are routinely recited in job specifications as the major requirements of the vice-chancellor's role, are unlikely to find obvious expression in the confines of a majority of these meetings. But the patterns of work are in a sense only the framework of working days. What really counts in terms of the social practice of managerial leadership is more likely to be found at a deeper level than the office diary. Our observations of leaders in action reveal some of the processes involved in their attempts to connect the vision and strategies with the day-to-day practice of leadership.

The first vignette exemplified the dynamics of senior management and vice-chancellor interactions in managing a mounting funding crisis. Here there was overlapping of concerns, the vignette illustrating the sort of constraints and impediments to the process of leadership in daily practice. It illustrated too how the vice-chancellor tried, not without some success, to engender a team spirit and develop the notion of shared 'ownership' of the decisions. Most importantly, it showed how the intertwining of strategic concerns with other issues, planned and unplanned, might threaten to push and pull policy lines off course. Again, the vice-chancellor was observed as the key initiator of action, the person most able to manipulate the various policy strands and keep the broad picture in view, despite the pressures. However, the task of moving the senior management of the institution towards collective development and ownership of funding strategies was complicated by other contextual forces. In this case, strategy was wrapped in the problematic of renegotiating accepted customs and practices in institutional budgetary allocations and working practices. Here the deans emerged as key players torn in this, as in other institutions, between loyalty to their faculties/schools and the demands of corporate responsibility. This is a theme to which we return in the next chapter.

The second vignette was an exemplar of the vice-chancellor's pivotal role in mediating between corporate/strategic and academic/operational demands. We have observed that the role of the vice-chancellor is in many key academic/professional areas formally circumscribed. The development of the academic curriculum as 'product', in terms of conception and design, delivery and assessment, is outside the direct control of the executive office. However, decision making about the broader academic structuring and market position of the institution is a key role. This vignette, concerning the assessment of a new opportunity to develop a new academic 'product', shows the vice-chancellor taking soundings and monitoring information from the key professionals involved. Even then the limitations to authority of the office to act without reference to other institutional players was revealed. Though the vice-chancellor decided to support the project, the next phase would be to convince the board and its chair.

The third and fourth vignettes revealed more graphically how the broader policy lines were worked on, monitored and amended in conjunction with key colleagues. As these final vignettes confirm, leadership, if it is to be successfully accomplished, can rarely be a solitary activity and involves constant interaction with colleagues in the pursuit of a 'shared' version of reality consistent with broader institutional goals. The need to work in unison with key colleagues in order to harness expertise, gather and monitor information was evident in all the case studies. It was apparent that each chief executive faced broadly similar problems, often funding-driven, requiring them first and foremost to challenge established behaviours and patterns of thinking, particularly in the ranks of senior management.

Taken together, the vignettes demonstrate two essential features. The first is further confirmation of some essential similarities in the operational patterns of work of the three vice-chancellors. Engaging in vision and strategic thinking with colleagues, setting priorities and agendas, and coping with scarce resources or diverse activities were part of the daily ritual of the chief executives' days. The layout of their work, the meetings culture, the formal and not-so-formal briefings, the long hours and demanding schedules and, as we shall see, their external ambassadorial and representational roles are in essence very similar. However, the second feature of the vignettes is evidence of important differences in the behaviour of the chief executives. Despite the core similarities in the nature of their work, chief executive behaviours reflected certain situation-specific factors. Although some of the issues – budgetary constraints, corporate spans of control to name but two – were essentially the same, the job retains considerable room for vice-chancellors to interpret and execute their role in distinctive ways or styles.

6

External Accountability:
Governing Bodies, Networking and
the Policy Community

The external dimensions of the role of vice-chancellor have become increasingly important in recent decades. Wider changes in society have, it is suggested (Bargh *et al.*, 1996), tilted the balance of university business away from internal, essentially academic, issues, to those of institutional positioning, mission and even survival. Vice-chancellors in consequence spend an increasing amount of time explaining the university and promoting its activities to the wider community both nationally and locally, and in turn reflecting inwards external demands and developments which require a response. As chief executive officers they also hold ultimate responsibility in the increasingly complex range of accountability checks to which universities are subject. These external demands have created internal changes as universities have developed planning and control systems to enable the university to respond. The complexity of these interrelationships with a growing number of stakeholders makes it increasingly difficult to distinguish internal from external dimensions. The system as a whole is becoming more permeable. As we argued in Chapter 1, the most difficult task is how to reconcile the institution's increasingly open intellectual engagement with its enveloping environment(s) and its need to retain normative focus and managerial coherence.

The vice-chancellor is both a conduit and a filter between the institution and the wider community and state. Once the external role might have largely been symbolic, town-and-gown links, for example, being primarily confined to ceremonial and dignified occasions, or conducted discreetly in periodic meetings with ministers and civil servants. Now there is much greater public involvement with local and regional enterprises, whether private or public sector, as well as cultural and social activities. The university as a business is now a critical dimension of any institutional profile which the vice-chancellor must both promote and exploit.

This increased emphasis is of relatively recent origin. The sixties proved a watershed in a number of ways. Initially, public and therefore political concern in the late fifties and early sixties had been to secure a sufficiency of student places to meet the rising aspirations of young people and their parents for higher education. The sector developed a highly visible public profile. Once expansion had begun to deliver higher education opportunities to a larger proportion of the population, and a greater diversity of institutions and higher education qualifications existed, public interest expanded from a simple focus on the number and availability of places to the nature of the provision available. What did a university offer as opposed to a (then) polytechnic? Was a degree from The Open University the same as a degree from other universities? Why did only some institutions provide part-time courses? Universities individually and collectively began to define and justify their patterns of provision – not only to the UGC and Parliament but also to the wider community of potential students and their families. Vice-chancellors became more visible public figures.

The government was acutely interested for two reasons. First, a newly elected Labour government, emphasizing the importance of science and technology, wanted to see a more commercially and industrially responsive higher education system. One result was the decision to create a more vocationally oriented higher education sector, with newly established institutions, polytechnics, as alternatives to universities. Second, the financial crises which beset the government made them sharply aware of the resources being poured into higher education. Their concern to achieve value for money resulted in a publicly expressed interest as to whether changes to patterns of delivery might result in significant savings to the Exchequer. This ongoing search for cost reductions led the government to take a more direct interest in those matters that had hitherto been seen as the private domain of universities. Vice-chancellors were forced on to the defensive and a long running public debate about higher education ensued. Universities and consequently vice-chancellors found themselves not only justifying a diverse range of university practices hitherto of little interest to anyone but academics, but also having to persuade an often reluctant academic community of the need for change within relatively short time-scales.

The search for economies has remained a constant problem. In the ensuing decades successor bodies to the UGC have increasingly found themselves implementing a government agenda with little room for manoeuvre. University grants have now become funding contracts, with performance targets and penalties for failure to deliver. Both research and teaching are explicitly assessed, with significant financial consequences in the case of research at least for any institution with declining or inadequate performance outcomes. All vice-chancellors keep an eye on their institutional ranking in the numerous performance league tables which are now constructed and published. These are the formal and visible dimensions of the accountability process, particularly in relation to the state, and in Chapter 1 we discussed the reasons for this growth of an 'audit society'. As head of the institution the vice-chancellor must take ultimate responsibility for performance rankings, and increasing amounts of time are spent directly or indirectly on these issues.

However, the vice-chancellor also invests time and energy mediating in more informal but equally important ways between the institution and the wider community. In particular, the relationship with the governing body has become more complex. Both have to be taken into account in any assessment of whether the external role and responsibilities have significantly changed as a consequence of the wider changes in higher education described above.

Balance of activities

Vice-chancellors were asked about their external role in terms of both the balance between internal and external activities and how they prioritize activities. While there was evidence of tension between some chairs and vice-chancellors on this issue, overall there was widespread agreement that external activities are an essential part of a vice-chancellor's role. One reported that this was an item discussed at interview and 'it was made clear to me before I came that the university wanted a vice-chancellor with a certain sort of public profile, both locally and nationally'. Another had definite views about the importance of 'the ambassadorial and representational role' and consequently had a high personal involvement and time commitment in trying to raise the public profile of the university.

However, there were interesting variations in the assessment made by different vice-chancellors as to the balance of time they allocated to external and internal activities. These ranged from one estimate of half and half, with the balance tilting in favour of the external, to more typical estimates of 20 or 25 per cent of time spent externally. There is some evidence from the interview sample that vice-chancellors who have been longer in post spend more time on external activities. Perhaps this simply reflects the fact that initially, as one vice-chancellor put it, 'I felt I had to know a lot of what went on in the university, the broader questions I'd be dealing with, so I devoted myself internally.' However, there is also evidence that increasing volatility, particularly in relation to the financial climate, causes even experienced vice-chancellors to reassess their priorities periodically. One recounted how in previous years, encouraged by the board of governors, the role had been 'to act as an ambassador, an icon, a totem, an image-maker for the university'. Now, however, because of rising financial and political pressures on the institution, both felt it necessary to adopt a more 'domestic or hands-on role'. Some chairs of governing councils expressed strong reservations about the time spent externally. 'If you're going to be a chief executive you've got to really run the business, which means spending time on the business and not on other things', as one put it. This chair remained unconvinced by arguments about the importance of the ambassadorial role, but this may partly be a reaction to the fact that the vice-chancellor of this university was among those who spent a high proportion of time externally. Others thought there might be a tendency 'to overplay the external relations bit', but generally such differences of view do not appear to result in outright disagreements.

While these reactions may simply reflect a pessimistic phase concerning the financial climate for universities, it also underlines the importance of disentangling the various dimensions of the external role. Some activities are seen as relatively prestigious and beneficial to the institution; membership of one of the funding councils tends to be viewed in this way. About others there is more disagreement; the benefits of active involvement in the CVCP are sometimes queried both by vice-chancellors and chairmen. The relative importance attached to local as compared to national activities varies according to the university's mission. What is clear is that external activities are now rarely viewed as a simple extension of civic responsibility; a more direct pay-off to the institution has to be identified if the vice-chancellor's time is to be committed. The test applied by one vice-chancellor was fairly utilitarian, namely 'whether they are going to contribute directly to the well-being or purposes or reputation of the university, or whether they are going to equip me to be a better vice-chancellor in some way'. A recent reassessment had led this vice-chancellor to curtail several national and European activities. Another suggested there were some activities that 'just had to be done'.

> An example would be the Training and Enterprise Council. In terms of the volume of paper and time it's quite a pain. But a vice-chancellor of a university with a particular regional and local commitment, with an enormous army of part-time students, which is comprehensive in nature – well it's quite clear to me that it's something you should do as part of the job, so I do it.

This view of the importance of an involvement in local and regional activities is perhaps not so surprising for a new university, but it is apparent that even pre-1992 universities are conscious that local and regional networking has become increasingly important. As the registrar of one such university remarked, 'over the last ten to fifteen years things have changed dramatically. I mean we do now try to work closely with the city.'

The governing body

Writing in the mid-fifties, a distinguished commentator on university affairs suggested that 'one of the great virtues of lay governors is that they can represent the modern patron of universities: the taxpayer' (Ashby and Stout, 1956). More recently doubts about the effectiveness of that 'representation' in terms of delivering value for money were publicly aired by government and steps were taken, particularly in the eighties, to strengthen accountability. The relationship between the vice-chancellor and governing council has been particularly affected by changes in governance culture. In the old universities the effect of the Jarratt Report was to strengthen the role of council and vice-chancellor, particularly in relation to strategic planning. The Education Reform Act (1988) replaced the more politically representative governing bodies typical of the former polytechnics, with smaller executive boards having a majority of independent governors, particularly reflecting those with business interests and expertise. Both developments were intended to promote a change in governance culture, to ensure universities not only became better managed institutions, but also displayed greater sensitivity to industrial and commercial interests while themselves becoming more entrepreneurial and responsive to external markets. In particular, the newer executive style boards would, it was hoped, prove more successful in ensuring a greater measure of accountability in the university sector. For the vice-chancellor, therefore, handling relationships with council/governors is a critical part of managing external relations and accountability.

A decade later, it is possible to assess more clearly how the process of accountability is managed and what impact this has had, in particular, on the role of the vice-chancellor. The change wrought by Jarratt (1985) and the ERA (1988) has given governing bodies a clear surveillance task. The report of the Nolan Committee (1995) also made it clear that in carrying out this task the governors are to reflect the interests of consumers and employers. The university is also accountable, through governors, to the relevant funding council for the appropriate and efficient use of public funds, and ultimately to central government and scrutiny by the Public Accounts Committee. But the transition from an elite to a mass higher education system has also transformed the nature of accountability. Higher education is no longer a system regulated exclusively by public policy, but one in which market and quasi-market forces play an important role. Institutions must not only meet the formal requirements of accountability, however important, but to be successful they must also be perceived as engaged with the wider community, responsive to changing demand and clear as to mission. Governors are intended to be an important means of helping institutions to delineate new markets and become more responsive to existing ones.

Our analysis confirms many of the findings of the study of governance by Bargh *et al.* (1996), which stresses the increasing importance of senior management teams, headed by the vice-chancellor as chief executive, and their working relationship with the chairman of council and one or two key members, usually those who chair the important committees. One vice-chancellor summarized it in the following terms

> The council as a whole is not, I have to say, a very effective body. But individuals on the council are very important to me. I've got some good lay members I use as sounding boards, they chair small committees, get involved in enterprises.

Vice-chancellor and chair: a complementary relationship?

In the guidance which the funding councils issue to councils or boards of governors, and the advice which the Council of University Chairmen (1995) has circulated to its members, there is little consideration of the relationship with the vice-chancellor. Yet the relationship is important to the successful management of the institution and effective working relationships with council or governors. Several chairs we interviewed had been responsible for appointing more than one vice-chancellor, sometimes at more than one institution. They were all convinced that role was becoming more complex and that a smooth working relationship built on mutual trust and respect was essential. It was an important part of the (unstated) appointment criteria that the vice-chancellor and chair should get on, should be on the same wavelength. One indicated that for a recent appointment he had individually lunched with all the candidates to ensure he felt comfortable he could work with them. This complementary relationship, as one researcher has suggested (Stewart, 1991), raises many issues. It strengthens the top leadership but at the same time poses problems from a corporate governance perspective, raising questions as to whether and how the chair can actively retain and represent the interests of external stakeholders while simultaneously enjoying a close working partnership with the chief executive. One example of this ambiguity is the question of who chooses whom. When a chair on behalf of council takes the lead in the search for a new vice-chancellor, this accords with constitutional theory. In practice a vice-chancellor often 'chooses' the chair, taking the initiative on those occasions when a new chair is required, since he or she too is concerned to secure a good working relationship. As one chair recounted:

> We lunched in March and he told me the chairman wished to retire. I expected the next question to be whether I knew anyone who could be a candidate, but he asked me if I would consider standing. We lunched again in May and he asked the question again. I said, if this is serious you and I had better get to know each other properly. We then spent a lot of time together in the summer and I took the chair in September.

The motivation of the vice-chancellor on this occasion was not only to secure an effective working relationship, but also because the chair was an accountant and 'I knew we needed a strong financial manager. I needed skills available at council level that I knew I personally didn't have.' This also illustrates the complementary relationship to which Stewart refers. Both, however, believed they had a robust relationship: 'certainly not a duo that is tweedle-dee and tweedle-dum', according to the chair.

While most chairs and vice-chancellors have formal pre-council meetings, and some chairs intermittently attend senior management team meetings by invitation, it is the unscheduled but regular meetings which are clearly most important both in terms of the personal accountability of the vice-chancellor and in setting the general direction of the university. Most spoke of these informal sessions as laying the foundations of their relationship, and they typically happen once a week 'or more frequently if necessary'. Clearly difficulties can arise when the chair is not available for informal discussions either with the vice-chancellor or with other council members. At one university where the chair was not a local figure there were many reservations among council members because 'he's not part of the local scene and therefore there's no possibility of having informal discussions about university related matters. He's a key figure in the university and he breezes in and breezes out and gets on the train and he's gone.' Members of council, whether lay or academic, want to be able to use the chair to express concerns or raise issues outside the formality of the meeting itself. The chair provides an important channel of communication, particularly with the vice-chancellor.

Informal meetings provide opportunities to discuss not only agenda items in advance of council, but also those issues which need to be monitored even though specific decisions are not required immediately. Both parties seem equally concerned that there should be no crossed wires arising from lack of communication. As one vice-chancellor put it, 'we absolutely need to discuss any matter that significantly affects our public position locally. For example, there's a proposal here for a major development by the local football club. And there are completely divided views both in the university and in the city. So we're in a very hot spot.' There is a substantial investment of time and energy to ensure that the relationship works smoothly and a recognition that both partners need to acknowledge the boundaries and limitations of their mutual responsibilities. For some this relationship mirrors that between council and senate and 'it would be a very serious occasion, and a sad day for this institution, if council were at loggerheads with the senate', as one chair put it.

While this may suggest a mutually supportive relationship, rather than a directly accountable one, it reflects the fact that accountability is increasingly a process jointly managed by the chair and vice-chancellor. Their relationship holds the key to that process. Several chairs spoke of their experience in industry where, if the chair of the board is at odds with the chief executive, one or other usually has to go. There is therefore a strong incentive to seek solutions to problems that both parties, and their respective 'constituencies', can live with. However, it is also clear that frank discussion does occur and disagreements are aired. 'At times the chairman can be very critical indeed. In private, that is. As a result of which I've often refined or changed things', one vice-chancellor acknowledged. A chair recalled the time 'when I realized the new management information system was wrong. The VC and I sat down privately and I said we must cut the cackle, I'm not prepared for this any further. I made it quite plain I wanted it dealt with.' While most chairs make their views known on a wide range of issues, only in exceptional circumstances will they insist on their view prevailing, usually in relation to a major financial issue. As one recounted:

> About five years ago the governing body dug its heels in because we were very worried we were going into the red. We said we're not going into the red, we're going to put aside £1 million a year and build up a

small reserve. The academics did not like that at all. I mean we did dig in and faced them down.

In practice, most consultations at the informal meetings are a mutual sounding-out exercise resulting in compromise, both parties deciding any disagreement is not sufficiently serious to jeopardize the relationship. However, the relationship is not without difficulties, as one vice-chancellor, concerned at how isolated the university had become from its local community, openly acknowledged. In consequence, 'there's certainly a debate between the chair and other senior governors and myself about institutional leadership, the ambassadorial/external role and the hands-on elements of the job.' Both the chair and vice-chancellor described it as 'a creative tension' but it was clear that it was sometimes more of the latter than the former. Vice-chancellors have to learn to manage upwards as well as downwards in the system.

The most difficult area for the chair and council to monitor is probably that of academic standards, primarily seen as the business of senate. Audit and assessment reports now provide council or governors with some information and occasionally this provides an opportunity for intervention. One vice-chancellor indicated that in the light of their recent audit report, the chair had indicated that 'I haven't pressed down hard enough on the system. It's probably right that I need to do that if I'm going to evaluate how well we're doing against our own stated targets.' However, as we noted in Chapter 1, in many ways the university's core activities of teaching and research are the least amenable to being managed and the structural separation between council and senate makes it even more difficult for council to exercise its scrutiny on behalf of external stakeholders in these areas.

Governors and the external community

Governors have links with the wider community which are important to vice-chancellors in the delivery of institutional mission. They provide key and sometimes critical contacts with the world of industry, the professions and wider external networks on which the university seeks to capitalize. There is a desire to include representatives of major local industrial and business interests, particularly if there is already an education or training link with the university. Just as industrial companies put major shareholding interests on the board, so many universities include major industrial or corporate interests on the governing body. One chair recounted that the original invitation to join the board of the (then) polytechnic was a direct consequence of being managing director of a company which was also a major client of the business school, which validated in-house company training courses. It is the vice-chancellor's responsibility to make sure the relationship actually works to the university's benefit and that membership of the governing body is not simply seen as an honorific role. One recounted that the governing body representatives of a major international company, whose headquarters were in the region, 'originally did very little for the institution. A few industrial placements, that's all. I've had to go in at a very senior level and sort this out.'

Some universities establish a sub-committee to draw up lists of individuals who might serve as governors, so enabling vacancies to be filled smoothly. People may be sounded out informally about their willingness to serve if invited. It is a sign of the increasing concern, following the Cadbury Report, to attract governors with appropriate skills and experience. Securing a mix of relevant skills and experience to promote the university's interests, and harnessing those skills to steer the activities and vet proposed developments within the institution, is a key part of the task vice-chancellors have to manage. 'We've been very careful to try and pick the people with the skills we need', one said, pointing out that they had a former merchant banker chairing the athletics committee raising money for new sports facilities, and an estates committee run by 'a distinguished ex-surveyor from one of the big London firms'. Other members of the management team simply want governors to 'apply external standards to what we're trying to do; tell us if what we're coming up with sounds silly in business terms'.

Vice-chancellors are also conscious of the need to make positive inputs into local and regional schemes, whether to tackle urban regeneration, improve staying-on rates in local schools, aid local charitable causes, make joint research and development contracts with local firms or just promote the region more widely. Sometimes this is viewed as general public relations and image building, with the added advantage of making the kinds of contacts which can prove useful: for example, when the university wants to smooth out a planning problem. In other cases university and regional interests are seen as very closely integrated. More than one university had contributed money or resources in kind to local initiatives which were certainly not in the short-term or narrowly defined interests of the university: for example, a feasibility study for reintroducing light rapid transit (LRT) to the city streets. A survey conducted for the Committee of Vice Chancellors and Principals and Centre for Urban and Regional Development Studies (1994) uncovered links both with local economic development and more generally into wider social network and development schemes. Our own research confirmed both these aspects with vice-chancellors involved with Common Purpose and various City Initiatives, typically public–private partnerships aimed at promoting and supporting regeneration schemes. One pro vice-chancellor involved with knowledge transfer had played a key role in securing joint bids with local industry for European funding. Another had developed an innovation centre, bringing together representatives of companies that had benefited from their teaching company schemes. These were asked to 'talk to invited audiences of local industrialists and businessmen to tell them what the university has done for them. It gives the university a better local profile.' Some vice-chancellors recognized that improving recruitment to the university is inextricably bound up with improving the profile of the region. 'We are a new university in a low profile region in an unfashionable part of the world', one vice-chancellor acknowledged. It was therefore 'important for the university and the vice-chancellor to be seen to be committed to the region, to be active in it'.

Networking: locally, regionally, nationally and internationally

The vice-chancellor is also expected to be involved in networking to promote the university and its image, even when no immediate outcome is in prospect. These occasions are constantly overlapping, particularly locally and regionally. The opportunity to have a word with people of influence is one that is seen by many vice-chancellors as critically important. In some cases the networks an individual developed were a factor in their appointment to the post. Particular roles may be undertaken because of the opportunities for networking they bring. It is difficult to gauge the effectiveness of these occasions since general image building is not easy to assess and the number of occasions on which contacts gained in this way are utilized, and to what effect, is impossible to determine. What is clear is that the networking process is widely valued and seen as an essential attribute of a successful vice-chancellor. One chaired the regional arts board because of the excellent networking and lobbying opportunities this offered. Although he was personally both interested in and committed to the arts, the regional arts world was also important for the faculty of arts at the university, both as a source of students and as an arena for enhancing its reputation. Being chair of the regional board also resulted in ex-officio membership of the Arts Council nationally, which in turn offered further networking opportunities.

Others focus entirely on the region or locality, 'because the test has to be what's the benefit for the university', and as head of a new university this vice-chancellor saw little benefit in national networking. There was a widespread view, particularly prevalent in old universities, that 'overseas it often has to be the vice-chancellor. It's a status thing. If it's not the vice-chancellor you won't be taken seriously by foreign governments or other universities.'

Other aspects of networking are much more intangible. Several vice-chancellors mentioned the need to cultivate a group of 'friends of the university': 'good people with time on their hands who would involve themselves in occasional missions on behalf of the university', as one put it. Universities need 'to find distinctiveness and celebrate it with friends; not just alumnae but highly placed friends of the university, people to say the right word at the right time in the right place'. Another vice-chancellor had used contacts in the world of theatre and TV to enhance the university's image. An edition of the *South Bank Show*, filmed in front of the main university building and talking about the university, was 'public relations on quite a grand scale. I'm using it essentially to promote the university, promote its image. You know I'm using these people, I don't mean improperly, but I'm using them to make things happen here.'

Two contrasting examples can be drawn from the periods of observation undertaken during the course of the research. One involved a lunch, arranged at the invitation of the vice-chancellor to take place in the university dining room, with the archdeacon of a nearby cathedral. There was no specific purpose to the meeting; instead it was part of the vice-chancellor's attempts to get to know all the constituent elements of the local community and build bridges and networks which might come in useful. The archdeacon, in turn, was interested to learn more about the university and its multi-ethnic community. The two discussed the similarities and differences in their respective roles and organizations, the role of prayer in a university, the values an academic community espouses and the work of the university chaplains. The second example was a local event, a community fun-run in which several members of the university were participating. The vice-chancellor presented one of the prizes and one of the deans commentated on the race(s). The entire evening was spent showing a positive public face to the local community, while also talking to the chief executive of the local radio station about sponsorship deals and getting the local council to agree to sponsor a reception for new overseas students in September. These were among a number of relatively minor, but nonetheless important, local links forged during the course of the evening.

Managing the knowledge boundary: the vice-chancellor's role

In Chapter 1 we argued that the boundaries between the university and other knowledge-producing institutions as well as other types of post-secondary education are being eroded. The vice-chancellor must lead and shape the way the university handles this interface, which involves important challenges to many traditional academic values and sometimes the need to reassert those values in the face of increasing pressures to differentiate the system. One example can be found in the links with further education institutions cultivated by an increasing number of universities with the support of the funding councils. Chapter 4 explored the negotiations between one vice-chancellor and the principal of a local further education college, illustrating the tensions which can arise. The university had an agreement to collaborate with the college, allowing it to run a limited range of courses validated by the university. Such agreements help universities to achieve their wider access mission by drawing on new student constituencies, and also help to secure recruitment targets, since most students start their course in a college but complete it in the university. Managing such agreements and deciding which are appropriate strategically for the university can be both time-consuming and complex. With fears of dumbing-down never far below the surface, the vice-chancellor must ensure that strong quality controls and monitoring arrangements are in place, as otherwise externally provided courses could undermine the university's reputation.

Externalizing the delivery of courses always involves risk. One old university had developed a number of entrepreneurial centres to offer distance learning provision at postgraduate level both in the UK and overseas. The registrar estimated this produced about £7 million turnover annually for the university. But it also involved considerable financial risk since markets, particularly those overseas, could collapse, leaving the university carrying overheads, including staffing costs, it was unable to recoup. Consequently, 'the VC was very proactive in certain areas' to minimize the risk both financially and to quality.

Examples of the flow in the opposite direction abound, with provision such as nursing and other health-related professions coming formally within the universities' boundaries, where these were previously located in separate schools of nursing attached to hospitals or in specialist training units. Consequently, vice-chancellors have spent increasing amounts of time in negotiations with area health authorities and NHS trusts; many are members of trust boards, which is a further demand on time. One vice-chancellor was convinced the university would never have secured the contract to deliver nurse training, and a centre for medicine, if the relationship had not been deliberately nurtured by the creation of a health partnership and by three of the senior management team taking up membership of local health trusts.

There is also a growing need to ensure that what is available internally is clearly understood and acceptable to the different external constituencies. What you can do, as one vice-chancellor put it, 'is to fashion or package what you have internally so that it's attractive externally. It needs coordination, management and presentation from the top.' The presentation is to industry and the professions as well as to potential students; certainly the student interface is being transformed. Meeting recruitment targets is a constant concern for some universities, particularly in less popular curriculum areas. At certain times of the year vice-chancellors may well get involved in detailed debates or management of this area. One had 'toured all the admissions offices at the critical period' to talk to people about how things were going and whether the university could do more to assist. 'I need to be seen to be involved' was the message. At one senior management team meeting which we observed, the head of recruitment spent a considerable period of time discussing the need for a specific prospectus targeted at different categories of student and how to ensure the schools in the university complied with a common format for recruitment. Another university was concerned not primarily about numbers but the quality of its student intake, as reflected in the 'A' level points score. The vice-chancellor had consequently 'chaired a small group that met in August when the actual decisions were taken. I looked into that in a lot of detail.'

Relations with government

The growing importance of the regional dimension, further enhanced by devolution in Scotland and Wales and the establishment of the Scottish

Parliament and Welsh Assembly, now means that all vice-chancellors, not just those from new universities, are keen to have a local and regional profile. When the CVCP survey (1994) was conducted shortly after the end of the binary system, the authors noted that 74 per cent of new universities recorded links with the locality/region as having a high priority, whereas only 47 per cent of old universities expressed similar views. Several vice-chancellors from old universities suggested this had now changed. 'I don't think there would be the same feeling now,' one said, noting that local contacts would be essential, 'particularly if there comes to be a regional layer of government which has some responsibility for higher education.' For universities in Scotland and Wales the importance of the local/regional relationship has been enhanced. Having had both separate funding councils and sometimes distinctive higher education policies even before the formal establishment of separate legislatures, vice-chancellors regard the more intimate environment positively. 'We are fortunate that the government is just there across the road and we maintain very close relationships with them', one acknowledged. Another noted the ease with which an informal word could be had with key people, because 'if there's a function on at the Bank of Scotland I can go along knowing the chairman of the funding council is likely to be there and the under secretary from the Scottish Office.'

Not all are convinced that higher education is able to represent its own interests successfully, because so few people in the system perceive how they are viewed by the external world. One vice-chancellor, with direct experience of the interface between government departments and higher education, believes that this lack of awareness is a fatal weakness. 'Academics are only interested in their subject and research whereas on the whole the country does not care about research. It is seen by the Treasury as an overhead that has to be carried, and therefore minimized, and unless you realize this you're sunk.' This vice-chancellor in consequence queried the effectiveness of much of the lobbying undertaken by higher education. Most collective promotion of the sector is organized through the CVCP. However, individual vice-chancellors also take every opportunity to influence ministers and civil servants. If a vice-chancellor is a member of a national committee or agency, then opportunities often arise for informal discussions. Some chairs and council members also have contacts of this kind which can prove useful. There were few signs of regular and systematic contacts, however; instead, there were periodic events such as speaking engagements by politicians, degree ceremonies, the occasional dinner or lunch, perhaps in conjunction with local business leaders or perhaps to mark the opening of some new development at the university. Higher education does not presently have a high political profile, although more students from a greater diversity of backgrounds now participate. During the past two decades the government has devolved many of its detailed decision-making powers and responsibilities to bodies such as the funding councils and other quangos. In consequence, many of the issues on which, in the past, lobbying government would have been an obvious course of action now have to be addressed elsewhere.

The vice-chancellor's network: the CVCP

Now seen as the collective voice of the university sector, the CVCP has undergone several metamorphoses over the years in both its constitution and its staffing. Post-war vice-chancellors were adamant they could neither speak on behalf of their university nor commit the institution to a particular course of action. This perception of the role, however, became increasingly untenable. The establishment of the Robbins Committee and the subsequent expansion of both student numbers and the number of university institutions was something of a watershed. Responsibility for the UGC was transferred from the Treasury to the Department of Education, as recommended by Robbins (Committee on Higher Education, 1963), which made vice-chancellors increasingly aware of the need to represent university interests more proactively.

As a result the CVCP was placed on a more professional footing, with increased staffing, and came to be seen as the collective voice of the university sector. The increased dependence on state funding which has characterized higher education in the post-war era raised fears of a possible threat to university autonomy and hence implicitly to academic freedom. Again there was a heightened concern at the time of Robbins. A paper to the CVCP suggested that 'effective autonomy is only likely to be maintained by adopting a positive policy and putting it forward to the Government and the public'. The establishment of the binary policy, post Robbins, and the effects of the Woolwich Speech (Crosland, 1965), in which the new public sector was identified as being 'under social control, directly responsive to social needs', was a further indication of the need for a clearer public articulation of the role and contribution of the university sector in relation to national needs. Individually and collectively via the CVCP vice-chancellors began to give more systematic attention to this dimension of their work.

More recently the ending of the binary system in 1992 and the consequent increase in membership as university institutions doubled in number has changed perceptions once more. Interviews revealed a considerable diversity of view among both vice-chancellors and chairs as to the usefulness of the organization. Nonetheless, while many believe it to be less efficacious than in the past, most accept it serves a function and is the only existing organization to fulfil this essential role. As one sceptical chair put it, 'I accept that if the CVCP didn't exist there would be a need to create something for lobbying and PR, if nothing else.' Many chairs also believe that the vice-chancellor must be part of the network picking up information about trends and developments. Additionally, as a more supportive chair suggested, 'the vice-chancellor has got to be exposed to the thinking of other vice chancellors.' A third viewed it, reasonably sympathetically, as 'a support unit for vice-chancellors. Inevitably it's a pretty lonely job.' Vice-chancellors themselves had very diverse views of the organization and the extent of its effectiveness as a network through which to promote their own institution as well as the interests of the sector generally. At the iconoclastic end are those who almost never attend meetings but who nevertheless realize that occasionally attendance is essential precisely because the organization is the collective voice of universities: 'Last year when that debate about top-up fees took place, I decided I'd better go because otherwise the troops would think I wasn't taking life seriously.'

Others feel that 'just because it's there' a vice-chancellor has to go: 'otherwise people would wonder, you know, did this university actually exist.' Some clearly feel that enlargement and the consequent diversity of interests across the sector has made the CVCP lose its way. 'It's a very curious organization these days. I suspect my reaction today is very different to what it might have been a dozen or fifteen years ago.' This vice-chancellor, while mildly supportive, is not prepared to give any of his time to its activities. He has what he describes as a minimal involvement but 'wants to keep in touch'. In complete contrast are the views of two vice-chancellors who have taken an active role. One believed that such an involvement 'raises the profile and reputation of the university if it's successful'. While the interests of individual institutions have to be subordinated to the common cause, clearly the CVCP opens up new contacts which can be subsequently utilized on an individual basis. Indeed, as the different interest groups within the CVCP coalesce more permanently, sometimes the collective interests represented may be those of the Russell group or the modern universities group rather than the university sector as a whole. Another vice-chancellor acknowledged that the biggest drain on his time had been the CVCP, but 'the chairman accepted there would be some potential benefits to the way I do the job here because I'd be more aware of trends and developments and opportunities.' Nonetheless, he found it difficult to weigh the gains and losses.

No longer a club of like-minded individuals with common interests ('the gossip is not of the same quality these days'), the CVCP has inevitably become more of an umbrella organization promoting broadly based interests. Much of the networking, including that of a supportive nature, takes place among the self-organized university interest groups, such as the Russell group, which promote particular segments of university interests. All this might be more familiar in, say, the American system, where universities with very distinctive profiles and missions are the norm. In the UK, in contrast, despite the attention given to developing institutional missions, universities are still broadly expected to share common characteristics by virtue of which they are clearly identified as universities. The diversity of views concerning the CVCP clearly reflects this confusion, which betokens a British system in transition. Nonetheless, it does provide networking links to an important range of different policy communities, including, of course, the government. When key issues are at stake – for example, the question of fees, which has a clear public interest dimension – the CVCP is the only organization able to develop a policy to which the sector as a whole can subscribe irrespective of the views and interests of particular institutions. In this respect it remains an important network for vice-chancellors, although the extent of any involvement varies widely.

Accountability and the rise of the quangos

The past decade has seen a rapid increase in the number and range of monitoring and assessment checks throughout the system. The complexity of returns to the funding councils have increased. The assessment of both teaching and research has become quantified so that criteria are clearly specified even if they remain contested in the academic community. Almost all institutions have a number of teaching assessment visits each year and research is assessed on an agreed cycle, which is currently four years. The assessment culture has permeated the university system and, being distinctly unpopular with most academics but of great importance to the future of individual institutions in terms of funding and reputation, has to be sensitively managed by vice-chancellors and occupies a significant proportion of their time at critical periods. The research assessment process has probably caused the greatest anguish and resulted in the most far-reaching change as the generalized contractual requirement to undertake research has become quantified in terms of the number and type of publications required. Substantial sums of money are at stake and, as is clear, several vice-chancellors believe their own reputation and perhaps continued tenure turned on the outcome for the institution. One result was their extensive hands-on involvement, particularly in the period immediately prior to submission. 'Between March and April myself, the pro vice-chancellors and four other senior academics spent every Saturday here. We went through every submission and looked at every member of staff and I would just weed them out.' Another agreed that although the RAE, like most other areas, was formally devolved to a pro vice-chancellor, 'I felt this was sufficiently critical I had to be equally involved', and he too had spent a lot of time on the detail of the submission.

This, however, only illustrates the vice-chancellor's role in the final phase of the process. In those universities with a significant research profile, vice-chancellors have often been involved in serious restructuring of the institution by combining/merging departments into larger units or, in some cases, abolishing departments which were unlikely to contribute effectively to the RAE. Many universities have sought to secure the early retirement of older staff who are no longer considered research-active in order to appoint younger lecturers building new research careers. Such restructuring can often, of course, be highly controversial, especially if the policy is identified with the vice-chancellor personally. Other vice-chancellors have gone to major lengths to achieve academic support, putting their own prestige on the line. One described how the need to close a department on grounds of quality shortly after taking up the post was put to senate, with 'all the cards put on the table to seek their support. I said you mustn't shirk this by abstaining or whatever and they voted in favour. If they hadn't, I would have had serious concerns about going on.'

Teaching quality assessment is more pervasive because all institutions are equally affected but, to date, it has had a greater effect on reputation than finance in terms of outcome. However, vice-chancellors feel they must take these exercises seriously and try to build up a strong profile of excellence in teaching. It was clear to the old universities that it would be dangerous if the new university sector developed a reputation for excellence in teaching at their expense, since teaching is likely to be of far greater interest to potential undergraduate applicants than research reputation. As most universities want to improve the quality of their intake as reflected in 'A' level points scores, teaching reputation is important. Many chairs are alert to these points because, as one put it, 'particularly in a research-based university, teaching is not all it is cracked up to be'. Another was clear that 'initially we didn't focus enough on the teaching and we started to get a worrying number of satisfactory grades instead of excellent. We learned our lesson and the vice-chancellor has now given the matter his attention so we are now getting excellent in our recent assessments.' It is the vice-chancellor who signals to the university that these issues are being given increased priority and who will normally find time to greet assessment teams.

Interpreting external demands

As well as representing the university externally and identifying its skills and programmes to appropriate groups within the wider community, the vice-chancellor must also interpret the demands of government and perhaps highlight wider trends affecting the ability of the institution to realize its goals. Part of this depends on the way in which the vice-chancellor chooses to spend time externally – which invitations are accepted, particularly where they involve long-term commitments. Whatever the specific motivation, the general information gathering which takes place is equally significant. This is fed back to the senior management team, who, in turn, feed appropriate elements into other meetings. Clearly this is not simply information but an interpretation of events, whether these be current trends, government reports or changes in emphasis as new initiatives unfold. One vice-chancellor who was chairing a CVCP committee on research and technology transfer was invited, as a consequence, to a seminar run by the Royal Society. 'I could pick up from that certain threads, the way the argument is moving about research selectivity. That's very relevant to the way the university has to develop in order not to be left high and dry.' As a result, this vice-chancellor had lengthy discussions with the management team but also with those directly responsible for research policy internally within the university.

Information must be used to help members of the academic community to make realistic assessments about the chance of achieving particular objectives. Most vice-chancellors have found this a challenging task, since they believe that many academics have little understanding of the external world. One clearly did not expect to succeed but nonetheless felt it essential to keep trying. 'I certainly see myself as trying to understand and represent feelings on the ground. While at the same time being prepared to say to people "look, do you actually expect me to put that case to the Secretary of State".' Another took an equally robust view when faced with academic views he believed were politically naïve: 'I tell 'em, tell 'em – you're all wet. You know – this is not the way the world is, brother!'

Personal interaction is not always involved. One way vice-chancellors influence the permeability of the organization is via the organizational structures they establish to act as a gateway to the university. These influence the extent to which the university is receptive to information flows from various communities. The CVCP survey of universities and communities notes that only four universities did not refer to the region in their strategic plan. But there were significant differences between old and new universities as to the weight accorded to international and regional links, with the former laying significantly more stress on international connections. The latter are more likely to have established a regional office, with a member of the senior management team having regional responsibilities as part of their portfolio. New universities were significantly more likely than old universities to regard themselves as proactive in relation to the region. This involves not only vice-chancellors but other members of the university who may be encouraged to take on key roles in local or regional organizations or on national bodies. The CVCP survey noted that many universities fail to capitalize on their links simply because information is not coordinated and shared.

Conclusions

Chapter 1 explored the changing context in which higher education is delivered and the implication of these changes for institutional leadership. One important dimension is the extent to which the external impinges on the internal or core elements of the university as these institutions lose their monopoly over knowledge production and therefore the internal–external boundaries no longer have the same meaning. In such circumstances the role of the vice-chancellor also changes. In addition to carrying out some of the traditional external functions, many of which still persist, the vice-chancellor must now steer the institution in managing and redefining its boundaries and opening up the institution to challenging new influences and developments, without creating a collapse of morale. Moreover, as governments increasingly steer higher education at a distance, an array of new bodies and agencies have been created to assess or oversee the internal processes of the institution, so that research and teaching and learning are directly scrutinized. The interface with this network of agencies must also be managed, placing further demands on the time of the vice-chancellor. Finally, the relationships with the governing body or council have become more complex following the Jarratt reforms, which strengthened their role, and the vice-chancellor has to pay more attention to managing the relationship with the chair and other key members of council.

Most vice-chancellors and chairs believe that the external pressures have increased significantly and that the external dimensions of the role are correspondingly important. Simultaneously, however, the financial pressures on the system are leading to demands for a more hands-on approach, 'spending time on the business', as one chair of council put it. Too often 'the business' is seen as internal and there seemed less awareness on the part of chairs and councils of the import of some of the wider transformations that are now occurring. The change from recruiting overseas students to developing delivering and credentializing provision overseas is a change which councils tend to discuss in terms of financial risk rather than its wider implications for the university as a knowledge institution. The vice-chancellor has to interpret such developments for the internal community and council or governors, while steering the university to a flexible but responsive position.

Universities now collaborate both formally and informally with a wider range of organizations than in the past. As part of the lifelong learning agenda that list seems likely to expand as the periphery increases in scale and importance. All universities now want to secure links with the locality and region, to play a part in regional development networks and to consult with industrial and professional organizations, whether in the development of new products or company training schemes. In consequence, the vice-chancellor and other members of the senior management team are invited to sit on a growing number of boards and committees which proliferate at the interface. These pose constant pressures in terms of time and require sensitive handling to avoid causing offence.

The research uncovered substantial variation in the time allocated by vice-chancellors to their external role. By their own account, some spend over half their time on external affairs, whereas others spend a fifth or less. It was not easy to identify common factors influencing externally oriented vice-chancellors, or their institutions, which could account for such variations. Moreover, some vice-chancellors who define their external role as extremely important appear to spend less time on external affairs than others who perceive themselves as internally focused. This might reflect both a semantic problem in classifying activities and genuine confusion about shifting internal and external domains. Further research is clearly needed to shed light on this changing aspect of the role and the shifting boundaries which define it.

7

Cultures of Leadership:
Styles and Approaches

Introduction

The previous three chapters have described some of the key tasks and activities of the university chief executive: the 'corporate' leader responsible for charting organizational direction and destination; the 'internal' governance or managerial leader dealing in a huge ebb and flow of information and interpersonal roles, a conflict resolver and resource allocator in a regime of scarcity; and the 'external' representative acting as a conduit between the internal and external worlds of the university, connecting academe through various networks, alliances and relationships with funders, stakeholders and other users of the universities' outputs in knowledge creation and transfer. For all the 'intense busyness' (Shapiro, 1998: 91) of the vice-chancellor's office, however, what has emerged is an ambiguous and at times confusing picture of being a university chief executive. The role appears to be constructed around a series of bipolar descriptions, making the job simultaneously powerful and powerless, ordered and chaotic, crushingly mundane and challengingly creative. Despite the patterns of similarity across the landscapes of chief executives' days, lurking beneath the surface features of their interactions with the university lie more opaque yet immensely important elements of differentiation and specificity.

One of the main sources of such opacity is the relationship between the vice-chancellor and organizational context. This chapter concentrates on this relationship. While the general theme is still the behaviours of university vice-chancellors, attention is switched to their explicit styles of managerial leadership. The intention is to explore the relationship between their approaches to the job and differences in organizational cultures and expectations of leadership found in specific institutional contexts. Clearly there are core similarities of task and time expended in a system of higher education driven by formula funding and other universally applied measures of performativity. However, even ostensibly similar institutions in terms of size, history, mission and operating infrastructure can exhibit multiple personalities. To understand the priorities and approaches of vice-chancellors, therefore, requires exploration of these sometimes less tangible relationships between university and leader. This is wrapped up in the notion of organizational culture and refers back to earlier references to questions about how far vice-chancellors are affected by and can, in turn, influence the often contrasting academic/professional and managerial/administrative paradigms found in the modern university. The purpose of this chapter, then, is to explore the influence of some of the most salient variations in terms of organizational cultures and contexts found within the sector and to relate these to the approaches, or styles, of our case study vice-chancellors.

The map of the chapter reflects these themes. The first section expands some of the references in the opening chapters of the book to the operating paradigms of the university. These are the key, but unwritten, rules and practices which define the boundaries of leadership behaviour. If we are to discover anything meaningful about vice-chancellors' leadership styles and the reasons for differences in approach to the job, then we need to establish the contexts and cultures which define the scope for leadership activity. The second section focuses on narratives of leadership activity derived from our empirical research in a broad range of university settings. These narratives serve two purposes. One is to help us to unpack the relationship between organizational contexts and leadership styles. The other is to illustrate how certain key themes in leadership styles – transformational, symbolic and charismatic – are played out in practical situations. Accordingly, the narratives are intended to exemplify how the particular vice-chancellors in the study interpreted and explained their approaches to key elements of their work. In the final section, the evidence is reviewed and conclusions are drawn about the relationship between styles and organizational states and cultures.

Operating paradigms

The operating paradigms of universities exert important influences on the nature and scope of the vice-chancellor's leadership function. Some of these paradigms are shared across the higher education sector: the autonomy of the academic labour process; the limits to managerialist intervention in key areas of academic design, delivery and quality assurance; and the existence of partially eroded but still extant structures of collegiality and democracy. As we have already argued, these critical areas in terms of the actual 'products' and services delivered by the university are effectively insulated from direct executive intervention by a series of internal processes and practices derived from systems of peer review, examination, validation and assessment procedures. These are rarely found in other fields of business, where the chief executive can interfere and determine standards (although in practice this might be rare) in even the finest details of product design and delivery. In the setting of the university, however, the boundaries which define the ways in which it is possible to act as a chief executive have to take into account the various constituencies of power and interest represented by the executive (management), the professionals (academics) and the accountable body (council or board of governors) – 'the three ringed circus', as one vice-chancellor described it.

The scope for vice-chancellors to exercise their power, as well as the nature of their interactions with the university community, have changed only slowly over time, despite the post-Jarratt emphasis on the chief executive. Academic freedoms and institutional autonomy have been progressively compromised, yet important restraints remain in place which, in the academic/professional domain at least, continue to circumscribe executive control over processes and products. Although formal job titles routinely incorporate the terms vice-chancellor *and* chief executive, inside the system of higher education there is still a temptation to see the vice-chancellor's role in largely symbolic terms. Nevertheless, the shift in universities towards a 'business' model of organizational control and direction has made the boundaries between the academic/professional domains and the managerial/administrative less clear and more contestable. There are tensions arising from these shifting frontiers. The expectation is that the vice-chancellor, as institutional chief executive, takes on a sharper leadership role, but what of the old constraints exerted by traditional (academic) power bases and institutional cultures? Do these tensions manifest themselves equally in all institutions? How does the vice-chancellor work through the tensions and seek to exert influence and broad managerial steers on the social practices of both the academic/professional and managerial/administrative domains of organizational life?

Although there are limits, both formal (statutes and articles) and informal (unwritten customs and practices), to their direct influence on academic matters, our research indicates that vice-chancellors share a focus on operating paradigms (transactional approaches) and reframing existing ways of thinking and doing inside the university (transformational approaches). Their potential to influence and change is exercised through two main arenas: organizational culture and the design of operating infrastructure. Both relate in diffuse ways to the core academic activities of the institution and neither area is uncomplicated as an arena of leadership practice. But it is in the vice-chancellors' interventions in these two areas that we are most likely to be able to discover patterns of similarities and differences in leadership styles and approaches. Before examining the empirical evidence on vice-chancellors' leadership styles, we explore the nature of, and linkages between, organizational culture and context.

Organizational culture and context

In Chapter 2 it was noted that the culture paradigm advocated the strengthening of organizational culture as the key to achieving excellence and, hence, competitive advantage. Originating in an obsession with declining standards in manufacturing quality compared to Japan, the culture of excellence school did far more than simply repackage vague ideas about 'atmosphere' or 'ethos'. As Willmott has pointed out, the culture perspective embraced a powerful set of ideas about the theory, practice and discourse of management and leadership (Willmott, 1993). Such concerns may have peaked in the 1980s, but corporate culturalism in its various guises has retained such a powerful hold in the literature, spreading far beyond its original manufacturing/quality focus, that it would be unwise to ignore its principal tenets if we are to begin to make sense of the styles and approaches of university leadership.

In the setting of the university, though, the concept of culture is complicated by fine and, outside the academy, often misunderstood notions of academic freedom, autonomy and collegiality. As a result, academic culture is sometimes used as shorthand to describe distinct and often complicated elements of universities as social institutions. Insofar as the roles of vice-chancellors are defined formally in university statutes, it is in reference to having oversight of the general education character of the university. This intriguing reference to 'culture' has transatlantic resonances. In the nineteenth century American university presidents also took responsibility for what Shapiro (1998) refers to as the 'ethical dimension' of leadership, exemplified in their teaching of moral philosophy. By the late twentieth century, American presidents no longer retained this specific role. But in the USA, as in Britain, the 'moral' tone, or educational character, of the institution appears to have been subsumed into a more diffuse role of protecting and projecting academic vision and intellectual culture (Shapiro, 1998: 92).

As we argued in Chapter 4, vice-chancellors in our UK study interpreted culture less as a moral imperative and more in terms of its visionary and intellectual components, often referring to the university's ethos or atmosphere. More than one associated cultural (or visionary) leadership with a determined effort to structure the academic effort of the institution in ways that gave meaning (and satisfaction?) to the role of academic labour and the university's relationship with the wider community. This was encapsulated in ideas such as running a 'happy' organization (admissions of running an unhappy organization were not heard from the vice-chancellors at least). These references are related to the notion of cultural adaptation and renewal. The need to shape the university in order to meet changing expectations of external and internal constituencies as environmental circumstances shift represents a different kind of leadership challenge.

Despite the problematic nature of corporate culture, however, there is little doubt from our research data that vice-chancellors frequently frame their views of the university and their place in it in terms of a cultural perspective. Their views about their roles and the ways of achieving their goals were often explicitly contextualized in the discourse of culture and the achievement of cultural change as both an end and a means to an end. For these reasons, incorporating a cultural perspective into the analysis of leaders' styles and approaches may assist in unpacking the ways in which leaders' styles might be influenced by their perceptions of their own (and other) university's culture. However, our data also made clear the imprecision of the term organizational culture. Frequently, and not without justification, vice-chancellors collapsed notions of culture into awareness of leadership as a political act.

The particular strength of a culture perspective (as distinct from corporate culturalism) is that it draws attention to key elements of the university's internal organizational configuration, including how the leader imagines the organization in relation to its external and internal constituencies. Although we are dealing with organizations within a specific field, there are clearly important variations between different types of institution. As we suggested in Chapter 2, more recently established institutions are likely to possess relatively immature (though possibly less intractable?) transactional and bureaucratic systems. The assumption is that leadership styles in such settings will be more likely to be transformational, symbolic and charismatic. Older institutions with firmly embedded systems and cultures are possibly less amenable to such approaches. Here the association is likely to be more with transactional and bureaucratic styles. However, variations are not simply a reflection of maturity and, by implication, the inheritances associated with position within the former binary divide. It was also suggested in Chapter 2 that scale is an important variable. Larger organizations pose potentially greater problems in terms of devising suitable communications systems and need greater care in locating the boundaries between the key functional elements of the organization. Both are intimately related, since in larger organizations the boundaries between different areas of specialization and function tend to proliferate, with important implications for ensuring communication across the interfaces. When organizational infrastructure is 'restructured', old interfaces and patterns of communications will be changed and new ones created.

The extent to which the variables of age and scale of institution appear to influence the approaches of vice-chancellors is complicated by a further dimension of the leadership task. This is the relationship between organizational state and the broader external environment within which it operates. We also noted in Chapter 2 that this relationship can be described in terms of two dichotomous states: divergent and convergent (Burnes, 1996). Divergence occurs when organizations operate in turbulent and challenging environments. Under these conditions, existing goals and the established paradigms – structures, rules and ways of working – may come to be increasingly inappropriate and inflexible. Convergence, in contrast, is most likely when the internal and external environment is conducive to stability. Under these more stable conditions established modes of working, and existing structures and goals, are more likely to suffice. From a contextual perspective, the organizational state determines the most appropriate style of leadership. The theory is that under divergent conditions the leader requires a more change-oriented style, one that challenges existing ways of thinking and doing, one that is more creative, innovative and entrepreneurial. In convergent conditions, however, the organizational leader's style needs to be in tune with prevailing goals and practices, nurturing and accommodating by degrees, rather than questioning and challenging.

Narratives of transformation and transaction

A contextual perspective is helpful mainly because it draws attention to the place and role of the institutional leader in relation to both internal and external conditions. However, we do not believe that these variations can be related mechanistically to perceived differences in leaders' styles. Accordingly, in the accounts which follow we have attempted to capture from our data how vice-chancellors (and others around them) perceive the variables which might condition their leadership, rather than impose a rigid categorization of context in relation to leadership style. Following the approach in previous chapters, the focus is far more on how leadership is socially and culturally constituted in the institutional context of universities (Knights and Willmott, 1992: 762).

It is important to recognize that vice-chancellors still operate in two broad worlds: managerial/administrative and professional/academic. These worlds are notionally distinct – one representing the closed, self-referential domain of professional and collegial structures, the other the more open organizational world of management/administration. The connections between these worlds are as diffuse as the boundaries between them. The notion of organizational culture embraces both the academic and managerial domains, yet the powers of the vice-chancellor to engage in the two domains are formulated and applied in very different ways. In effect, vice-chancellors are required to engage simultaneously with both, and much that becomes the art of executive leadership is in knowing and understanding the operating paradigms which characterize the two. The implication is that each demands of vice-chancellors not just knowledge of how to 'manage' these boundaries, but an ability to adapt leadership styles as appropriate. But what evidence is there of such differences in styles and approaches? The following narratives attempt to construct from our research data a more comprehensive picture of what vice-chancellors appear to be doing in specific institutional contexts and the style or approach they adopt in order to achieve their objectives. In the final section we will review the evidence and draw some conclusions about the much vaunted notion of leadership styles.

The managerial domain: designing the infrastructure

As part of our research we consulted a range of documentation detailing the institutional vision and mission, strategic thinking and corporate planning of our case study universities. Contained somewhere in these documents, often as an appendix, was a diagram presenting a schematic representation of the management structure of the university, providing (sometimes out-of-date) information about the committees, sub-committees and personnel heading up the main functional areas of activity. Helpful though such documentation was for obtaining a rapid picture of the organization, we soon began to appreciate that such diagrams presented only a fraction of the story. Essentially, such schematic representations were no more than historical artefacts, for the simple reason that job redesign and restructuring in relation to the managerial domain has become an almost endemic state in the modern university. Some redesign is merely tinkering at the edge, changing by small degrees subordinates' individual roles and responsibilities as new or unexpected opportunities or problems arise. In such circumstances job titles may remain the same, even though the balance of functional tasks may change, sometimes substantially. More systematic changes, including changes to job titles in the management structure, may be made following end-of-year staff reviews when new tasks are allocated to deputies and pro vice-chancellors to reflect the vice-chancellors' perception of shifting priorities. Shuffling the 'cabinet' pack also reflects the politics of work and power, as some individuals are quietly sidelined and others 'promoted' to membership of the 'in' group.

The paradox of this process is that vice-chancellors appear to take soundings only from members of the 'in' group. For example, in one of our case studies the vice-chancellor and senior pro vice-chancellor were becoming concerned that one of the chairs of a key university committee was increasingly becoming 'off-message' as far as the corporate university was concerned. It was also known that the particular individual was also applying for jobs in other universities in order to achieve promotion. The decision was to 'shift him out', to be replaced by a steadier hand. Although enacting the change would be handed to the pro vice-chancellor, the vice-chancellor was concerned: 'Be diplomatic, thank him for his input and tell him we'd like to concentrate on [another area] now.'

Relatively minor in terms of the broader management infrastructure (though perhaps not for the individual concerned), this episode needs to be interpreted within the broad range of day-to-day adjustments, or transactions, of leadership. It was a classic case of 'management by exception' as described in the Bass (1985) model of transactional leadership. Once someone was appointed to the chair of the committee in question, the vice-chancellor expected performance in line with corporate policy. Provided things did not go wrong the leader would not intervene. In this case, however, performance was assessed as unsatisfactory and intervention deemed necessary. The ultimate form of negative feedback – demotion – was accordingly metered out. The interesting aspect of the episode was that it took place in an institution struggling to reconcile its corporate identity and sense of purpose with the operations of the core units, the faculties. This was acknowledged as a big problem, much more so than one individual stepping out of line.

Nor was the institution alone in this experience. Devolved management and devolution of budgets to key cost centres was the guiding principle of the majority of case study institutions in our research and most, it seemed, were struggling to find an effective solution to the perennial corporate problem of spanning the gap between centre and periphery. In the same case study institution, recent experience of some faculties going out of control had been sufficient to promote a review of devolution policy by outside management consultants. For one of the pro vice-chancellors, the problem clearly lay with the balance of power leaning too heavily in favour of deans of faculty. In his view there was always a danger of operating units running off course because:

> The average dean doesn't spend enough time running his faculty. He's given too much of an opportunity to help run the university. Not many of my colleagues will agree with this, but we have had cases in the past of extremely badly run faculties ... and often the reason for this is that the dean has spent too much time participating in university-wide activities – giving up time to various committees, working groups ... Of course, a lot of people like to do this, but at the end of the day if that happens then their faculties can suffer.

At the time of the research, the vice-chancellor was still considering the conclusion of the consultants that while devolved management had provided the incentive for the faculties to develop vigorously since incorporation, it had been at the expense of the corporate well-being of the university as a whole. Action to remove any isolationist tendencies in the faculties was recommended, together with seeking a clearer definition of, and commitment to, the university's corporate objectives. A key part of this would be a review of leadership roles in operating units and the instigation of a system of evaluating 'outputs' as part of a more rigorous system of performance indicators. Alongside these measures, the consultants recommended that the university critically examine the support structures necessary to enable budget holders to 'manage', rather than merely 'administer', effectively and introduce new methods of quality control and service pricing.

Blood on the carpet?
Two further case study institutions, similar in terms of background and age but smaller in size, provide evidence of recent histories of interaction between organizational context and leaders' concerns with changing the infrastructure. In the opinions of their vice-chancellors, these institutions had entered the university 'system' in 1992 without deeply rooted local and regional presence. They spoke in similar terms about the need to develop and diffuse throughout their organizations a clear vision of how they should grow and establish distinctive roles in their geographical hinterlands. Although they did not use the language of a context-style approach to leadership, the narrative of each vice-chancellor articulated a strong sense of the institution

being out of alignment with the external environment. In each case the response had been radical, with a deliberate intention to transform.

At one, the University of A, the vice-chancellor had perceived a need for major restructuring designed to 'break the baronies' – the faculties. In the vice-chancellor's view, the deans of some of these faculties were too strongly entrenched in the existing college culture and represented an alternative, potentially subversive, power base to the authority of the chief executive. The object of breaking the baronies, therefore, was to bring the operating units into closer alignment with corporate aspirations. Through a combination of restructuring and early retirements, some key deans were removed and new players brought in. The governing body was persuaded that such 'restructuring' was an essential prerequisite to achieving the rapid organizational growth necessary to consolidate as a new university. Only through growth could the institution reach a viable income base and greater critical mass in key academic areas. With new deans in place, the organization underwent a period of sustained staff recruitment in the early 1990s, most of those in senior positions being hand-picked by the vice-chancellor. In interview, the chair of governors concurred that the vice-chancellor had redesigned the management structure to give it the capacity to tackle the scope and scale of changes envisaged in the vision for the organization.

Underpinning the radical changes in size and structure was a conscious attempt by both vice-chancellor and chair of governors to align the institution with the emerging characteristics of the market for mass higher education. Accordingly, the culture and discourse of the institution was purposefully placed in tune with concepts such as flexibility, modularity, credit accumulation, equal opportunities and Europeanization. Restructuring, therefore, was seen as a prelude to developing degrees as 'product lines' and to rebadging 'products' in order to ensure they are in step with the state of the market. The metaphor of the market and business was used consciously and without apology.

A similar approach was discernible at the University of B. Like the previous case, this is a relatively small institution with a focused portfolio of mainly teaching-related activity, though with pockets of successful, mainly applied, research. The vice-chancellor saw one of the main challenges of his leadership as being to give the university a much higher profile in the regional and local community. Redesign of internal practices and rules in order to 'deliver' a vision of the university at the heart of regional social and economic development was considered essential. Most radical was the introduction of business planning procedures. Under this system all budget centres had to develop plans which were demonstrably connected to the corporate plan for the institution as a whole. Resources were assessed and allocated in line with the robustness of the business plans.

The vice-chancellor recognized the culture shock caused by this practice. It was, he claimed, justified by the need to ensure that the corporate plan remained at the core of activity and provided a touchstone against which operating unit activity could be measured and budgets allocated accordingly.

Again there were palpable tensions between corporate intent and control, on the one hand, and the problem of variable practice related to devolution of large budgets, on the other. Like the opening case study, history and inheritance set important parameters for leadership action. For both these former polytechnics, initial routes out of the control (interference) associated with the local authority era included a move towards greater devolution and freedom of action. Later, as external monitoring of quality began to bite, there had been a shift of the balance internally in favour of a centralized system of regulation and monitoring.

So far, the institutions reviewed were recently designated (post-1992) universities. Each vice-chancellor had developed a strong vision of the university's place in the firmament and had redesigned structures, personnel and operating practices in radical ways. There is, then, some support for the notion of vice-chancellors leaning more broadly towards transformative rather than transactional styles of leadership, with a specific focus on the development of robust corporate control systems. Equally, there is evidence to suggest that these vice-chancellors perceived their organizations as out of alignment with their external environments and so had become deeply engaged in radical changes in order to produce better convergence. However, our research evidence suggests that even older institutions, typically the civic universities established in the late-nineteenth century or the more modern 1960s 'plate-glass' institutions with much more embedded systems and established corporate memories, could struggle with similar problems of control.

Restructuring for research
Two institutions provide illustration, the Universities of C and D. The drivers in these cases were provided by the Funding Council's policy of promoting research selectivity. At the University of C, recent history, predating the present vice-chancellor, had been dominated by financial difficulties. The previous incumbent had concentrated primarily on devising and implementing suitable financial control procedures. With the finances under control the need was to transform the culture of the institution to be far more research oriented. A fundamental redesign of the management structure had recently been put in train. Faculties had been abandoned in favour of a two- (rather than three-) tier model of departmental cost centres. Critical to the success of this model would be devolution of responsibility to the departments, underpinned by the facility to hold balances and carry forward any surpluses. To service this new structure the chief executive had increased the number of pro vice-chancellors to five, describing them essentially as academics who act functionally as part- rather than full-time administrators. The early retirement of the registrar had been used as an opportunity to test working with a senior executive rather than a direct registrar replacement, an experiment which would be reviewed subsequently.

It was suggested by the vice-chancellor, and reinforced by other senior academics, that he adopted a fairly light touch approach. He saw his role as 'setting the standards of [the university's] interactions with outside bodies'.

Included in this was the need to take 'hearts and minds' with him, particularly the collective view of senate. Convinced that effective leadership would be impossible without senate support, the vice-chancellor had sought to ensure full information flow and discussion of difficult 'restructuring' decisions, including closures of departments. Decisions, he stressed, had to be collective. Above this, however, was the steer and influence exercised by the vice-chancellor and the senior management team (SMT) through the university's standing committee. As one respondent observed, the chief executive was undoubtedly an iron fist in a velvet glove and was determined to introduce new operating paradigms and an infrastructure to match.

The second 'old' university exemplar, the University of D, exhibited strong similarities to the previous narrative. This was also a multifaceted (but larger) civic institution, unable to lean too heavily towards research to the exclusion of teaching or vice versa, and the problem of leadership was concurrently to give a sense of direction while enabling diversity to thrive. Here, though, there was rather stronger evidence of how a vice-chancellor's style might not exhibit an overtly transformational approach but, like the previous case, attempt to restructure gradually in order to adjust the institution to a changing environment. Through a series of in-house lectures the chief executive had promulgated the message that the future environment of higher education and the history/strengths of the institution precluded any substantial shift towards part-time students, HND and vocational courses. In these niches, he argued, competition from new universities was too strong and capable of beating the university. It was far better to concentrate on its historical areas of expertise, exemplified in a move in the direction of postgraduate schools.

Reflecting the difficulty of steering the institutional course was an acknowledged issue of ensuring that constituent parts of the university stay on message rather than be tempted by new development opportunities. As in the case of the new universities above, it was a problem of encouraging entrepreneurialism in the operating departments without losing control and sight of the corporate plan. The vice-chancellor explained: 'You've got a very delicate line between the guy who was trying to be developmental and the guy who's actually driving down the wrong track. And you have to stop external decisions driving the direction in which you go.'

A key part of spreading the message was bringing lower tiers of university management into the ambit of strategic thinking and delegating responsibility downwards. In this case, the vice-chancellor had decided to restructure management by giving to his immediate deputies functional rather than subject responsibilities. This move had freed immediate line management responsibility for the next tier of management, heads of planning units. According to one interpretation, this gave the deputies functional oversight over all faculties and, at the same time, provided greater autonomy to the faculty-based planning units, which became directly responsible to the vice-chancellor; hence there was a more direct line between the latter and the faculties. Although this had freed up the subject areas from interference by deputies, the danger was that the planning units might try to by-pass the strategic review process and appeal directly to the chief executive. The vice-chancellor rejected this as a problem, stressing that if it occurred he would merely refer any culprits back to the appropriate channel. But he did admit that part of his agenda was 'not to be tempted in a paternalistic way to take on their [the deputies'] responsibilities'. The important points about the reorganization were: (a) it built on changes initiated by the previous chief executive (the creation of planning units); and (b) it gave senior managers greater strategic control, particularly in the sense of being better able to steer in the right direction and guide errant faculties back on course.

Cultural change

The foregoing examples illustrate the difficulties attached to terms like academic and managerial leadership. In reality, none of the redesign of the managerial or functional infrastructure involved direct corporate interference in academic affairs. To be sure, the vice-chancellors were involved in decisions to go modular, to adopt CAT systems or to connect better with regional needs and demands of higher education. In each case, redesign of the infrastructure had been intended to secure better connections between the corporate entity of the university and the work of the operating units: departments and/or faculties. But intervention in quality control matters or the design of new courses, the development of new approaches to teaching or the organization and execution of research remains strictly off-limits, protected by the panoply of checks and balances of the academic domain.

How then do we explain the much vaunted, and highly traditional, role of providing academic leadership? If vice-chancellors are proactive in transforming operating infrastructures in order to promote corporate control and renewal, are they, by contrast, merely transactional in their dealings with the academic domain? Our research suggests that to understand the concept of academic leadership requires a more oblique focus on vice-chancellors' roles in defining and changing organizational culture broadly defined. This is a process of accretion and renewal, rather than transformation and control. Given the hands-off role determined by the academic–managerial divide in terms of job design and control, vice-chancellors seek to influence the academic enterprise through a series of sometimes quite remote levers, both formal and informal. In this final empirical section, then, we investigate these levers. The context is the highly political, often tense, relationship between the academic enterprise, culture and the vice-chancellor's leadership style. Two specific areas of activity are highlighted: senior appointments and the academic fraternity.

Changing faces

Most of the vice-chancellors in the study were strong advocates of devolution of powers to academic units. There were various admissions that such a policy needed constant monitoring and that achieving a balance between corporate and operating units was easier to say than achieve. And, as we have suggested above, the balance between centre and periphery might shift in an attempt to match changes in organizational priorities. However, despite their chief executive status, the levers of change available to vice-chancellors are limited. In this respect influence over senior staff appointments represents an exceptional opportunity to exert influence in the academic domain.

The vice-chancellors in our study were actively involved in all appointments at the level of professors, deans and other senior staff. Decisions about appointments are invariably the 'collective' responsibility of the panels involved, but the presence of the vice-chancellor may exert considerable steer on eventual choice. For example, at the University of C the vice-chancellor was clear that achieving the goal of a radically improved position in the next RAE required the appointment of eminent academics in key areas of activity with a mission to transform the research cultures in the operating units:

> It's building up the research image and expertise of the university . . . bringing in big names, reorganizing the departments, merging and closing departments. That is at the heart of what I do . . . There are many important things, but then none of them are as important as that.

Although the RAE provided clear targets to aim for, the same vice-chancellor saw his approach to changing the research culture as being underpinned by a deeper conviction about achieving quality, about moving 'from moderate to being excellent'. He continued:

> I mean everyone is expected to say if he hears of any distinguished person who's unhappy where he is or would like to move, or whose mother was born [here] or heaven knows what would make them a target for bringing them. We've done this with moderate success and will keep on doing. And this is nothing to do with the RAE. I'd have done that whatever institution I'd have gone to . . . We've brought in some pretty big names . . . The first appointment I made was an FRS . . . who has given us a big chance of [that] department going from a fading 3 to within reach of a 5. There are many other ones there, but I mean he was the key figure to come in to show that we really meant business and it's really those sorts of appointments.

Other vice-chancellors in the study concurred about the importance of appointments in the academic units. At another civic institution, concern about fading research performance was also at the forefront of the vice-chancellor's approach. As one of the PVCs put it, 'It is important that we take a very clear view of where the [research] game is and what the competition is.' The vice-chancellor and chair of council concurred that the demands of achieving quality, reduced funding and research selectivity required ever more efficient management. Despite the deeply embedded collegial and professional cultures of the institution, the vice-chancellor saw his role through the metaphor of managing director. Such a role was necessary simply because of the way the state distributed its resources.

Exerting influence on top appointments was also seen as an indispensable tool of the job. As in the previous example, big names with top research reputations were sought. In addition, it was stressed that great care was taken in appointing very good professors to key internal roles, at both departmental and senior management levels. The vice-chancellor had no inhibitions about admitting the purpose of such appointments: 'I have certainly appointed professors who have caused horror and dismay in departments, because I wish to cause horror and dismay.' Apart from safe stewardship of the finances, departments, in his view, were the key facet in transforming a large and somewhat sprawling civic university into something with a much clearer focus. Although the broader organizational framework can be adjusted incrementally in order to facilitate the contribution of the constituent units, departments could be turned round in much shorter time-spans. This vice-chancellor, then, saw the task essentially as rebuilding the organization from within, adjusting departments (radically if necessary) to their own particular environmental changes. To this end, a focus on human resource management was essential.

Influencing the fraternity: academic hearts and minds
Collegiality is a problematic notion in the modern university. It retains a powerful symbolic role in the internal governance of the institution and a potentially powerful brake on the actions of the vice-chancellor. Academic boards and senates in new and old universities represent in essence the collective will of the academics. Although they are nominally chief executives, vice-chancellors pay great attention to the hearts and minds of these academic collectivities. The relationship is formally expressed in the role of the vice-chancellor in chairing meetings of academic board/ senate. Technically this is a formal expression of academic leadership. What does it mean?

The University of E, another old university, exemplifies the approach of vice-chancellors to the problem. Its vice-chancellor was clear that there was a need for quite radical processes of renewal of the academic culture. In his view, academic leadership involved him in articulating, facilitating and focusing activity. An integral part of this was educating the academics themselves in the political realities of the environment; guiding them towards the facility of being able to decentre and see themselves as the rest of the world sees them. It also involved redefining what was understood by collegiality. Although the vice-chancellor acknowledged the importance of collegiality (like many of his peers he still saw himself essentially as an academic), he was clear that in its traditional guise it was no longer appropriate to the environment. In its place the vice-chancellor wanted the culture of collegiality to embrace that part of the tradition giving opportunity to discuss an issue prior to making a decision. Thereafter, however, collegiality required redefinition to mean that colleagues who disagreed nevertheless accepted collective responsibility for the final decision.

The vice-chancellor acknowledged that this redefinition of collegiality represented a major challenge to the traditional culture of the university. This was being tackled by openly sharing information with colleagues unless there were good reasons for maintaining confidentiality. Improved communications at a formal level were considered vital to the process and link back to our discussion above of the ways in which vice-chancellors attempt to manipulate boundaries between functional areas and engage in a process described as 'massaging the interfaces' between them. This 'massaging' is an important dimension of leadership style. It comprises the ability to work outside the confines of the formal structures of power and engage in extensive informal lobbying and opinion forming with leading figures inside the university. This, in essence, was what they meant in referring to the need to take hearts and minds of academic boards and senates with them. Referring to his relationship with senate, the vice-chancellor at the University of A captured the importance of this element of the job:

> Senate is absolutely crucial. I believe that if a vice-chancellor loses control of senate, they will go . . . If you look at all the vice-chancellors who've gone, they've gone because of a specific reason which may or may not have been sufficient, but they have lost control of their senate. And I regard keeping control of senate and making sure they understand the problem, even when they don't like the decisions one has to take, understand it and totally take them seriously. It's a most essential part of the job.

Academic boards, the ex-polytechnic equivalent of the old university senate, are less embedded within long-established traditions of collegiality. Nevertheless, evidence from the research reinforces the view that even in the more 'managerialist' cultures of new universities, vice-chancellors are sensitive to the views of academic boards and perceive a need to take them with the executive. But whether the context is academic board or senate, our observations suggest that preparation for a meeting with academic board or senate is taken seriously. Briefing meetings were arranged in order for agenda items to be discussed with senior team members, for policy lines to be finalized and for any divisions of labour to be agreed in terms of speaking to specific items. Not surprisingly, contentious issues would be discussed in greater depth, with care taken to ensure unanimity prior to the meeting.

Perceptions of the strengths and weaknesses of senates and academic boards varied. Two vignettes illustrate the approaches typically adopted in the meetings themselves. The first, again at the University of C, is drawn from a vice-chancellor's own account of how he 'managed' the difficult case of closing a department within the confines of the collegial body. Once he had determined to close the department, the decision had to be approved by his peers. He explained:

I suppose I could have bulldozed that through by tricks and timings and things, but I mean I really felt I had to go to them and say look, this is what we're going to do and this is how we're going to do it – put all the cards on the table and say, you know, this needs your support. And if we don't have your support, it will be chaos . . . Obviously, this affects their colleagues and things [but] you mustn't shirk this by abstaining, you have to think about this. And, they voted in favour of it.

The vice-chancellor in this case admitted that had the vote gone against him he would have had serious misgivings about going on without senate's confidence. Later, another problem arose about restricting the growth of a department. In this case, senate was unhappy about the course being proposed by the executive and was divided. Without a reasonable chance of winning the vote by a clear margin, the vice-chancellor agreed to report back later with a revised plan. The expectation was that the executive would then carry the day.

The second short vignette, drawn from the University of F, illustrates more clearly the inner dynamics of meetings of boards or senates. In this case, the vice-chancellor was in the throes of a major academic reorganization. Pivotal to the plan would be the appointment of new deans, required as a first step in developing a system of stronger budgetary delegation to academic units. The agenda item was introduced with a report by the leader of the implementation group responsible for paving the way for the appointments process. The report stressed that all outstanding areas of demarcation and possible disputes between the faculties had been settled. The vice-chancellor followed the report with a personal intervention to reassure colleagues of the lengths to which the university was prepared to go to ensure that the appointment panels were conducted in a scrupulously fair manner. Instead of short-listing, it had been decided to interview every candidate and take up all references suggested by the candidates themselves. Prior to the next meeting of the governing body the vice-chancellor promised to write formally to members informing them of progress. This, he hoped, would ensure that they felt the process had been as open as possible. A member asked if there would be an opportunity to respond in due course and transmit views from members to the governing body. The vice-chancellor reassured the member that he would be punctilious in ensuring that all views would be drawn to the governors' attention.

These examples emphasize the vice-chancellors' attempts to ensure open communication with the academics. Observation of meetings of senates and boards confirm that such meetings demand of the executive leader abilities not just to argue a case and persuade, but to be sufficiently sensitive to know when to push an issue and when to withdraw. These more charismatic and political elements of leadership style constitute one example of the actual practice of transformational styles of leadership. However, it should be stressed that formal and collective settings of boards and senates provide only a partial view of the development of the vice-chancellor's approach to specific leadership issues. Much preparatory work was done in more intimate and informal one-to-one or small group interludes. It was in these sessions that we found clearer expressions of the three elements of transformational leadership suggested by Bass (1985). Hence, a vice-chancellor, even if capable of effectively chairing meetings of senate or the academic board, would not survive for long without the ability to work in the spaces between formal meetings. It was here that they demonstrated a capacity to inspire academics in line with their own vision and interpretation of what needed to be done, or to demonstrate their ability to see colleagues as individuals and treat them in line with their particular capabilities and needs. And it was in the informal, off-the-record sessions, often over a drink in the vice-chancellor's office, that they worked to focus the attention of colleagues on problem solving in line with the sets of beliefs, vision, etc. encapsulated in the leader's approach (Bass, 1985).

Conclusions

Whether for cultural, personal modesty or other reasons, few chief executives in the case study institutions admitted to explicit theorizing about leadership style. As one leader put it, 'I don't really think about these things frankly. I just try and get on with the job. Basically I don't read books about it, I just get on with it.' There is no denying that this statement contains more than a grain of truth. If nothing else, it reinforces the notion of leadership as a practical art and the importance of previous experiences in extending the repertoire of approaches and responses to particular situations. And, as we have seen in Chapter 3, across the cohort of chief executives in any era, those experiences are remarkably similar in terms of previous posts, exposure to common academic and institutional cultures, problems and responsibilities.

But there is more to university leadership than merely playing it by ear. Implicit theories of leadership and management abound in the case studies, in the words and deeds of the chief executives, their deputies and senior colleagues, as well as chairs of councils and governing bodies. Awareness of institutional context, the place of the organization in the broader environment of higher education and the firmament of economic, social and technological scale is high. Contact with the outside world is extensive, as is exposure to a range of externally generated views about the institution and the academics (and students) inside it. Leaders in our case studies were acutely aware of the need to transform or not, to introduce radical changes or to peddle more softly; they were constantly thinking about the place and nature of the internal organizational boundaries, whether they could or should be changed and what this might do to the key interfaces internally and externally; they shared a common perception of the problem of devising appropriately robust yet flexible spans of control between corporate centre and operating units, how best to delegate and to balance autonomy with direction; and they were forever grappling with the problem of culture and institutional personality, how to change something but not everything, to challenge but not destroy.

For these reasons, the categorization of leadership styles as either transformational or transactional provides some insight into leaders' approaches. Equally relevant is the attempt by vice-chancellors to establish the degree of congruity between an ever-changing external environment and the organizational state, its ways of doing and thinking. Their interpretations are important since, right or wrong, they exert a powerful influence on why vice-chancellors seek to adjust and change. But the picture of how they seek to lead is necessarily complex. We have suggested that the two broad domains of leadership action – academic and managerial – present rather different patterns of opportunities and constraints. The boundaries between the two domains remain in place, but they are shifting, tenuous and at times imperceptible. It is evident from the research that university vice-chancellors have to be capable of using both transformational and transactional styles of management over time (though we acknowledge that appointments to the top job may be associated with expectations of the need to transform or consolidate, at least in the initial phases, and that subsequent changes in style may have to wait until the appointment of a successor). The complexities of the organizational context may be such that different parts of the organization may require different styles of leadership at the same time. We would have been surprised if this were otherwise, but the case studies confirm that although the transformational–transactional paradigm is useful, its application in practice is highly nuanced and sensitive to local or micro-level conditions.

It is also evident that categorizations of universities as either new (ex-polytechnic) or old (established prior to 1992) are not especially correlated with particular leadership styles or approaches. History and inheritance are undoubtedly important, but many key tasks and the approaches adopted straddle the former binary divide. Certainly, the case study institutions reflect the diverse backgrounds and traditions of governance and management which characterize the two broad groupings of old and new universities, and the former binary divide remains a powerful indicator of institutional difference. Missions and governance structures, as we have seen, as well as positions in the learning and research market place locally, nationally and internationally, remain heavily skewed by this binary inheritance. However, if we are to understand facets of leadership styles it is important to avoid getting locked into an old and new dichotomy.

Implicit assumptions about differences between old and new universities make it difficult to see the things that do not belong within the paradigm (Clarke and Clegg, 1998). For example, it is generally assumed that new universities are more managerial, less collegial and, hence, less democratic than old universities. Such perceptions are derived from the ways in which new universities were 'converted' from polytechnics and from a set of assumptions about the influence exerted by their generally smaller and more commercially oriented governing bodies. In fact, our research failed to uncover any significant differences between old and new institutions in this respect. True, governing bodies in our case study new universities were smaller than their old university counterparts; academic boards were less entrenched in the constitutional framework of institutional governance than senates in old universities; and senior managers (deans, pro vice-chancellors and deputy vice-chancellors) in new universities were invariably 'permanent' appointees rather than 'temporary' or fixed term tours of duty in the old. But there was no evidence that a chief executive could not seek to transform the situation simply because the governing body was too large or because pro vice-chancellors were not permanent appointments. Some of the sharpest managerial teeth and more extensive use of the discourses of managerialism were found in the apparently more 'collegial' confines of some of the oldest universities in our study.

Nevertheless, there are some important differences in institutional contexts which impacted on leadership styles. Sharp divergences exist in the need to compete for resources (whether from the state or elsewhere), in the need to reposition in terms of markets for students and research income, and in relationships with local and regional stakeholders. New hierarchies, reflected in their crudest forms in league tables, are creating new sets of tensions which all institutional leaders have to manage. As Martin (1999) has observed, the task is to balance tensions between 'vision and reality, individuality and collaboration, reward and accountability, valuing the past and being open to the future'. Such tensions emerge within organizations in different ways and in different locations. A simple old–new university dichotomy explains some, but by no means all the variations between institutions. Nor can such a dichotomy explain or predict how leaders will respond to environmental challenge. In short, the system as a whole is in the throes of an important paradigm shift from elite to mass forms of thinking and this shift is creating new sets of problems and new sets of rules or games. Our case study analyses reveal vice-chancellors and other senior managers reconceptualizing problems in similar ways, deploying similar sets of tools to deal with them and redesigning organizational boundaries and infrastructures along similar lines in order to deal with emerging complexities in the higher education business.

Our final point, then, concerns the multifunctionality of the modern university and the problem of information flow. The scale and scope of activity and the location of boundaries and interfaces are important influences on the effectiveness of leadership styles. When chief executives decide to restructure their teams or operating units, they shift boundaries in order to align the organization and its operations better with its environment. The primary reason for doing this, documented time and again in our case studies, is to improve communications across and between organizations. It is about facilitating better access to knowledge and information both downwards and upwards through the organization. In this sense, leadership style is a reflection of the big picture or vision of the organization and how information is structured and shared in order to translate the vision into something more than a dream. In leadership style, therefore, there is, or at least should be, a clear connection with organizational vision and the steps that are taken to translate it into practical reality.

8
Comparative Models: Europe and the USA

In order to refine our thesis about the vice-chancellorship we need to locate it in the wider context of developments in university leadership in other cultures. In Chapter 1 we argued that demands for more and different forms of teaching and research, the abandonment of traditional state planning regimes and the adoption of market-like principles as the ultimate arbiters of resource allocation and roles are transforming the university's traditional role as knowledge producer. Although these pressures are global in scale and shape, historically they have produced rather different responses across higher education systems on either side of the Atlantic: the American universal but stratified model being one approach; the maintenance of European binary systems being another. However, the challenges facing national higher education systems obviously have major implications not just for policy makers at state level but also for institutions of higher education and those who lead them. The question arises as to whether the British vice-chancellorship is following the pattern of the American presidency, the European rectorship or some alternative approach. Indeed, it is legitimate to ask whether convergence is occurring in leadership models on both sides of the Atlantic despite the differences between American and European higher education systems.

This chapter tackles these important questions. It provides a comparative focus, placing the evolution of the vice-chancellorship in the wider context of developments in university leadership in the United States and other European states. It draws on a combination of secondary source materials and the results of four survey questionnaires sent to university rectors in Sweden and the Netherlands (as exemplars of European trends in leadership) and to university presidents in the states of Georgia and California in the United States. These survey studies, conducted during the period between spring 1997 and winter 1998, provide broadly comparable sets of national data (issues of survey design and response rates are discussed in the Appendix). Each questionnaire was designed to elicit from the leaders of university and other equivalent higher education institutions information with respect to two broad sets of questions. The first comprise basic biographical details of those in post at the time of the questionnaire, including age, sex, qualifications, previous career and other relevant experiences; the second concern perceptions of leadership roles and responsibilities. The biographical data provide comparable information to that held in our databases of British vice-chancellors and enables a cross-national view to be constructed of typical career progression routes to the top job in each system. The aggregated results of leaders' views of their leadership roles, priorities and approaches provide valuable benchmarks of European and American practices compared to the evolution of the British vice-chancellorship. In order to refine our thesis about the vice-chancellorship further, however, we need first to locate it in the wider context of developments in models of university leadership in other cultures.

The rectorship and presidency

The contrast between the presidency and the rectorship, like the larger contrast between market-oriented American higher education and state-dominated European systems, may underestimate the powerful global forces of convergence which are impacting on the evolution of executive leadership. Concepts such as academic 'capitalism', 'entrepreneurialism' and 'commodification' have been advanced by various authors in an attempt to describe and explain the ways in which the power and pervasiveness of these convergence forces are being played out (Shumar, 1997; Slaughter and Leslie, 1997; Clark, 1998). However, if the forces for change have been global in scope, there remains a need to identify local and regional differences in the way they have been worked out in practice. As Deem (1998) has pointed out, important sources of economic, social, political and cultural differentiation persist with regard to higher education policies and funding regimes, as well as the organizational and leadership practices of higher education institutions. Leadership functions are intimately connected with variations in organizational and cultural practices in different countries.

Most accounts of the American model of university leadership concur that the president is traditionally subject to the outer-directed influences of lay trustees, state appointed regents or coordinating boards depending on whether the university is located in the public sector or is a private institution. The power of the governing boards over the president is considerable, not just in terms of hiring and firing, but in the actual direction of leadership activity. Generally speaking the American president, especially of multi-campus systems, is more preoccupied with questions of financial planning (particularly fund-raising) and external representation (particularly political lobbying) than with academic policy. However, some private universities and liberal arts colleges expect their presidents to interpret their responsibilities in more holistic terms, as academic and even pastoral leaders (Giamatti, 1988). These roles are reflected in Kerr's (1964) classic description of the American university president as a multitalented individual performing a multifaceted task:

> The university president in the United States is expected to be a friend of the students, a colleague of the faculty, a good fellow with the alumni, a sound administrator with the trustees, a good speaker with the public, an astute bargainer with the foundations and the federal agencies, a politician with the state legislature, a friend of industry, labor, and agriculture, a persuasive diplomat with donors, a champion of education generally, a supporter of the professions (particularly law and medicine), a spokesman to the press, a scholar in his own right, a public servant at the state and national levels, a devotee of opera and football equally.
>
> (Kerr, 1964: 29–30)

For all this, not all studies of the American president concur that the president can make a difference as a change agent. Cohen and March (1974) and Bennis (1976) tend towards the view that such are the inconsistencies and uncertainties about the purposes and goals of universities as organizations that leadership (in an anarchy) is inevitably both confused and compromised. Other analysts, however, point to the pivotal role of institutional leaders in specific organizational circumstances. For example, Baldridge (1971) has argued that dynamic presidents at Reed, Swarthmore and Antioch were critical agents in taking the institutions forward. In a penetrating study of organizational change at New York University, he cites one published tribute to the university's president, James Hester:

> One is left with the impression that, even in this very large place, the influence and contribution of its president are unique and life size. He is a capable, agile administrator and a consummate fund raiser finely attuned to the sensitivities of his faculty. In these days of tight finances he could carry a big stick, but he does not. Instead, he gives much of each day to the infinite process of consensus building among his 5,450 full- and part-time faculty, and in doing so he seems to be succeeding where many others have failed. It may be the new miracle on Washington Square, and an eloquent testimonial to the ability of complex universities to spring back to life.
>
> (Baldridge, 1975: 447)

The notion of the university president as a critical change agent is consonant with recent analyses which portray American education as increasingly commodified (Shumar, 1997) and driven by market-based, supply side economics (Rhoades and Slaughter, 1997). From this perspective, higher education is increasingly focused on employers (rather than students) and more on the needs of large, private, transnational employers than the needs of either medium or small, public and private employers (Rhoades and Slaughter, 1997). These market needs demand institutions that are more managerial in configuration and leaders able to respond to multiple masters.

In this model, there is space for the exercise of vigorous leadership functions, sensitive to faculty certainly, but ultimately free to make top-down decisions in a way that some analysts suggest would not be recognized by traditional elected rectors (Trow, 1985). Although this model of leadership is not likely to be free of faculty resistance to change, ultimately the effective leader is able to discharge the role of change agent because there is access to corporate styles of chief executive leadership, with the president expected to restructure and stratify faculty and initiate changes in the production process. The president, as chief executive, is not unfettered by notions of collegiality which embrace the concept of participation by various constituencies in important decisions. However, the appointment of presidents by 'outsiders' in the form of the boards described above is premised on the expectation that the president is appointed to initiate and effect change. It is expected that the formal powers and authority of the job can be used by the president for this purpose. According to Green (1997), the chief executive model of leadership is gaining in appeal even though corporate styles of management do not sit well with the traditional core values and purposes of the academy. The momentum towards adopting the corporate chief executive, rather than the elected rector model, is clear: 'as pressures mount for institutions to be more relevant to economic development, to be more accountable to the public, to find alternate sources of funds, and to take a more active role in developing linkages with external groups, it will be difficult for academic leaders simply to be first among equals' (Green, 1997: 139).

In continental Europe and other parts of the world, the alternative to the American presidential style of executive leadership is the rectorship. Rectors are normally elected to the post by senior members of the academic institution and there is an assumption that the leader is appointed from these ranks. There are clear political overtones, with prospective rectors running campaigns to build up their bases of support prior to the election. Since the student 'troubles' of 1968, the notion of the rectorship as a 'political' office has been reinforced by a process of university democratization. Frequently, the rector is one leader in a tripartite leadership 'act' comprising the chairman of the university council and university director (equivalent to the British registrar) as well. In Trow's (1985) description of the office, the power of the elected rectors to make decisions is circumscribed much more heavily than that of the university president. Decision-making councils are a key part of the often complicated structures which impinge on the process of leadership. According to Green, in its traditional form the system of elected rectors 'seems to guarantee that vigorous leadership will be thwarted' (Green, 1997: 140). It is conceded, however, that because the rector is elected from the ranks of the academics, the system gives to the leader advantages of stature and credibility among colleagues.

Although there are clear contrasts between the chief executive and rectorship models of leadership, in practice there may be greater convergence between the two approaches. In several systems (for example, Sweden and the Netherlands) the collectivized and democratized leadership role has been subjected to growing pressures towards a more executive style as state controls have been relaxed and demands for more efficient institutional stewardship increased. As we suggested in Chapter 1, in several European countries, discourses of contracting, accountability and entrepreneurship have begun to make inroads into the language of supervision and regulation traditionally deployed to monitor state–university relations. This liberalization of 'state' systems (and the constraining of the 'autonomous' British universities) has refocused attention on the role of leadership in reconfiguring university missions and responsiveness to changing economic and social demands. It also re-emphasizes the convergence thesis, with the emergence of a new model of state–university relations based on the often competing needs of supervision and control with freedom and entrepreneurship (Maasen and van Vught, 1994).

Both the European rectorship and the American presidency offer persuasive approaches to institutional leadership. However, the question arises as to whether they remain as distinctive as the models imply. The diversity and market-responsiveness of the American model resonates increasingly with a unified and stratified British system of higher education, with expectations that the vice-chancellor functions more like a corporate chief executive than a traditional vice-chancellor. At the same time, the European approach remains influential, not least because of the ever-closer links between British and other European universities within the regional trading bloc incorporated in the European Union. In the next section, therefore, the evidence from our surveys of European and American leaders is interrogated with a view to comparing and contrasting the British model of the vice-chancellorship within a broader framework describing the nature of the leadership task in other higher education systems.

Career routes to leadership: international comparisons

It will be recalled from our study of vice-chancellors' careers that one of the most enduring trends of the British model was the consistency over the decades in the average age of appointment. Although there are slight differences between old and new university practice ('old' universities tending to appoint older candidates than new universities), the average age at appointment for those in our study was 52 years. We concluded that despite the shift towards a more corporate executive model, the vice-chancellorship still tends to be regarded as a prestigious end of career appointment: a capstone to a successful academic career. It will also be recalled that these were overwhelmingly academic careers. Recruitment to the vice-chancellorship was typically from the ranks of the professoriate, the pro vice-chancellors and deputy vice-chancellors, i.e. the next layers down of senior academic management. Experience outside higher education in the earlier careers of those making it to the top was extremely limited and then largely confined to bouts in the civil service or some other form of public sector activity. The British vice-chancellor then, conforms to the well established pattern of leadership by 'insiders'. Typically they may have been appointed from another institution (though of a similar type), but they are academics who, if they have learnt anything at all about management, have done so 'on the job' as their careers have advanced.

Against this pattern we might hypothesize some subtle differences in European and American approaches. Elected rectors would typically be academics from the same institution, again with little or no 'outside' experience and possibly older on appointment, since, as in Britain, there are connotations of the rectorship as a career pinnacle. The profile of the corporate executive styled American president, on the other hand, might be expected to be somewhat different: possibly younger on appointment, since the post is not necessarily seen as an end of career promotion; less immediately connected with the work of academic faculty, because there is an assumption that the United States has developed a cadre of experienced 'academic' managers who may have begun their careers in faculty but relatively early on have decided to specialise in administration; and almost certainly more experienced in the wider world of politics and business in preparation for a presidential career devoted primarily to fund raising, public relations and political lobbying.

Capstones of careers?

The results of our surveys, however, provide only limited support for these ideal-typical leadership representations. In the USA (remembering that we sampled higher education in two states, California and Georgia) the average age of presidents at appointment was 49 years – with the youngest president being 39 and the oldest being 60 years old at appointment. In the Netherlands, too, the average age at appointment was 49 years (youngest 36 and oldest 61). In contrast, at 52 (youngest 37, oldest 59), Swedish rectors tend to be older than their American and Dutch counterparts at appointment but the same average age as the British vice-chancellor. As in Britain, though, these sectoral averages conceal some subtle differences between the different 'ranks' of higher education institutions in each system. Presidents appointed to doctoral-awarding American universities tended to be slightly younger on average (44 years) than those in masters (average 49 years) and research (50 years) universities. The prestige of leading one of the top Dutch universities also appears to be associated with the appointment of slightly younger candidates than in the more numerous Hogeschools – typically 48 in the former, 51 in the latter. In contrast, the Swedish system seems to mirror British practice, where leaders of new universities have been consistently younger in age than in the old. In Sweden, university sub-sector appointments average 53 years old, compared to 50 in the university college sector.

Analysis of leaders' previous educational experiences suggests that European rectors are more likely to have spent time studying at the same institution. Just under a third (30 per cent) of Swedish rectors had previously been undergraduates at the same institution; in the Netherlands, the proportion was much lower, at 13 per cent; in the USA the proportion was lower still at just 10 per cent. Tested by previous association as a student, these results confirm the hypothesis that American executive style higher education leaders tend to be much more catholic appointments than their European (especially Swedish) counterparts. If we examine the extent to which American leaders are 'internal' appointments from within the ranks of the same institution, then only a fifth of respondents came from this inside route, compared to just over a third (35 per cent) of British vice-chancellors.

Recruitment strata

In both the American and European models there is strong replication of the British pattern of appointment from the higher education recruitment pool. Swedish rectors, like British vice-chancellors, were overwhelmingly career academics. In total, 87 per cent came directly from career positions within the university sector. If those with civil service experience inside higher education state agencies or research councils are included, the proportion increases to 93 per cent. In the Netherlands, academia was less pervasive as a recruiting ground, though still highly important. Over 80 per cent of Dutch rectors came directly from career positions within the higher education sector. American presidents, despite the apparent differences between the presidential and rectorship models, conform to the same pattern, with at least 80 per cent in our survey having been recruited from career positions within the university sector. Of those presidents coming from outside the sector, the largest recruiting ground appears to have been professional practice (6.5 per cent). Only 3 per cent were actually recruited from the corporate sector, the same proportion as recruited from state higher education agencies.

These headline figures about the principal avenues of mobility in European and American higher education conceal some subtle 'internal' variations, however. In the Netherlands, a high proportion of rectorships were shown to be held by those who had previously held the same or a similar leadership post. A third (31 per cent) of Dutch rectors had previously been university rectors or heads of other higher education institutions. In the USA just 16 per cent of presidents had made horizontal (accepting that there may be differences of prestige associated with different types of institutions) moves from an existing presidential post. At the opposite end of the scale, only 7 per cent of Swedish rectors had previously been head of another higher education institution. Evidence of differences in the 'spacings' of rungs on the academic career ladder are also suggested in the figures on promotion from the immediately lower rung. In the USA nearly a half

(45 per cent) were recruited from the ranks of vice-presidents (6 per cent of these achieving promotion in the same institution). In Sweden, a quarter (23 per cent) came from this career stepping stone (a similar proportion to Britain, where 24 per cent were previously pro vice-chancellors or deputy vice-chancellors). But in the Netherlands this lower rung is virtually non-existent as a career stepping stone, with just 5 per cent being recruited from the post of vice-rector in a Dutch university.

Educational and other employment experiences

There are a number of important variations in the educational backgrounds of those in these recruitment pools.[1] American university presidents are predominantly qualified in the arts. Over half (58 per cent) have their highest degrees in arts disciplines, and another quarter (21 per cent) in social science. Men (only 6 per cent of American survey respondents were female) of science were in the minority by some margin at 14 per cent, and technology even further behind at 7 per cent. Dutch rectors, in contrast, were just as likely to be qualified in the social sciences as the arts. Each accounted for just over a third (36 per cent) of the rectors in the survey, with science and technology at similar proportions to the Americans (15 and 12 per cent respectively). Sweden offers a variation on the Dutch pattern. In this case arts are joined by science as the leading backgrounds, each accounting for around a third each. Slightly more Swedish rectors had social science qualifications than had technology. In terms of the different leadership models there are apparently no consistent cross-national guides. The key differences seem to be national, between an arts-dominated American presidency, at one end of the spectrum, and a predominantly science-oriented British vice-chancellorship at the other. In Britain we found that nearly half the vice-chancellors possessed a science degree, the remainder being fairly evenly distributed between the arts, technology and social science. The European rector, if Dutch and Swedish experience is typical, tends to be split fairly evenly between arts, sciences and social sciences.

Our final set of comparative data in this section concern the wider career experiences of presidents and rectors. Just over half the American university presidents (55 per cent) claimed previous career experience outside higher education (though this should not be confused with post held immediately prior to appointment as president). The largest proportion (39 per cent) of presidents had been in private-sector employment at some stage in their careers. Around a quarter had been directors in the private sector and almost 30 per cent claimed non-salaried and/or salaried public-sector experience. Rather surprisingly in view of our earlier hypotheses about differences between the presidential and rectorship models, a higher proportion of Swedish and Dutch leaders claimed previous employment experiences outside higher education. In both countries, 70 per cent fell into this category. In the Netherlands, 51 per cent had salaried other public-sector experience and 10 per cent non-salaried experience. A quarter had private-sector experience as company directors, while nearly a third had been employees in the private sector. Swedish rectors followed a similar pattern: 53 per cent had worked in other public-sector salaried posts, 37 per cent had been employees in the private sector and 20 per cent had held directorships in the private sector.

We also have some evidence on the range of relationships maintained by rectors and presidents with external agencies and organizations whilst in post. Involvement in industry was measured by the holding of company directorships. The highest proportion occurred in Sweden, where 43 per cent of rectors held directorships while in their posts. In the USA the proportion was around a third (36 per cent) and in the Netherlands much lower still (10 per cent). Not only did a greater proportion of Swedish than American leaders hold directorships, but typically they held more such posts: in Sweden the average number of directorships was three; in the USA it was two. Respondents were also asked to indicate their wider involvement in other areas of educational, professional, government or voluntary activity. Typically between a half and three-quarters in each national group recorded some commitment, often heavy, in each of these areas. The largest proportion of American presidents and Swedish rectors (both 70 per cent) were members of academic or professional bodies, while in the Netherlands the largest proportion were involved in other educational bodies.

Leadership roles and responsibilities

The literature of managerial leadership and our own investigations of the work of vice-chancellors guided our thinking about which issues and problems are seen by university leaders as priorities and why? Reflection on the perceptions of vice-chancellors and the actual landscapes of their days enabled us to identify six fairly distinct, though interconnected, categories of activity designed to encapsulate their work in a meaningful way and form an appropriate comparative framework for leadership roles in the USA and Europe. These include (in no particular order of priority):

- *Human resource management*: defined as the range of tasks associated with the appointment of senior individuals and developing commitment to institutional goals and values; representation, lobbying and ceremonial activities; ensuring the institution is respected by, and reflects its regional, national and international communities and lobbying on behalf of university interests.
- *Control systems*: designing and implementing procedures to control and direct institutional activities and monitoring academic and financial performance.

Figure 8.1 Areas of university policy ranked in terms of importance

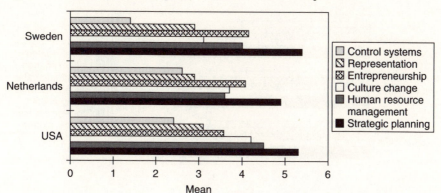

- *Entrepreneurship and competitive advantage*: positioning the institution within the higher education sector and engaging in successful competition with other institutions.
- *Strategic planning*: creating a clear institutional vision or mission in relation to present and future developments in its external environment.
- *Culture change*: encouraging staff to embrace change and innovation throughout the university.

Presidents and rectors were asked to rank these policy areas by their perceived importance to their own leadership role. The results are shown in Figure 8.1. Leaders on both sides of the Atlantic were clearly unanimous that their first priority area was strategic planning. This is entirely consistent with the results of our qualitative investigations of vice-chancellors in Britain, where the notion of strategic leadership, defined broadly but also incorporating the formal requirements of the funding councils with regard to strategic planning, is taken very seriously. At the opposite end of the scale, again consistently in Europe and the USA, were representation, lobbying and ceremonial activities, and corporate control and monitoring, in fifth and sixth places respectively.

More surprising, perhaps, was the greater emphasis placed on entrepreneurship by Swedish and Dutch rectors (both second in importance) compared to American presidents (fourth place). Issues of human resource management were clearly of more pressing concern to presidents after the broader strategic function. Given the apparent 'retreat' from planning discussed in Chapter 1, perhaps the importance placed on the free market rhetoric of entrepreneurship is consistent with recent priorities in European higher education systems rather more than American, where the market model has deeper roots. We can only speculate, of course, though some support is offered from the British context, where the drive towards segregation poses the dilemma of how to retain control over the direction of change without overtly planning it. At institutional level, too, we saw some of

Figure 8.2   Areas of university policy ranked in terms of time spent

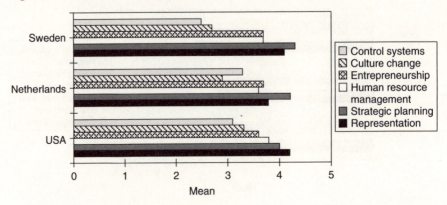

the consequences of this policy being played out in the competing paradigms of centralized versus (sometimes radical) decentralization and how to balance control with entrepreneurship. Entrepreneurship is possibly considered less of a novelty in the American context. More pressing apparently is the issue of relations with faculty and appointing senior individuals, much more so than issues of public relations and representation, despite the literature cited above (Kerr, 1964; Green, 1997).

Apart from the unanimity about the importance of the strategic role, there is an apparently sharp contrast in British, compared to European and American, perceptions about the importance of representation activities. Our observations of vice-chancellors indicate significant amounts of time and energy being devoted to developing links with various communities, as well as extensive lobbying in a variety of arenas (though part of the research coincided with key phases in the preparation of the wide-ranging Dearing review of British higher education, which may have skewed our findings in this respect). Vice-chancellors also express often grave concerns about the development and impact of various systems of quality monitoring and controls. Again, our observations suggest that monitoring the organization's key operating and quality signals, and the preparation of statements for the various systems of internal and external audit and assessment – being, in effect, accountable – consume significant amounts of vice-chancellors' working time.

Accepting that our different research methodologies might account for discrepancies of this kind, we also asked university presidents and rectors to rank the same areas of university policy in terms of the time expended on each. In this way we hoped to be able to measure perceptions of importance against perceptions of time spent on each activity. Figure 8.2 shows there is a clear mismatch between the two assessments.

American presidents may have thought that representation, lobbying and ceremonial activities was one of the least important policy areas in terms of importance, but in terms of time spent they ranked it first. Swedish and Dutch

Figure 8.3 Predicted importance of roles: Sweden

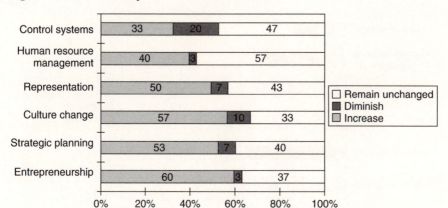

Figure 8.4 Predicted importance of roles: the Netherlands

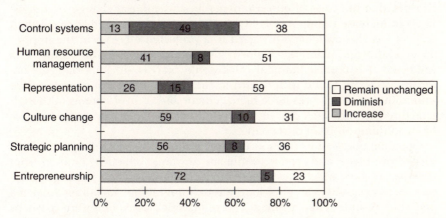

rectors presumably thought along similar lines, although strategic issues remain in first place in terms of time spent. Other shifts in rankings are perhaps less clear-cut. However, cultural change stands out as third most important in the roles of American presidents, though it ranks next to control in terms of time spent. The ranking of culture change produced by Dutch rectors may also be interpreted as evidence that despite its importance as a role, not enough time is spent on the activity. Across all three systems, control was ranked as the area of policy least important and taking the least amount of time.

Respondents were also asked whether they thought these roles would increase, diminish or remain the same in terms of importance. Figures 8.3, 8.4 and 8.5 show these results for Sweden, the Netherlands and the USA.

Figure 8.5   Predicted importance of roles: the USA

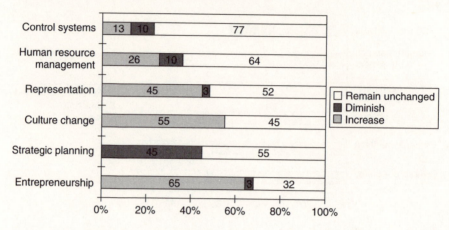

There is a high degree of congruence in perceptions on both sides of the Atlantic. A majority of American presidents and Dutch and Swedish rectors thought that the roles of entrepreneurship and cultural change were most likely to increase in importance. Convergence between Swedish and Dutch leaders was also evident with regard to a projected increase in the import-ance of strategic planning. Majority opinion among Swedish rectors also predicted that representational roles would increase in importance. Con-sensus was again found with regard to the predicted lack of change in the importance of human resource management and control systems (although Dutch rectors indicated that they thought that the latter role would be most likely to diminish in importance).

Our final question in relation to these policy areas was open-ended, and invited presidents and rectors to indicate any areas of activity omitted from the questionnaire which they believed to be important. The most frequent re-ference among American presidents was to 'fund-raising', including 'financial and other resources management'. More maverick statements were (perhaps inevitably) included, such as 'healing past wounds and creating a civil envir-onment', 'understanding legal dimensions of the job' and 'campus cheer leader'. Rectors in Sweden and the Netherlands were more circumspect in proffering opinions, although two Dutch rectors considered knowledge management (policy in the field of information and communication tech-nology) and interaction with private business (technology transfer and cor-porate learning perhaps) were discrete areas omitted from our categorization.

Organizational characteristics and the leadership task

These perceptions provide a valuable first indication of how top university leaders in different national systems tend to view the nature of universities as organizations. They suggest strong cross-national agreement that they are not really amenable to a control perspective and that the primary objectives of the leadership task are focused first on strategic direction, followed by the needs of organizational and cultural renewal. Further evidence that presidents as well as rectors tend to prioritize renewal over control is provided by their views of universities as organizations and the type of leadership they think appropriate for such organizations. Four alternative propositions were offered describing universities:

- Higher education institutions are *complex organizations*: the rector's or president's leadership role is to manage this complexity to enable the institution to survive and flourish.
- Higher education institutions are *managerial organizations*: the rector's or president's role is to create a clear sense of corporate purpose and direction.
- Higher education institutions are *creative organizations*: the rector's or president's role is to create an ethos and environment that stimulates innovation.
- Higher education institutions are *collegial organizations*: the rector's or president's role is to protect the procedural integrity of her or his institution and to build consensus.

The pattern of American and Dutch perceptions were most consistent in response to these images. Nearly half (45 per cent) of the Dutch rectors concurred that higher education institutions are essentially creative organizations and that the rector's role is to create an environment and ethos that stimulates innovation. These perceptions are consistent with their views (discussed above) about the importance of entrepreneurship and competitive advantage. A third (37 per cent) of the American presidents concurred that 'creativity' is the key organizational attribute of the institution. A further third of both presidents (37 per cent) and Dutch rectors (34 per cent) identified complexity and its management as the key characteristics. Equal proportions of presidents (both 13 per cent) preferred the descriptions of managerial and collegial organizations. While a fifth of Dutch rectors identified with the managerial view, rather starkly none felt inclined to signal the collegial organization as being most important.

Swedish perceptions were different except in one respect. Nearly two-thirds (60 per cent) thought higher education institutions were creative organizations. A further 27 per cent supported the notion that they are complex organizations, but only 13 per cent associated themselves with the managerial image. As in the Netherlands, however, the collegial organization was not seen as important: only one rector identified with this image. According to these results, therefore, rectors in both countries do not identify with collegiality and building consensus above other descriptions of the organizational and leadership characteristics of higher education institutions. Rather more American presidents did identify with collegiality and consensus. However, there is a fairly strong transatlantic message that the donnish dominion, if it ever existed at all, is no longer cherished as the principal characteristic or purpose of higher education, at least by university leaders.

Reinforcement that collegiality and consensus is not a top priority is provided by responses to a separate question about the primary role of the president or rector. Respondents were asked whether they agreed or disagreed with two separate statements. The first suggested that the rector's or president's role is to maintain consensus and balance the competing demands of academics, students, politicians and industry. Nearly two-thirds (64 per cent) of American presidents, but only a half of Dutch and Swedish (55 and 53 per cent respectively) could agree with this statement. Far greater agreement was evident with regard to a second statement that the rector's or president's role is to set clear goals and make firm decisions in the interests of the university. An overwhelming majority of respondents in each country agreed with this statement: over four-fifths (87 per cent) of Swedish rectors and a similar proportions of Dutch rectors (80 per cent) and American presidents (77 per cent) agreed with this statement. The weight of the evidence on both sides of the Atlantic is clearly in the direction of firm leadership through clear goal-setting and firm decision making.

Leadership skills and constraints

In terms of the actual performance of the leadership task, leaders were invited to rank four categories of generic skills in terms of importance. Again these were derived from our empirical work with British vice-chancellors and included interpersonal skills, decision making, teamwork and information management. The results demonstrate considerable transatlantic agreement on the ranking of these leadership skills. Both rectors and presidents considered interpersonal skills as most important, followed by decision making, teamwork and information management. Leaders were also given the opportunity to specify other skills deemed important but omitted from the pre-selected list. Between a quarter (the Netherlands and America) and 40 per cent (Sweden) specified other skills. However, some of the skills suggested may be subsumed under the four pre-given ones. Examples include: 'communication (oral and written)', 'political', 'inspire a sense of vision/purpose', 'leadership'(!), strategic planning and implementation, and marketing skills. Figure 8.6 incorporates the skills rankings of leaders in each country.

Our focus on the positive attributes required of presidents and rectors was counterbalanced by an understanding from fieldwork, with vice-chancellors indicating four possible constraints on leadership effectiveness. The first, a universal concern in the British context, was the shrinking unit of resource given by the state to a higher education system pressurized into expanding and diversifying. At the same time that government rehearses the general 'retreat' from the welfare state, it develops a variety of strategies

Figure 8.6   Skills ranked in terms of importance

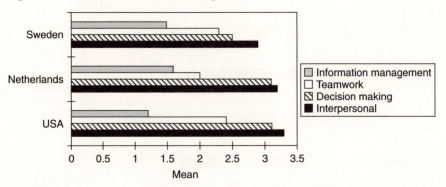

designed to promote value for money and greater accountability. We know that globally other systems face similar problems as educational restructuring and diversification take place side-by-side. Second, and closely linked, particularly in the British context, is the encroachment of the state (despite the 'retreat' from planning) into the once autonomous spaces of the university in the name of national competitiveness, social cohesion, etc. The third possible constraint arises from the broader relationship with colleagues. We have seen that vice-chancellors concurred on the importance of taking the 'hearts and minds' of colleagues with them. But this is a broad constituency comprising several key groups. Lose any one of them, collectively or individually, and the consequences for effective leadership (and harmonious working relationships) can be catastrophic. A final, more personal, constraint is excessive workloads. Our own and other research concurs on the sheer scale of both the leaders' and their immediate subordinates' workloads. To be sure, we did not find evidence to suggest that most vice-chancellors did anything other than (broadly) enjoy their jobs, but it was clear that the regime for all in top management posts could be extremely punishing.

Presidents and rectors were asked to indicate how strongly they agreed or disagreed with four statements designed to capture these concerns. The results reveal few cross-cultural consistencies, other than a general perception that lack of cooperation from colleagues is not a major problem (although a third of Dutch rectors thought it was). For American presidents, the major constraint on personal leadership effectiveness was seen as declining resources, followed closely by excessive managerial workloads. Swedish presidents reversed this ranking, two-thirds of respondents citing excessive managerial workloads as the most important constraint on effectiveness. Rectors in the Netherlands, in contrast, saw intervention by the Dutch state as a clearer impediment to action than workloads. These results are presented in Figures 8.7, 8.8 and 8.9. Invitations to specify other factors which influence or impede their approach to university leadership produced a small but interesting selection of responses. American presidents nominated

Figure 8.7   Constraints placed on effective leadership: Sweden

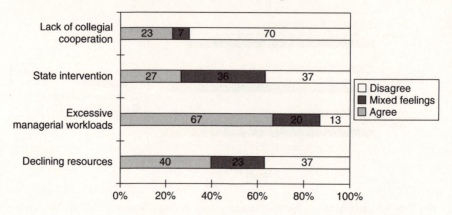

Figure 8.8   Constraints placed on effective leadership: the Netherlands

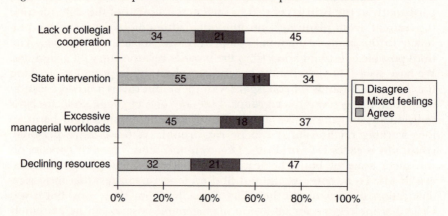

Figure 8.9   Constraints placed on effective leadership: the USA

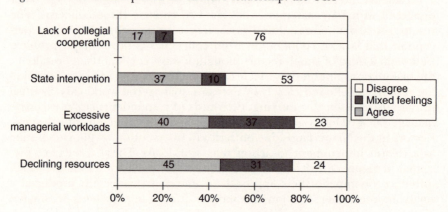

the 'university structure', the 'unions', 'interaction with the community', 'federal and court intervention' and 'continually team building'. Among the responses from Dutch rectors were concerns that 'feminine leadership styles can't be effectively appreciated as long as the number of women at the top doesn't increase' and more generally that history and the 'culture of rules and procedures' and the 'culture of rights' were particular obstacles.

Conclusions

The leadership post continues to carry different titles in different countries – typically vice-chancellor in Britain and some Commonwealth countries, president in the United States and rector in many European countries. The question is whether these are merely differences in semantics, or whether they remain important indicators of variations in who can serve as university executive leaders, in selection and appointment processes and, most importantly, in leaders' roles and responsibilities. The European rectorship and American presidency offer persuasive approaches to institutional leadership and the literature on each constructs a robust set of contrasts between the two. The presidency is associated more strongly with the marketized model of higher education and the style of corporate leader, rather than the collegial-style first among equals. Such leadership is associated with more vigorous, top-down decision making, certainly not unfettered by the concerns of academic faculty, but the expectation is that presidents initiate and effect change. The presidency is also linked with a conception of leadership more distant from faculty, exercised by an emerging cadre of 'professional' rather than 'amateur' leaders. The rectorship, in contrast, is traditionally associated with the state, rather than market, model, a political appointment from the academic ranks: an academic leading the academics whose power to change is circumscribed. These images risk an element of caricature, but do they remain valid descriptors of rectorship and presidency in their historical forms? Do they remain as distinctive as the ideal–typical models imply?

Our data on the rectorship in Sweden and Holland and the presidency in the American states of California and Georgia, however, provide some valuable sightings on the broad issue of transatlantic convergence in leadership practices. While the evidence is far from conclusive, it is suggestive of a broad drift towards a less distinct 'transatlantic' leadership model. In terms of career routes there are no significant differences. The profiles of leaders and how they arrived in the top post are remarkably similar. They are of similar age on average, though slightly older in Sweden and Britain than the Netherlands and America; most are appointed from other higher education organizations (though there is usually a minority with some previous connection with the institution); and, as in Britain, they are overwhelmingly career academics. The career ladder to the leadership post is essentially the same, though we found some variations in the rungs of promotion. A greater proportion of American presidents than elsewhere are recruited from the vice-presidency or its equivalent posts. In contrast, in the Netherlands there is a much stronger willingness to appoint rectors from other leadership posts – nearly a third of Dutch rectors came from leadership of other institutions. However, the disciplinary backgrounds of leaders reveal no distinct transatlantic differences. Arts backgrounds were predominant in the USA, compared to sciences in Britain. But Dutch and Swedish rectors were fairly evenly split between social sciences and arts, and arts and science backgrounds, respectively.

There is no evidence that the corporate-executive model of leadership associated in our earlier discussion with the American president is fashioned on extensive exposure to wider business practices or methods, whether in the private or public sector. Indeed, the European rector is far more likely to be exposed to such influences and therefore less reliant on previous careers purely inside academia. British vice-chancellors appear much closer to European practice in this respect, with around 70 per cent having had previous employment experience in the public sector (broadly defined to include the civil service), the private sector (including the holding of a non-executive directorship post) or both. If American postholders do behave more like chief executive officers than their elected or appointed counterparts in either mainland Europe or Britain, it is not because of their experiential learning in non-higher education settings. Nor are presidents more likely to be involved in industry as directors than their European counterparts. The highest proportion of leaders holding directorship was among Swedish rectors, who on average also held more such posts than their American counterparts.

In terms of leadership role there is evidence of both convergence and divergence, though the latter is not in the direction one might have anticipated. Convergence centres on the universal top ranking assigned to strategy in leadership roles. Whatever the sources of the pressures impinging on higher education systems, institutional leaders interpret the requirement to think strategically, engage in strategic planning and chart organizational direction as a top priority. After this there are some differences. Swedish and Dutch rectors, surprisingly, place more emphasis on entrepreneurship than American presidents. All placed cultural change higher in ranking than either representation, lobbying and ceremony or control systems. In terms of time actually spent on these activities there was some reordering, although strategy remained in first place. In each system, leaders promoted representation, broadly defined, to a higher place according to time spent. This would accord with our observations of British vice-chancellors, who spent significant amounts of time interacting with local, regional and international communities and in lobbying at various levels.

The emphasis on renewal rather than control was also evident in perceptions of universities as organizations. The strongest tendency was to see universities as creative organizations, followed by complex organizations. Association with the idea of the university as a managerial organization was much weaker. However, there was a surprising reluctance, particularly among

European rectors, to identify universities as collegial organizations. No Dutch and only one Swedish rector agreed that the university was a collegial organization and that the rector's role is to protect procedural integrity and build consensus. In contrast, 13 per cent of American presidents felt able to identify with the collegial description of the university. The lack of commitment to collegiality as an organizational and leadership characteristic was reinforced on both sides of the Atlantic in a vision of leadership predicated on setting clear goals and making firm decisions. There was also clear convergence across the Atlantic on the priorities attached to various leadership skills. However, there were no clear patterns with regard to constraints to effective leadership. Dutch rectors thought the state problematic; Swedish rectors were worried by excessive workloads; American presidents were more concerned about declining resources (as were Dutch rectors much more so then Swedish).

The pattern of these results provides some interesting comparisons with the perceptions of British vice-chancellors and our observations of their work and leadership styles: the emphasis on strategy; the importance attached to devising suitable methods of linking control with entrepreneurship and competitive advantage; the concern with dwindling state resources for higher education stand out as obvious points of comparison. The paradoxical nature of the leadership task so evident in the British context also lurks in the more sublime messages from the survey of rectors and presidents: universities as creative organizations; the focus on renewal rather than control; the apparent lack of identification with collegiality. These provide confusing messages for a British vice-chancellorship still steeped in the values and experiences of academic careers and the structures and cultures of universities as relatively autonomous and protected places. Like their British counterparts, it would seem that European and, to a lesser extent, American university leaders are still struggling to come to terms with the contradictions of free-market rhetoric, the apparent retreat of the state from planning and the competing demands of corporate control versus creativity and entrepreneurship. In this respect, at least, the distinctive characteristics attached to notions of the vice-chancellorship, the presidency and rectorship are being eroded in material if not symbolic importance by the same forces of convergence.

Note

1. Academic backgrounds were not directly comparable across all three countries since categorization of academic discipline was by highest degree for leaders in the United States and the Netherlands and discipline now involved in for Swedish leaders. Data for British vice-chancellors were taken from analysis of first degrees.

9

Conclusions: the Paradox of Executive Leadership

This book grew out of an interest in whether the Jarratt recommendation that vice-chancellors should be seen as the chief executives of their institutions has actually resulted in a significant change in their role. Specifically, we wanted to explore whether the culture of universities has been transformed, with institutional leadership now more clearly based on managerial and entrepreneurial skills and operational competencies rather than collegial or charismatic authority. Has the vice-chancellor become the dominant figure in defining institutional culture and shaping university mission? This interest stems not only from a concern with university leadership but also from a wider interest in what such a change might imply for the development of higher education. In short, changes in the role of the vice-chancellor might signify that some of the wider developments, which critics and enthusiasts alike suggest are occurring in higher education, are actually becoming embedded in the system.

The conclusions fall into three parts. The first deals with institutional context and considers whether changes in the nature of university organization and culture have fundamentally altered the role of the vice-chancellor. The second analyses roles and work: what vice-chancellors actually do and to what extent this post can be conceived as a classic managerial role. Is the vice-chancellor a chief executive in the sense understood in other organizational contexts or does the university remain a special case? Finally, we consider whether the role of vice-chancellor in the UK remains contingent upon specific institutional and national contexts, or whether convergent patterns are emerging throughout other European countries and the USA.

Universities as organizations: continuity and change

Chapter 1 explored the wider context in which institutional leadership is now exercised, noting that vice-chancellors have been closely bound up with the various transformations in higher education: as initiators or inter-preters of the wider mission adopted by higher education; as mediators between their institution and national and international systems and mar-ket forces; and as managers of complex organizations. This analysis ques-tioned whether universities remain recognizably the same organizations or are being transformed; in particular, whether the traditional organizational leadership and culture which has delineated universities hitherto is now in decline and being replaced by a more permanent and professional man-agerial system and culture.

The dominant image of the higher education system in recent years, as portrayed by most observers, has largely been one of turbulence and change. Vice-chancellors and other senior figures also readily identified changes in the system. Notwithstanding the scale of such change, there is also evidence of continuity and much that has characterized universities in the past re-mains. Part of the complexity, therefore, is assessing the balance between continuity and change. Four elements in particular help to underpin con-tinuity in the role of vice-chancellor. First, despite extensive changes in university organization, key structural elements, particularly those which underpin professional autonomy, continue to circumscribe and define the powers of the vice-chancellor. Second, there is little evidence of broadening recruitment patterns, and those appointed to the post of vice-chancellor continue to come from similar, predominantly academic, backgrounds. Third, the pattern of days and styles of work also offer evidence of stability in organizational culture. Finally, despite the decline in national planning and the impact of marketization, planning objectives continue to be pur-sued through quasi-market bidding and competition. The system remains one in which planning priorities – albeit now pursued by government and funding councils at arm's length – place significant constraints on the free-dom of institutions and institutional management.

Universities have proved themselves highly adaptable organizations, chang-ing size and shape, extending missions and realigning boundaries in re-sponse to political and social change. They remain distinctive organizations and their core task of knowledge creation in the form of skills, credentials and research remains intact despite the many changes discussed in Chap-ter 1. Their expertise lies in the exercise of academic judgements which their organizational structure is designed to protect. These judgements are undertaken by academics, externally by peer review in the case of new know-ledge and research, by internal peer evaluation exercised via examination boards in the case of credentializing students or by validating committees in the case of the approval of new courses. This central focus of much univer-sity business, which Trow (1973) referred to as the private life of institu-tions, is largely impervious to the managerial power of the vice-chancellor.

This continuity of collegiate/professional authority was never threatened during the binary system, since the requirement that polytechnics offer equivalent academic standards to the university sector led to these struc-tural features being replicated from the outset – indeed, the Council for

National Academic Awards (CNAA) was extremely vigilant in ensuring there was no managerial encroachment on academic authority. More significantly, in terms of future developments, there is no evidence that vice-chancellors actively seek to extend their managerial authority in these areas. This balance of powers, which lies at the constitutional heart of higher education institutions in the UK, is as much endorsed by vice-chancellors and chairmen of council as by academics. Indeed, it is regarded as an essential safeguard of quality. In one recent example the deputy vice-chancellor, acting on behalf of the vice-chancellor, was alleged to have attempted to adjust the overall grades in the examinations because of problems experienced by students. The subsequent outcry shows just how strong this boundary remains.

Vice-chancellors regard keeping in tune with senate or academic board thinking as crucially important – more than one mentioned in interview that those who lose their jobs do so because they have ceased to command the support of senate – and the chairs of council regard 'senate business' as outside the remit of university councils. They are also concerned to ensure that council and senate are not at loggerheads. The link rests with the vice-chancellor as chair of the senate or academic board, and vice-chancellors take many decisions on the basis of their role as chair of senate or its sub-committees rather than their formal powers as chief executive of the university. Their formal powers as set out in university statutes remain deliberately vague. The donnish dominion view of the vice-chancellor as 'senate's man' may no longer be an adequate description, but it continues to have resonance in the system, even in the context of the post-1992 universities.

There is no evidence that the shift towards a more executive interpretation of the post of vice-chancellor has resulted in major changes in the career preparation and professional profiles of those appointed. Instead, the data in Chapter 3 show that vice-chancellors are much the same people they have always been, namely academics who have predominantly enjoyed an academic career prior to appointment to their present post. Nearly a third have no history of previous employment outside higher education, whether in the private or other parts of the public sector, a further third had experience elsewhere in the public sector and the remaining third had experience of salaried employment in the private or both sectors. This latter category, however, includes non-executive directorships, some of which are in enterprises established by universities themselves. Most significantly, the proportion of vice-chancellors with previous career experience outside higher education has not changed in any major way over time.

One reason for this profile is that, despite an increased emphasis on managerial competence, chairs of university councils or governing bodies seem unanimous in their view that universities have to be run by academics or those with academic backgrounds, because universities are 'distinctive', 'different', 'not line-management organizations', so 'people can't be brought in from outside to run them'. If these views are as pervasive as the interview data suggest, there seems little danger of managers from commercial or other professional environments being appointed. For all its designation as chief executive, the post of vice-chancellor seems, at present, to be almost exclusively reserved for academics. Nor has the emphasis on managerial competence led to any attempt to secure managerial training for those on a potential career path to a vice-chancellorship or to systematize their managerial experience. It remains, in large measure, a 'catch-as-catch-can' approach, which reinforces the argument that managerial expertise is not the major factor in the selection process.

Although predicting the future is a hazardous enterprise, the data indicate that at present there is not a single recruitment market for vice-chancellors. While pro vice-chancellors and deans from old universities are being appointed to head new universities, the converse is not the case. Yet vice-chancellors in new universities are nearly twice as likely as their counterparts in old universities to have experience in the private sector, again suggesting that such experience is less highly valued than other attributes. One interpretation is that managerial experience is viewed as additional to a strong academic track record, rather than a substitute, and an important aspect of this experience lies in knowing how to draw upon and work with collegial and professional authority; so managerial experience needs to be allied to collegial authority and therefore to be acquired in an academic context.

The vice-chancellor as chief executive

The Jarratt designation of the vice-chancellor as chief executive presupposes that the role is essentially managerial, with typical managerial functions. Vice-chancellors and chairs of council identified two key tasks associated with the role: strategic planning and academic leadership. The former illustrates clearly the multilayered nature of much university activity at senior management level, and Chapter 4 analyses what one vice-chancellor called 'this messy networking process' in operation. Typically there is no full-time formal planning directorate or team modelling options for the university and vice-chancellor to consider. Nor is the distinction between strategic and operational planning that characterizes many large-scale organizations in the private sector of apparent significance. The strategic planning process as it operates in universities is not exclusively (primarily?) a professional planning activity (although clearly it results in a strategic plan as required by the funding council), but is used by many vice-chancellors as an opportunity to (re-) establish the style and culture of the organization: that is, the way the university relates to its mission. Some see it as an ethical document reflecting the values of the organization and an opportunity to enter into a dialogue with staff about these aspects of university and academic life. It is not the managerial dimension, a world of hard strategic choices, which the vice-chancellor typically emphasizes in discussions at various levels of the institution. Instead, it is a question of core values and 'what the university stands for' that is the focus of debate. So strategic planning, which sounds hard-edged and an aspect of a new managerial culture, is more typically presented soft focus, involving the kind of discussion in which earlier generations of academics and vice-chancellors might well have engaged.

Academic leadership, which includes such activities as appointing professors, securing appropriate facilities to support teaching and research and recognizing and supporting excellence, was clearly central to many vice chancellors' views of their role. Chairing appointment panels and sounding out senior academics whom the university would like to attract is one of the most time-consuming activities, but many vice-chancellors continue to prioritize this aspect of their work. One estimated that five or six professorial appointments are always in the process of being filled and the vice-chancellor's role as chair of the panel is crucial. Other tasks revolve around academic services, what one called 'the straight operational nuts and bolts – how you make the place work'. This area of work is probably the most managerial and bureaucratic and in recent decades has increasingly been handled by pro vice-chancellors, assuming particular responsibilities for estates, staffing, academic services, external relations and marketing and their associated committees. Yet even here a vice-chancellor sometimes intervenes personally to deal with detailed issues: for example, to smooth the path for an incoming professor needing specific facilities.

Recognizing and supporting excellence covers diverse activities reflecting different institutional missions. Many vice-chancellors mentioned the RAE, describing their role as one of 'detailed scrutiny' and 'very much hands-on'. In conjunction with deans and professors who have the relevant subject expertise, many have spent time trying to develop, realign or restructure curriculum areas – and therefore departments – to make them more attractive to students and/or to maximize research funding opportunities. Finally, undertaking departmental visits to encourage staff and also 'ask the occasional awkward question' is seen as an activity for which there is never enough time. In particular, those vice-chancellors who were internally focused described these tasks as 'at the heart of what I do'.

The meetings culture still prevails in universities, as Chapter 5 makes clear. Vice-chancellors may now work longer hours, and at a more frenetic pace, than many of their predecessors, but the round of meetings – formal and collegial, interspersed with informal personal interaction with key personnel, particularly professors, and external representational/networking – is a pattern that has persisted over time. This range of activities would have been thoroughly familiar to vice-chancellors in earlier decades, and a straightforward comparison of work diaries would reveal many similarities. Most vice-chancellors also continue to prioritize their work with senate or academic board, citing the need to align these key academic decision-making bodies with their view of where the university should be going. Despite a healthy dose of cynicism, and not infrequent exasperation, they take this aspect of their work seriously. In some of the new universities the academic board is perceived as a slightly less powerful body, but few vice-chancellors seek to override widespread and strongly held objections to proposals under discussion. Instead they seek to defer debate to a future meeting – and probably undertake more preparatory discussions with key staff. As one study of British universities suggested, 'there is a special premium upon securing consent by persuasion' (Moodie and Eustace, 1974).

Two things are worth noting about these aspects of vice-chancellors' activities. First, many of the examples of academic leadership were also advanced as evidence of strategic management in operation. So working to reshape or refocus departments or appoint good professors is both an exercise in academic leadership and an aspect of strategic management designed to enhance performance and secure for the institution its place as a top research university. There is no clear distinction, operationally, and this blurring of boundaries is reflected in the language vice-chancellors use when describing what they do. Disentangling rhetoric and reality has proved a difficult task. Vice-chancellors like to tell a good story, and accounts that emphasize academic leadership, strategic management, encouraging entrepreneurial activity or promoting excellence sound appropriate to a chief executive's role and responsibility. Our observations suggest a more mundane world, which some vice-chancellors also reflected in their accounts of what they do. 'I delegate most things and then interfere – dip in and out', was one approach. Another described constant forays into detail, sometimes on apparently minor issues. The result, suggested another, is that 'I end up from time to time doing things which could just as easily be done by a junior clerical officer.' Clearly this is a less heroic account of life at the top, but it is consistent with our observations. In Chapter 5 we noted the different approaches to dealing with 'minor' issues, with many vice-chancellors struggling to achieve a balance. They often appear to oscillate between high-level strategy and minor housekeeping operations. A meeting with the chief executive of a hospital trust might be followed by discussion of a relatively minor problem with a member of the academic staff. One member of a senior management team described meetings with the vice-chancellor as 'a mish-mash of things, part high level strategy and part just day-to-day items'.

This is not an attempt to puncture or deflate the accounts given of the role and the key tasks vice-chancellors undertake. Nor do we suggest that this oscillation reveals a lack of effective organizational systems designed to ensure the chief executive is free to devote attention to more important tasks. It is an attempt to draw attention to the importance of these mundane or everyday tasks. First, it underlines the continued importance of personal leadership in the university context despite the enormous growth in institutional size. An apparently endless stream of people want to book time in the diary and demand to be heard. Second, it is often out of these forays into detail and personal interactions that strategy emerges.

Observational analysis allowed us to consider the styles of leadership adopted by vice-chancellors. In almost all cases vice-chancellors operate through and with others, whether individuals, small groups or formal committees. In short, the pattern is indirect. Simultaneously, it is also highly personal. Vice-chancellors need to be accessible and the right of access to the vice-chancellor is highly cherished. Many vice-chancellors seek to maximize opportunities for informal contact by joining colleagues for coffee and a chat in the senior common room, and some encourage email access. Perhaps the managerial style most frequently mentioned was 'management by wandering around'.

The search for consensus and balance also remains a strong driving force. Vice-chancellors need and seek allies. They work primarily through formal committees or informal meetings with groups or individuals whom they must persuade to adopt a particular policy and pursue it, or at a minimum not oppose it. Such committees are mostly composed of a powerful but relatively small group of individuals, usually professors, whose views are authoritative. In new universities these people will typically hold managerial posts (deans, heads of school); in old universities this is not necessarily the case. It is a world of shifting alliances on particular issues and the vice-chancellor must put together a majority to ensure desired outcomes. This is not a world where orders, memoranda or unilateral decision making will succeed in other than the most trivial areas. Networking and lobbying, whether internally or externally, are important skills.

Arriving at a balanced view of a role that is clearly in transition in response to the varied pressures and turbulent external environment currently being experienced by universities is far from easy. As Chapter 5 notes, the language and metaphors of complex political systems are more appropriate to understanding universities than engineering or cybernetic systems or simple linear models of command and control. One chair of council, discussing the role of universities, pointed out that 'universities are not a business; they just have to behave in a more business-like fashion.' Similarly, it is suggested that the vice-chancellor is not a manager or chief executive in the classical sense; while they now adopt a more managerial approach to many aspects of their work, the role is better conceived as a political one in the sense identified above. The role, in formal terms, remains opaque and relies on a set of implicit and negotiated powers. It is in this context that analogies with political organizations and processes seem relevant.

Convergence or divergence?

It is clear that there is a considerable diversity of approach to the job, which is highly sensitive to context in terms of institutional mission and culture, external circumstances and the particular strengths and inclinations of individual vice-chancellors. Universities differ from each other to a significant degree, and those differences have been extended following the ending of the binary system. Some are federal systems, such as Wales and London; pre- and post-1992 universities have different organizational structures and their working patterns still reflect their diverse origins; and collegiate universities founded in the 1960s wave of expansion differ in turn from large civic universities from the Victorian era. This may seem an obvious – even trite – point to make but it clearly underlines the extent to which the role of vice-chancellor also varies. Some spend over half their time on external issues, whereas others report as little as 10 per cent of time allocated in this way. Local and regional developments are central for some, whereas others concentrate on national and international issues. The diversity of institutional mission also affects the balance of work: for example, the importance attached to research. Clearly there is considerable latitude in the ways these tasks are approached, which makes the high level of consensus around the key tasks of strategic planning and academic leadership interesting but not wholly illuminating.

Despite these contextual differences, however, our analyses of vice-chancellors' external roles, their leadership styles or approaches and European and American models of university leadership revealed some strong threads of similarity. The reconfiguration of university–state relations across Western societies has impacted on the complex interface between internal and external processes at institution level. In Chapter 6 we noted that vice-chancellors have to pay careful attention to the interface with a proliferating network of external agencies and organizations. Most suggested that external pressures have increased significantly, demanding more hands-on approaches to internal managerial tasks, yet paradoxically creating more, not less, need to collaborate both formally and informally with a wider range of organizations than in the past. Expanding yet controlling the periphery to ensure connections and fruitful collaborations with locality and region, nation and economy is a key task of the executive leader.

As we emphasized in Chapter 7, university vice-chancellors are acutely aware of the often contradictory pressures on their institutions. Their leadership styles reflect these contradictions, moving between transformational and transactional approaches at different times and at different levels within the organization. And, across all the organizations, new and old, in our study, the patterns of opportunities and constraints for leadership action were broadly shaped by the parameters and cultures of the two main domains of leadership action, academic and managerial. The boundary between these domains, despite all the changes and turbulence of recent years, remains basically, sometimes uncomfortably, in place. If the boundary is shifting and at times tenuous, the expectations of what the executive leader can and should do when operating in each domain remain distinct and exert practical limitations on the scope of being the chief executive. The practice of executive leadership in universities, therefore, depends in no small part on the skilful manipulation, yet deep respect for, the maintenance of this historical and symbolic boundary. Leadership styles in universities are heavily influenced by this contextual factor in ways which are not generally experienced in other sectors. Inevitably, of course, some universities are led in a more 'managerial' style than others, but it would be a mistake to link managerial propensities simplistically with position on either side of the former binary divide. The inheritances, structures, cultures and position in the higher education firmament may be different, but leadership tasks are often conceptualized in remarkably similar ways in very different institutions.

If we are right in this conclusion, and there is compelling research-based evidence to support it, then it suggests that an adequate theory of management and/or leadership in academic institutions has yet to be developed and needs to be firmly grounded in the specific features of the higher education context. Managerial theories do acknowledge the importance of context, but most generalized theories of management and leadership are still based on business organizations and their sub-types and are consequently of limited usefulness.

An adequate theoretical framework would need to acknowledge the distinctive organizational features and cultural peculiarities characteristic of universities. Many processes have their origins in organizational forms whose functions have long been defunct yet which still retain a powerful symbolic force. Vice-chancellors have to understand and work with these ambiguities to achieve their objectives. This suggested that exploring the historical evolution of the role in the post-war period might provide greater illumination. Although universities have individually distinctive profiles, almost all have faced common challenges and problems arising from expansion and reductions in funding. It therefore seemed plausible that, at a minimum, different aspects of the vice-chancellor's role would be emphasized in particular periods and our analysis suggests that the balance of the role appears to be tilting, once again, to emphasize the academic. This is consistent with the emphasis in the interviews on academic leadership.

The Jarratt proposal to import best business practice into higher education and reposition vice-chancellors as chief executives would suggest a move to bring the British vice-chancellorship closer to an American presidential system. In Chapter 8 we suggested that traditionally the president has been perceived as more autonomous, at least from faculty pressure, and better able to take top-down decisions. In addition, the greater responsiveness of the American system to market forces, at a time when bidding and other quasi-market strategies were being introduced into the UK, added some persuasive gloss to the possibilities of greater transatlantic convergence in models of university leadership. In Europe a common feature has been the retreat from the welfare state and state planning exercised directly in many continental European systems and indirectly in Britain via the UGC and successor bodies. Some have posited convergence between the rectoral model of university leadership, as the state systems of continental Europe were liberalized, and the vice-chancellorship, as the UK system has become more constrained. The evidence in Chapter 8 provides some evidence of greater convergence towards a common transatlantic perspective – at least as far as perceptions of the problems to be faced. Or perhaps the models were never quite as divergent in practice as the theory suggested.

Seen in a broader context of globalization, it may well be that models associated with national systems are inevitably becoming less persuasive. The diversity of institutional profiles operating as universities in the USA has hitherto contrasted sharply with the more unitary models of university institutions in the UK and continental Europe, which in turn are becoming more diverse. As all these societies seek solutions to common tensions, and greater differentiation within and between higher education institutions is one solution to the tension between mass higher education and the demand for excellence, then models of universities and university leadership may be more sensibly viewed across rather than within national boundaries. On a limited scale this has always been partially true, with Ivy League universities having more in common with elite research universities in the UK and Europe than some universities in the USA. Nonetheless, national policies and their corresponding interpretations of higher education have proved powerful forces which continue to shape institutions and expectations of institutional leadership. It is part of the paradox that such competing forces affect both institutions and their leadership. The long-term outcomes, as yet, remain uncertain.

At present, however, this analysis casts doubt on the thesis that vice-chancellors have become chief executives in the classic sense and suggests that the new managerialist thesis about higher education needs to be inter-preted with caution. That extensive change is and has been taking place is undeniable, with the development of senior management teams and more professional managerial approaches to many aspects of university life includ-ing aspects of teaching and research which have not hitherto been subject to managerial systems. This has tended to distract attention from many equally important areas of continuity which have acted as shock absorbers in relation to the new trends. In particular, the role of vice-chancellor retains many of its important attributes – some would argue limitations – in terms of the style and approach to key tasks. It continues importantly to provide the critical link between the academic/professional and administrat-ive/managerial domains and, as such, is a role with tensions permanently at its core. The designation as chief executive may have focused attention on the need to strengthen managerial systems associated with the role, but it has not been at the expense of the academic domain. Moreover, the institutional context remains critically important. Key skills in the manage-rial domain are those of networking, lobbying and persuasion, rather more than traditional managerial or administrative skills. In this sense the role is highly political and is not, therefore, most effectively conceived as chief executive *tout court*. Some universities reflect this by designating the most senior post as vice-chancellor *and* chief executive. It is a role in transition and many of the forces which impinge are not merely national but global. In particular, more comparative studies are needed to help us to under-stand more clearly how far these important leadership roles are slowly developing common approaches to the task of leading universities in the twenty-first century.

Appendix: Research Methods

This book is based on research conducted by the authors at the School of Education, University of Leeds. The research into new leadership styles in mass higher education was funded by the Leverhulme Trust (Project Ref. F122AO) and carried out over a two-year period commencing in the autumn of 1995. Two broad hypotheses were tested: first, that new forms of executive leadership in British higher education have emerged based on managerial expertise rather than collegial or charismatic authority; second, that there has been a power shift in universities, with vice-chancellors becoming the dominant figures in defining their cultures and determining institutional missions and performance.

The development of the vice-chancellorship was approached from a range of perspectives. These included the historical evolution of the role of British vice-chancellors, the literature on institutional management, the development of theories of organization and notions of 'leadership' generated in other commercial and professional settings. The intention was to explore the evolution of new patterns of leadership in British higher education in the context of, first, the changing goals and organization (and demands on) universities, and, second, parallel developments in university leadership in the rest of Europe and the United States. Using a combination of desk and field-based methods, three main sets of data were collected. The details are given below.

Biographical data on vice-chancellors

One of the key aims of the research was to examine the changing career experiences and backgrounds of vice-chancellors. The intention was to build on the work of earlier researchers and compile detailed biographical profiles of those appointed to the top institutional posts in British higher education for the period since 1960. The completed data comprise 341 separate cases held in two independent but linked databases. The first contains up to 77 numeric variables per case. These variables provide key descriptors of the changing profiles of vice-chancellors in three broad categories: demographic details such as age, gender, honours and titles; previous education and career paths; and participation in wider higher education and non-higher education affairs, including public and private organizations. The second database provides more detailed qualitative data about patterns of participation, arranged in nine tables.

Both databases were constructed from published data, principally those recorded in successive editions of *Who's Who*. It was recognized that these data may be incomplete in some cases, but, supplemented by other published sources, they provide the only accessible and comprehensive social profile of higher education's elite occupational group. Only 32 missing 'cases' of vice-chancellors occupying office in the period covered were identified. However, the tail-end data on vice-chancellors in the 1950s and later 1990s may not be representative of the total populations for the decades in question, since the former cover only those in post in 1960 and the latter those in post up to November 1996. Wherever possible we tried to ensure compatibility between our categories of analysis and those used by previous researchers. We did not attempt to replicate those analyses focusing on the social origins of vice-chancellors, using type of school attended as a proxy. Although data on type of school were collected, we did not proceed with substantial analysis because of the problem of identifying changes in school categorization over the long term. Although analysis is technically feasible, the resources and time demanded were beyond the scope of our project.

International dimensions

A key aim of the research was to compile comparative data on executive leadership from Europe and the United States. In addition to literature reviews of leadership approaches in European and American universities, we conducted three questionnaire surveys of university presidents (or equivalents) in California and Georgia and rectors in Sweden and the Netherlands. The questionnaire was first drafted by the Leeds team, incorporating insights derived from the British-based fieldwork. While the intention was to devise a research instrument which would provide broadly comparable 'transatlantic' sets of data, there was clearly a need both to develop and to customize the questionnaires with the specific characteristics and contexts of the specific higher education systems in mind. The initial draft questionnaire was developed in collaboration with colleagues in the Department of Business Studies, Uppsala University, Sweden. The subsequent American and Dutch questionnaires were based on this model, the questionnaire to rectors and their equivalents in the Netherlands also benefiting from insights and refinements suggested by colleagues at the Centre for Higher Education Policy Studies (CHEPS) based at the University of Twente.

The final questionnaires had five broadly comparable parts. Respondents were asked in the first part to provide some basic information about themselves, time in office and their higher education institutions. The second part explored their educational and academic qualifications, disciplinary affiliations, academic and public honours. Questions in the third part focused on previous careers and wider higher education and public service records. The fourth part asked specific questions about the range of duties and commitments outside the university but undertaken while president or rector. A final part explored attitudes towards leadership roles and responsibilities and made provision for a number of open response alternatives.

Response rates achieved varied. Thirty rectors of Swedish universities, specialist colleges (except those devoted to arts) and regional university colleges collaborated in the Swedish element of the study. In this case the response rate achieved was 100 per cent, owing largely to the collection of responses through either telephone interviews or personal meetings conducted by members of the Uppsala team. Questionnaires to rectors in the Netherlands and presidents in the USA were sent simply with a request to complete and return the forms. Of the 75 Dutch rectors surveyed, 39 returned questionnaires, giving a response rate of 52 per cent. The American questionnaire surveyed a total of 67 institutional leaders (48 in California, 19 in Georgia) and received 31 completed forms (21 from Californian presidents and 10 from Georgian), giving an overall response rate of 46 per cent.

Case studies

The field-based phase of the research involved a quest for data with which to offer a more grounded view of the day-to-day work of university vice-chancellors. Two approaches were adopted. The first was interview-based and sought to explore the attitudes, opinions and expectations of vice-chancellors with reference to shifting institutional priorities, leadership 'styles' or approaches and relations between the executive, lay and bureaucratic elements of university leadership. The vice-chancellors (or their equivalents) of ten higher education institutions selected as representative of the sector (eight in England, one each in Wales and Scotland) agreed to participate in the interview-based case studies. In addition to extensive semi-structured interviews with the vice-chancellors, we were also able to interview key members of their staffs (deputy and pro vice-chancellors, registrars, etc.), as well as chairs of council/governing bodies. A total of 39 interviews were conducted across the ten case study institutions.

In addition, the vice-chancellors of three further institutions (one pre-1992 and two post-1992 universities) generously agreed to participate in the research by allowing non-participant observation of their work over extended periods of two to three weeks. Apart from a handful of meetings involving personnel/discipline or commercially sensitive negotiations, only minimal restrictions were placed on researcher access to the daily round of activities engaged in by each vice-chancellor. Extensive field notes were supplemented by analysis of institutional documentation and interviews with other members of senior management teams, deans of faculties/departments and other staff. These data provided comprehensive insights into the actual work of vice-chancellors, and their interactions with senior management teams, other staff and governors, as well as a broad range of external constituencies. Following conventional social science practice, we have not identified either individual participants or institutions involved in the research by their real names and have endeavoured at all times to ensure anonymity in any of the reconstructions of events or views of those observed or interviewed.

Bibliography

Adair, J. (1981) *Developing Tomorrow's Leaders: a University Contribution* (Inaugural Lecture). Guildford: University of Surrey.

Adams, J., Bailey, T., Jackson, L. *et al.* (1998) *Benchmarking of the International Standing of Research in England: Report of a Consultancy Study on Bibliometric Analysis.* Leeds: Centre for Policy Studies in Education, University of Leeds.

Ashby, E. (Sir) (1968) *Hands Off the Universities?* An oration delivered at Birkbeck College, London, 19 January 1968 in celebration of the 144th anniversary of the foundation of the college. London: Birkbeck College.

Ashby, E. (Sir) and Stout, A. K. (1956) Self-government in British universities. *Science and Freedom,* 7: 3–10.

Baldridge, J. V. (1971) *Power and Conflict in the University.* New York: Wiley.

Baldridge, J. V. (1975) Organizational change: institutional sagas, external challenges, and internal politics, in J. V. Baldridge and T. E. Deal (with the assistance of M. Zieg Ansell) (eds) *Managing Change in Educational Organizations: Sociological Perspectives, Strategies, and Case Studies.* New York: McCutchan.

Bargh, C., Scott, P. and Smith, D. (1996) *Governing Universities: Changing the Culture?* Buckingham: Open University Press.

Bass, B. M. (1985) *Leadership and Performance beyond Expectations.* New York: Free Press.

Bass, B. M. and Avolio, B. J. (eds) (1994) *Improving Organization Effectiveness Through Transformational Leadership.* Thousand Oaks, CA: Sage.

Becher, T. and Kogan, M. (1980) *Process and Structure in Higher Education.* London: Heinemann.

Beloff, M. (1968) *The Plateglass Universities.* London: Secker & Warburg.

Bennis, W. G. (1976) *The Unconscious Conspiracy: Why Leaders Can't Lead.* New York: Amacom.

Bensimon, E. M. and Neumann, A. (1993) *Redesigning Collegiate Leadership: Teams and Teamwork in Higher Education.* Baltimore: Johns Hopkins University Press.

Blake, R. R. and Mouton, J. S. (1969) *Building A Dynamic Corporation Through Grid Organization Development.* London: Addison-Wesley.

Blight, D. (1995) International education: Australia's potential demand and supply. Paper presented to the International Education Conference, Brisbane.

Bone, A. and Bourner, T. (1998) Developing university managers. *Higher Education Quarterly,* 52(3): 283–99.

Bowden, V. (1966) *University Finance.* Manchester: Manchester Statistical Society.

Bull, J. (1994) Managing change or changing managers, in S. Weill (ed.) *Introducing Change from the Top in Universities and Colleges.* London: Kogan Page.

Burnes, B. (1996) *A Strategic Approach to Organizational Dynamics.* London: Financial Times and Pitman Publishing.

Burns, J. M. (1978) *Leadership.* New York: Harper & Row.

Bussom, R. S., Larson, L. L., Vicars, W. M. and Ness, J. J. (1981) *The Nature of Police Executives' Work: Final Report.* Carbondale, IL: Southern Illinois University.

Cadbury, A. (Sir) (Chair) (1992) *A Report on the Financial Aspects of Corporate Governance.* London: Gee.

Caine, S. (1969) *British Universities: Purposes and Prospects.* London: Bodley Head.

Campbell, A., Devine, M. and Young, D. (1990) *A Sense of Mission.* London: Century Business and Economist Books.

Carlson, S. (1951) *Executive Behaviour: a Study of the Work Load and the Working Methods of Managing Directors.* Stockholm: Stombergs (reprinted in 1991 with contributions from H. Mintzberg and R. Stewart).

Carter, C. (1980) *Higher Education for the Future.* Oxford: Blackwell.

Chemers, M. M. (1993) An integrative theory of leadership, in M. M. Chemers and R. Ayman (eds) *Leadership Theory and Research: Perspectives and Directions.* San Diego: Academic Press.

Clark, B. (1998) *Creating Entrepreneurial Universities: Organizational Pathways of Transformation.* Oxford: Pergamon.

Clarke, T. and Clegg, S. (1998) *Changing Paradigms: the Transformation of Management Knowledge for the Twenty-first Century.* London: HarperBusiness.

Cohen, D. (1999) Universitas 2000. *Guardian,* Education section, 20 July.

Cohen, M. D. and March, J. G. (1974) *Leadership and Ambiguity: the American College President.* New York: McGraw-Hill.

Collison, P. and Millen, J. (1969) University chancellors, vice-chancellors and college principals: a social profile. *Sociology,* 3: 77–109.

Committee on Higher Education (1963) *Higher Education* (Robbins Report). Cmnd 2154. London: HMSO.

Committee of Public Accounts (1994) *Eighth Report. The Proper Conduct of Public Business.* House of Commons, session 1993–4. London: HMSO.

Committee on Standards in Public Life (1995) *First Report. Members of Parliament, the Executive (Ministers and Civil Servants) and Executive Non-departmental Public Bodies (Including NHS Trusts)* (Nolan Report). London: HMSO.

Committee of University Chairmen (1995) *Guide for Members of Governing Bodies of Universities and Colleges in England and Wales.* Bristol: Higher Education Funding Council for England.

Committee of Vice-Chancellors and Principals (1985) *Report of a Steering Committee on Efficiency Studies in Universities* (Jarratt Report). London: CVCP.

Committee of Vice-Chancellors and Principals and Centre for Urban and Regional Development Studies (1994) *Universities and Communities.* London: CVCP.

Cowling, M. (1980) *Religion and Public Doctrine in Modern England.* Cambridge: Cambridge University Press.

Crosland, A. (1965) *The Woolwich Speech.* London: Department for Education and Science.

Dainton, F. S. (1981) *British Universities: Purposes, Problems and Pressures.* Cambridge: Cambridge University Press.

Davies, J. L. (1987) The entrepreneurial and adaptive university: report of the second US study visit. *International Journal of Institutional Management in Higher Education,* 11(1): 12–104.

Dearing Report (1997) *Higher Education in the Learning Society: National Committee of Inquiry into Higher Education.* London: HMSO.

Deem, R. (1998) Globalisation, 'new managerialism', academic capitalism and entrepreneurial universities: is the local dimension still important? Paper presented at the Society for Research in Higher Education Conference, Lancaster, 15–17 December.

Drucker, P. (1974) *Management: Tasks, Responsibilities, Practices.* London: Heinemann.

Drucker, P. (1993) *Post-capitalist Society.* New York: HarperBusiness.

Duff, J. (1959) *Universities in Britain.* London: Longman.

Engwall, L., Levay, C. and Lidman, R. (1999) The roles of university and college rectors. *Higher Education Management,* 11(2): 75–93.

Farnham, D. and Jones, J. (1998) Who are the vice-chancellors? An analysis of their professional and social backgrounds 1990–97. *Higher Education Review,* 30(3): 42–58.

Fiedler, F. E. (1967) *A Theory of Leadership Effectiveness.* New York: McGraw-Hill.

Gee, R. (1997) Work shadowing: a positive management experience?, in H. Eggins (ed.) *Women as Leaders and Managers in Higher Education.* Buckingham: SRHE and Open University Press.

Giamatti, A. B. (1988) *A Free and Ordered Space: the Real World of the University.* New York: Norton.

Gibbons, M., Limoges, C., Nowotny *et al.* (1994) *The New Production of Knowledge: Science and Research in Contemporary Societies.* London: Sage.

Giddens, A. (1974) Elites in the British class structure, in P. Stanworth and A. Giddens (eds) *Elites and Power in British Society.* London: Cambridge University Press.

Green, M. F. (1997) Leadership and institutional change: a comparative view. *Higher Education Management,* 9(2): 135–46.

Guttsman, W. L. (1963) *The British Political Elite.* London: MacGibbon & Kee.

Halsey, A. H. and Trow, M. A. (1971) *The British Academics.* London: Faber.

Handy, C. (1994) *The Empty Raincoat: Making Sense of the Future.* London: Hutchinson.

Harvey-Jones, J. (1988) *Making It Happen: Reflections on Leadership.* London: Collins.

Heatherington, H. (1954) *The British University System, 1914–1954.* Edinburgh: Oliver and Boyd.

Higher Education Funding Council for England (1993) *Circular Letter 17/93: Strategic Plans and Financial Forecasts.* London: HEFCE.

Higher Education Statistics Agency (1999) *Students in Higher Education Institutions 1997/98.* Cheltenham: HESA.

Hosking, D. (1988) Organising, leadership and skilful process. *Journal of Management Studies,* 25(2): 147–66.

House, R. J. (1971) A path goal theory of leadership effectiveness. *Administrative Science Quarterly,* 16(1): 321–38.

House, R. J. and Mitchell, T. R. (1974) Path goal theory of leadership. *Journal of Contemporary Business,* 3 (Autumn): 81–97.

Izbicki, J. (1999) Universitas 2000, *Guardian,* Education section, 20 July.

Kaplowitz, R. A. (1986) *Selecting College and University Personnel: The Quest and the Questions,* ASHE/ERIC Higher Education Report 8. Washington, DC: ASHE/ERIC.

Kauffman, S. (1995) *At Home in the Universe.* Oxford: Oxford University Press.

Kerr, C. (1964) *The Uses of the University.* Cambridge, MA: Harvard University Press.

Knights, D. and Willmott, H. (1992) Conceptualising leadership processes: a study of senior managers in a financial services company. *Journal of Management Studies*, 29(6): 761–82.

Kogan, M. and Kogan, D. (1983) *The Attack on Higher Education.* London: Kogan Page.

Kotter, J. P. (1982) *The General Managers.* New York: Free Press.

Lewin, R. (1992) *Complexity: Life at the Edge of Chaos.* Oxford: Maxwell Macmillan.

Logan, D. (1963) *Universities: the Years of Challenge* (Rede lecture). Cambridge: Cambridge University Press.

Luthans, F., Hodgetts, R. M. and Rosenkrantz, S. A. (1988) *Real Managers.* Cambridge, MA: Ballinger.

Maassen, P. and van Vught, F. (1994) Alternative models of governmental steering in higher education, in L. Goedegebuure and F. van Vught (eds) *Comparative Policy Studies in Higher Education.* Utrecht: Lemma.

McNeish, S. (1997) Leadership, management styles and organisational effectiveness in a university administration planning unit. MBA dissertation, Department of Management Studies, Glasgow University.

Mann, R. D. (1959) A review of the relationships between personality and performance in small groups. *Psychological Bulletin*, 56(4): 241–70.

Mansfield Cooper, W. (1966) *Governments and the University* (Frank Gerstein Lecture). Toronto: Macmillan.

Martin, E. (1999) *Changing Academic Work: Developing the Learning University.* Buckingham: SRHE and Open University Press.

Martinko, M. J. and Gardner, W. L. (1990) Structured observation of managerial work: a replication and synthesis. *Journal of Management Studies*, 27(3): 329–57.

Middlehurst, R. (1993) *Leading Academics.* Buckingham: SRHE and Open University Press.

Middlehurst, R. (1997) Leadership, women and higher education, in H. Eggins (ed.) *Women as Leaders in Higher Education.* Buckingham: SRHE and Open University Press.

Miner, J. B. (1993) *Role Motivation Theories.* London: Routledge.

Mintzberg, H. (1973) *The Nature of Managerial Work.* New York: Harper & Row.

Mintzberg, H. (1975) The manager's job: folklore and fact. *Harvard Business Review*, 53(4): 49–61.

Mintzberg, H. (1990) *The Structuring of Organizations.* London: Prentice Hall International.

Moodie, G. C. and Eustace, R. (1974) *Power and Authority in British Universities.* London: Allen & Unwin.

Morgan, G. (1986) *Images of Organisation.* London: Sage.

Nowotny, H., Scott, P. and Gibbons, M. (2000) *Rethinking Science: Knowledge Production in an Age of Uncertainty.* Cambridge: Polity Press.

Perkin, H. (1969) *New Universities in the United Kingdom.* Paris: OECD.

Perkin, H. (1978–9) The recruitment of elites in British society since 1800. *Journal of Social History*, 12: 222–34.

Perkin, H. (1989) *The Rise of Professional Society.* London: Routledge.

Peters, T. and Waterman, R. (1982) *In Search of Excellence.* New York: Harper & Row.

Power, M. (1997) *The Audit Society: Rituals of Verification.* Oxford: Oxford University Press.

Price, C. (1994) Piloting higher education change: a view from the helm, in S. Weill (ed.) *Introducing Change from the Top in Universities and Colleges.* London: Kogan Page.

Rhoades, G. and Slaughter, S. (1997) Academic capitalism, managed professionals and supply-side higher education. *Social Text*, 15(2): 9–38.

Rosenzweig, R. M. (1998) *The Political University: Policy, Politics and Presidential Leadership in the American Research University.* Baltimore: Johns Hopkins University Press.

Rubinstein, W. D. (1987) *Elites and the Wealthy in Modern British History.* Brighton: Harvester Press.

Sarch, Y. (1997) Outside academia: the changing job market and its influence, in H. Eggins (ed.) *Women as Leaders and Managers in Higher Education.* Buckingham: SRHE and Open University Press.

Scott, P. (1989) Higher education, in D. Kavanagh and A. Seldon (eds) *The Thatcher Effect: a Decade of Change.* Oxford: Oxford University Press.

Scott, P. (1995) *The Meanings of Mass Higher Education.* Buckingham: Open University Press.

Shapiro, H. T. (1998) University presidents – then and now, in W. G. Bowen and H. T. Shapiro (eds) *Universities and Their Leadership.* Princeton, NJ: Princeton University Press.

Shimmin, A. (1954) *The University of Leeds: The First Half-Century.* Cambridge: Cambridge University Press.

Shumar, W. (1997) *College for Sale: a Critique of the Commodification of Higher Education.* London: Falmer Press.

Slaughter, S. and Leslie, L. L. (1997) *Academic Capitalism: Politics, Policies and the Entrepreneurial University.* Baltimore: Johns Hopkins University Press.

Sloman, A. E. (1963) *A University in the Making* (Reith Lectures). London: BBC.

Sloper, D. W. (1996) The work patterns of Australian vice-chancellors. *Higher Education*, 31: 205–31.

Stewart, R. (1967) *Managers and Their Jobs.* London: Macmillan.

Stewart, R. (1982) *Choices for the Manager: a Guide to Managerial Work and Behaviour.* London: McGraw-Hill.

Stewart, R. (1991) Chairmen and chief executives: an exploration of their relationship. *Journal of Management Studies*, 28(5): 511–27.

Stewart, W. A. C. (1968) *British Universities: Dilemmas and Opportunities.* Keele: University of Keele.

Stodgill, R. M. (1948) Personnel factors associated with leadership. *Journal of Psychology*, 25: 35–71.

Szreter, R. (1968) An academic patriarchate – vice-chancellors 1966–7. *Universities Quarterly*, 23(1): 17–45.

Thody, A. (1997) *Leadership of Schools: Chief Executives in Education.* London: Cassell.

Tregoe, B. (1989) *Vision in Action: Putting a Winning Strategy to Work.* New York: Simon & Schuster.

Trow, M. (1973) *Problems in the Transition from Elite to Mass Higher Education.* Berkeley, CA: Carnegie Commission on Higher Education.

Trow, M. (1985) Comparative reflections on leadership in higher education. *European Journal of Higher Education*, 20(2–3): 143–61.

Trow, M. (1989) The Robbins trap: British attitudes and the limits of expansion. *Higher Education Quarterly*, 43(1): 55–75.

Wakeford, F. and Wakeford, J. (1974) Universities and the study of elites, in P. Stanworth and A. Giddens (eds) *Elites and Power in British Society.* London: Cambridge University Press.

Willmott, H. (1993) Strength is ignorance; slavery is freedom: managing culture in modern organisations. *Journal of Management Studies*, 30(4): 515–52.

Wilson, A. (1994) The management of change in a large civic university, in S. Weill (ed.) *Introducing Change from the Top in Universities and Colleges*. London: Kogan Page.

Wilson, A. (1999) Strategy and management for university development, in P. Scott (ed.) *Higher Education Reformed: Shaping the Future*. London: Falmer Press.

Wittrock, B. (1993) The modern university: the three transformations, in S. Rothblatt and B. Wittrock (eds) *The European and American University since 1800*. Cambridge: Cambridge University Press.

Yukl, G. (1989) Managerial leadership: a review of theory and research. *Journal of Management*, 15(2): 251–89.

Index

*Page numbers in **bold** indicate main discussion.*

The Society for Research into Higher Education

The Society for Research into Higher Education (SRHE) exists to stimulate and coordinate research into all aspects of higher education. It aims to improve the quality of higher education through the encouragement of debate and publication on issues of policy, on the organization and management of higher education institutions, and on the curriculum, teaching and learning methods.

The Society is entirely independent and receives no subsidies, although individual events often receive sponsorship from business or industry. The Society is financed through corporate and individual subscriptions and has members from many parts of the world.

Under the imprint *SRHE & Open University Press*, the Society is a specialist publisher of research, having over 80 titles in print. In addition to *SRHE News*, the Society's newsletter, the Society publishes three journals: *Studies in Higher Education* (three issues a year), *Higher Education Quarterly* and *Research into Higher Education Abstracts* (three issues a year).

The Society runs frequent conferences, consultations, seminars and other events. The annual conference in December is organized at and with a higher education institution. There are a growing number of networks which focus on particular areas of interest, including:

Access	Learning Environment
Assessment	Legal Education
Consultants	Managing Innovation
Curriculum Development	New Technology for Learning
Eastern European	Postgraduate Issues
Educational Development Research	Quantitative Studies
FE/HE	Student Development
Funding	Vocational Qualifications
Graduate Employment	

Benefits to members

Individual

- The opportunity to participate in the Society's networks
- Reduced rates for the annual conferences

- Free copies of *Research into Higher Education Abstracts*
- Reduced rates for *Studies in Higher Education*
- Reduced rates for *Higher Education Quarterly*
- Free copy of *Register of Members' Research Interests* – includes valuable reference material on research being pursued by the Society's members
- Free copy of occasional in-house publications, e.g. *The Thirtieth Anniversary Seminars Presented by the Vice-Presidents*
- Free copies of *SRHE News* which informs members of the Society's activities and provides a calendar of events, with additional material provided in regular mailings
- A 35 per cent discount on all SRHE/Open University Press books
- Access to HESA statistics for student members
- The opportunity for you to apply for the annual research grants
- Inclusion of your research in the *Register of Member's Research Interests*

Corporate

- Reduced rates for the annual conferences
- The opportunity for members of the Institution to attend SRHE's network events at reduced rates
- Free copies of *Research into Higher Education Abstracts*
- Free copies of *Studies in Higher Education*
- Free copies of *Register of Members' Research Interests* – includes valuable reference material on research being pursued by the Society's members
- Free copy of occasional in-house publications
- Free copies of *SRHE News*
- A 35 per cent discount on all SRHE/Open University Press books
- Access to HESA statistics for research for students of the Institution
- The opportunity for members of the Institution to submit applications for the Society's research grants
- The opportunity to work with the Society and co-host conference
- The opportunity to include in the *Register of Member' Research Interests* you Institution's research into aspects of higher education

Membership details: SRHE, 3 Devonshire Street, London W1N 2BA, UK. Tel: 020 7637 2766. Fax: 020 7637 2781. email: srhe@mailbox.ulcc.ac.uk world wide web: http://www.srhe.ac.uk./srhe/ *Catalogue*: SRHE & Open University Press, Celtic Court, 22 Ballmoor, Buckingham MK18 1XW. Tel: 01280 823388. Fax: 01280 823233. email: enquiries@openup.co.uk

GOVERNING UNIVERSITIES
CHANGING THE CULTURE?

Catherine Bargh, Peter Scott and David Smith

The governance of higher education in the UK was regarded until recently as the 'dignified' element within the constitution of the academy. University councils were trustees rather than directors. But governance is now a contested area and, in particular, lay governors are seen as key change agents, responsible for reforming the old donnish culture of elite higher education. *Governing Universities* explores who governors are, how they conceive of their new roles, and what they think about higher education policy. It examines whether governing bodies have become more actively engaged in setting institutional policies; and whether governors have changed the old culture or gone 'native'. It sets university governance in the large context of the massification and 'marketization' of higher education; and draws comparisons both with other parts of the public sector and the private sector, and with governance in North America and the rest of Europe.

This is the first full-length research-based study of UK higher education governance and is essential reading for all those involved with and interested in university governance.

Contents
Preface – University governance: the historical and policy context – Governance and management in higher education – The Governors: backgrounds and perceptions of higher education – People like us?: the selection and appointment of university governors – Governing bodies: roles and organizational structures – Process of governance: roles and decision making – Key agents and relationships: vice-chancellors and chairs of governing bodies – Clashes of culture?: comparative perspectives on university governance – Changing patterns of governance? – Appendix 1: research methods – Appendix 2: additional results of the questionnaire – References – Index.

208pp   0 335 19538 5 (Paperback)   0 335 19539 3 (Hardback)

LEADING ACADEMICS

Robin Middlehurst

At a time of major change in higher education, the quality of university leadership is an issue of key importance. Whether heading a research team, planning curriculum innovations, managing a department or running an institution, effective leadership is required. Yet how well is the idea of leadership understood? How is leadership practised in the academic world? What special characteristics are needed to lead autonomous professionals?

This book, based on research in universities, is the first comprehensive examination of leadership in British higher education. Robin Middlehurst critiques contemporary ideas of leadership and examines their relevance to academe. She explores the relationship between models of leadership and practice and different levels of the institution. She argues for a better balance between leadership and management in universities in order to increase the responsiveness and creativity of higher education.

Contents
Part 1: Thinking about leadership – What is leadership? – The new leadership – Organizational images – Leadership and academe: traditions and change – Part 2: Practising leadership – Institutional leaders – Collective leadership – Leading departments – Individuals and leadership – Part 3: Developing leadership – Leadership learning – Endings and beginnings – Bibliography – Index.

224pp   0 335 09988 2 (Paperback)   0 335 09989 0 (Hardback)

MANAGING STRATEGY

David Watson

Higher education institutions are under increasing pressure to produce corporate and strategic plans, both for external audiences and for the internal purposes of setting and achieving goals. They are significantly dependent upon public investment and the expectations of public bodies, as well as upon a fast-changing market. David Watson sets out what strategic management can and should consist of in a modern, essentially democratic, university or college, and how to make it work. He examines:

- how universities and colleges should tailor corporate plans to satisfy external and internal requirements for their corporate plans;
- how they should maximize their strategic assets and opportunities and minimize their weaknesses and threats;
- the role of governance and management in setting and achieving a strategic plan.

This book demonstrates how the academy must adapt to the needs of its rapidly changing host society as well as of a more diverse and plural internal community, whilst maintaining historical commitments. The result is an account of strategic management that is simultaneously careful of traditional values, restorative of those that have fallen into abeyance, and genuinely innovative.

Contents
Introduction – External perspectives – Internal perspectives – Personal perspectives – Appendix – References – Index.

176pp   0 335 20345 0 (Paperback)   0 335 20346 9 (Hardback)